# Matthew Arnold

# MASTERS OF WORLD LITERATURE

## PUBLISHED:

## IN PREPARATION:

MASTERS OF WORLD LITERATURE SERIES

LOUIS KRONENBERGER, GENERAL EDITOR

# Matthew Arnold

## *A Survey of His Poetry and Prose*

### DOUGLAS BUSH

MACMILLAN

*First published in the United States of America 1971*
*First published in the United Kingdom 1971*

*Published 1971 by*
THE MACMILLAN PRESS LTD
*London and Basingstoke*
*Associated companies in New York Toronto*
*Dublin Melbourne Johannesburg and Madras*

Library of Congress catalog card no. 72–144817

SBN 333 13392 7

Printed by photo-lithography and made in Great Britain at
the Pitman Press, Bath

*To Hazel*

# *Contents*

# Preface

A SHORT SURVEY of Arnold's writings in several areas is necessarily limited to some main lines and attitudes and must forgo the amplitude of exposition that he deserves—and has had in larger general and special studies. Also, in such a book, it seems best to avoid spacious generalities about his variegated and complex world, to stick closely to his own utterances, and to try, so far as one can, to see him as in himself he really is.

During recent decades Arnold's poetry and prose have received a large and rapidly increasing amount of enlightened and enlightening criticism, from which of course this book has profited. Some books are listed at the end and some books and articles are recorded in footnotes; many other substantial things could not be mentioned, since in a sketch of this kind a river of text (to use Arnold's favorite poetic image) must not pursue a sluggish course through "a blacker, incessanter line" of notes. One primary debt is owed to Kenneth Allott's edition of the poems and R. H. Super's edition, not yet completed, of the prose works. (If, by the way, some readers are annoyed by the references given for quotations, others may not be; one can spend hours hunting for a desired item and its context.)

I am obliged, for permission to quote, to the following publishers and authors:

The Columbia University Press and Lionel Trilling for quotations from his *Matthew Arnold*;

Frederick Crews, *The New York Review of Books*, and Winthrop Publishers, Inc., for quotations from "Anaesthetic Criticism: II"

(*New York Review of Books*, March 12, 1970; repr. in *Psychoanalysis & Literary Process*, Winthrop Publishers, 1970);

Faber and Faber Ltd. and Harcourt Brace Jovanovich, Inc. for quotations from T. S. Eliot's *Selected Essays*;

The Harvard University Press for quotations from T. S. Eliot's *The Use of Poetry and the Use of Criticism* and from *Essays, Letters, and Reviews by Matthew Arnold, Collected and Edited by Fraser Neiman*;

Longmans, Green & Company for the use of *The Poems of Matthew Arnold*, ed. Kenneth Allott;

The University of Michigan Press for the use of *The Prose Works of Matthew Arnold*, ed. R. H. Super;

The Oxford University Press and the Clarendon Press for quotations from *The Letters of Matthew Arnold to Arthur Hugh Clough*, ed. H. F. Lowry, and *The Correspondence of Arthur Hugh Clough*, ed. F. L. Mulhauser;

St. John's College, Oxford, and the Hogarth Press for an extract from *Rainer Maria Rilke: Duino Elegies*, translated and edited by J. B. Leishman and Stephen Spender;

The Viking Press for quotations from Lionel Trilling's *Beyond Culture*;

The Yale University Press for quotations from *Unpublished Letters of Matthew Arnold*, ed. Arnold Whitridge, and René Wellek's *History of Modern Criticism*, vol. IV.

Finally, I may once again return thanks to Louis Kronenberger, most amiable and encouraging of general editors.

D.B.

# Abbreviations

Allott = *The Poems of Matthew Arnold,* ed. Kenneth Allott. London: Longmans, Green; New York: Barnes & Noble, 1965.

Culler = A. Dwight Culler, *Imaginative Reason: The Poetry of Matthew Arnold.* New Haven and London: Yale University Press, 1966.

Lowry = *The Letters of Matthew Arnold to Arthur Hugh Clough,* ed. Howard F. Lowry. London and New York: Oxford University Press, 1932.

Neiman = *Essays, Letters, and Reviews by Matthew Arnold, Collected and Edited by Fraser Neiman.* Cambridge, Mass.: Harvard University Press; London: Oxford University Press, 1960.

Russell = *Letters of Matthew Arnold 1848–1888, Collected and Arranged by George W. E. Russell.* 2 v. New York and London: Macmillan, 1895. This collection was issued in editions with different pagination.

Super = *The Complete Prose Works of Matthew Arnold,* ed. R. H. Super, in progress. Vols. 1–6, Ann Arbor: University of Michigan Press, 1960–68.

Whitridge = *Unpublished Letters of Matthew Arnold,* ed. Arnold Whitridge. New Haven: Yale University Press; London: Oxford University Press, 1923.

# Introduction

WE THINK, loosely but rightly, of the Victorian age as ending in 1914, and the magnitude and rapidity of events and changes since then have made even the First World War seem very remote. In the last few years legitimate causes of revolt have led extremists, conspicuously in the United States, to much destructive violence (a course of action inaugurated on an international scale, and stubbornly pursued, by the government); and extreme revolutionary zeal seems to be attended by antiintellectual, anticultural intolerance and a false notion of "relevance." In such times Matthew Arnold's voice of civilized reason may seem too far off and faint to reach us. But violence has not yet extinguished civility and reason, sweetness and light, which become all the more precious when threatened from both the right and the left; and, if we are willing to listen, Arnold still speaks to us more directly, in a larger proportion of his poetry and prose, than any other Victorian poet or critic. Further, to be more "relevant," we may think that he—who lived through a period of radical change—speaks more wisely of continuing problems than our fashionable prophets of moral and social revolution or their reactionary opponents or the liberals of the center. Arnold was, as he said, "a Liberal of the future"—a future which has not yet arrived.

Throughout his life, as poet and as literary, social, and religious critic, Arnold was a nonconformist, at odds with orthodoxies of his age; that is one large and vital attraction. In creative imagination and artistic power and virtuosity he rarely approached Tennyson or Browning, but he had a keener sense than his elders of the modern malaise; most of his good poems set forth unresolved tensions which, if not quite those of the 1970's, are near enough to win our sympathetic response. The problems that afflicted Arnold and other sensitive spirits are familiar enough: the loss of traditional religious faith and its moral imperatives; the loss of Wordsworthian joy in man's unity with nature; the overwhelming growth of knowledge, technology, and industrialism, with the consequent harvest of enlightenment and skepticism, faith in "progress" and fear of materialistic enslavement, rapid and bewildering change in outward and inward ways of life, the manifest gulf between wealth and privilege and poverty, misery, and social unrest, and, because of all these things, the immediate personal pressure of loneliness and uncertainty of direction.

The same oppressive and inescapable complexities evoked much of Arnold's later and far more abundant prose. He neither possessed nor desired the apocalyptic thunder and lightning of Carlyle, the dogmatism and occasional shrillness and eccentricity of Ruskin, the philosophical logic (and flatness) of Mill, or the religious beliefs of Newman (whose temper he so greatly admired); but his own blend of liberal, rational intelligence, urbane irony, and high-minded earnestness is, or should be, attractive and relevant now. It has far more than historical interest. Arnold's manner and much of his matter are relatively, or even absolutely, quite modern, or better than that. This memorable sentence might have been uttered about a number of later politicians: "Mr. Gladstone's powers of self-deception are so inexhaustible that he is never insincere."[1] We may think of our "know-nothing" segment of campus radicals, both the young and their retarded elders, when we meet a comment on W. K. Clifford, the brilliant mathematician who fulminated against "that awful plague," Christianity: "Compared with Professor Clifford, Messrs. Moody and Sankey are masters of the philosophy of his-

---

[1] Neiman, 368. In *From Easter to August*, reprinted from the *Nineteenth Century* 22 (September 1887).

tory."[2] (Sir Leslie Stephen looked back to his own frequent wish "that I too had a little sweetness and light that I might be able to say such nasty things of my enemies"—though in the same essay he affirmed, from personal acquaintance, that Arnold had an irresistibly lovable sweetness of nature.)

Arnold might be called an individual mixture of eighteenth-century rationality, Romantic idealism, Victorian skepticism, and, if we like the overworn word, modern existentialism, although such labels do not go far toward defining or explaining his complex mind and temperament. The central fact of his experience was the loss of traditional Christian faith. This, to be sure, was the lot of many Victorians, great and small, but every case had its special character. For Arnold, so far as we know (not that we really do know), the actual experience was not in itself agonizing, as it was for some other people; it appears rather that he quietly shed a set of beliefs which had never been a strong personal reality. But he felt the consequences with intense and lasting seriousness, as his poetry and increasingly religious prose demonstrate. Tennyson and Browning, though far from conventional orthodoxy, were able to retain some prime articles of faith, enough to provide degrees of reassurance; but Arnold the poet had no such sheet anchor. In spite of his occasional appeals to starry skies and rivers flowing seaward, neither external nature nor internal intuition gave clear or lasting intimations of divinity; whatever man's transcendental cravings, he was alone and self-dependent in an alien and indifferent universe. An earnest seeker of the good life for himself and others was likewise alone in a society busily intent upon selfish ends and largely indifferent to the misery of the submerged multitude. Arnold, by instinct and paternal inheritance, could not surrender to a naturalistic or "pagan" view of life and become a wayward creature of sense and impulse; he had to find a saving and working creed. In his troubled search for light and direction he found help in such heterogeneous guides as George Sand, Senancour, Goethe, Spinoza, Carlyle (whose influence survived repudiation), Emerson,

[2] *God and the Bible* (New York: Macmillan, 1883), xv. The following remarks from Stephen are from *Studies of a Biographer* (New York and London, 1898), 2, 78, 104.

the ancient classics and Stoics, the *Bhagavad Gita*, the Bible and Thomas à Kempis.

On the other hand, Arnold was, for a time, a young man and a poet, and he could chafe against the self-discipline which, however essential for an ordered life, exacted a high price; although so different in temper and training, he had something of Yeats's fear of withering into wisdom and of Lawrence's fear of the overintellectualizing and mechanizing of life. He could say that "rigorous teachers seized my youth," in lines where "youth" is opposed to its rhyme word, "Truth." In and between the lines of various poems the ideal of a life of disciplined reason encounters the ideal of youthful, spontaneous feeling, an emotional response to life and love and nature which, in its wholehearted intensity, may seem to validate itself as a better guide than conscious reason. Thus the main body of Arnold's verse, written during the decade of his twenties, 1843–53, reveals a conflict—to put it in abstract and here strongly ethical terms—between romanticism and classicism, Dionysus and Apollo. In the end classicism won, as it was bound to do, though in his later years and writings the rational liberal could still invoke feeling to inspire and strengthen the dictates of reason. It may be observed that W. H. Auden, in his short poem *Matthew Arnold*, saw the poet's gift imprisoned and killed by the pressure of his father's "Hebraic" legacy which he felt obliged to carry on—a simplistic view, as Louis Bonnerot says, not in accord with the evidence.[3]

The transition from the young to the elderly Arnold was the usual process of both continuity and change, modified of course by his character and circumstances. We shall be noting some early testimonies to his debonair charm and also to the worldly-wise flippancy and arrogant aloofness—in part self-protective, in part an enjoyable pose—which could sometimes ruffle his Oxford friends. Mrs. Humphry Ward, the daughter of his brother Thomas, described the later Arnold, the man of "strong and rugged" face, with a "large mouth, broad lined brow, and vigorous coal-black hair," the face, with the side-whiskers, familiar from the portraits. Since Arnold transformed his youthful flip-

[3] *Matthew Arnold Poète: Essai de Biographie Psychologique* (Paris, 1947), 515.

pancy and arrogance into a strategic and effective weapon in his prose, we might say that the young and the elderly Arnold are combined in Sir Max Beerbohm's picture of the little niece looking up at the relaxed but formidable figure with the quizzical expression and saying: "Why, Uncle Matthew, oh why, will not you be always wholly serious?"

For all his wit, Arnold was very serious in the several branches of criticism he engaged in. He worked his way out of the many-sided internal conflicts which had been the main source of his poetry, and on the threshold of middle age the troubled poet gave place to the critic who had counsel for his backward and misguided countrymen. But, despite his outward assurance, Arnold himself never ceased to be a seeker of truth and righteousness. Unlike many reformers of the past and notably of the present, Arnold believed that the improvement of society begins at home, with the individual's very difficult task of improving himself, his own ways of thought, feeling, and action; he did not believe in the kind of virtue, so popular nowadays, that grasps the world in a loving embrace while gratifying every impulse and "need" of the primitive and predatory self. This sort of modernism—which has been acutely diagnosed in Irving Howe's *Decline of the New*—is obviously not in advance of Arnold but far behind him. However, we cannot go on here with a preview of the literary, social, and religious writings that were—along with his exacting professional labors—to occupy the rest of his life. It was as a critic that Arnold came to exercise immense influence; far more than any comparable figure, he dominated, in both England and America, the last third of the nineteenth century and the earlier part of the twentieth. And many recent signs indicate a renewal of active interest in both the poet and the critic.

Some of our younger critics, who ignore or condescend to Arnold and what he stood for, are—notwithstanding a sometimes doubtful range of knowledge—much more arrogant, dogmatic, and solemn than he was. To link together assertive testimonies from several witnesses (whose several creeds are unrevealed or unimpressive), it seems that "the traditional humanistic values" function as "pure hypocrisy," are "fraudulent" anyhow, and are happily dead or dying; that Arnold's ideal of culture, whatever its theoretical virtues, is "not true" because it is "not grounded in any existential or psychological grasp of the actual human and historical situation." Arnold of course sought to preserve, balance, and refine those old values, the best that twenty-five centuries of human experience have evolved, and he was less concerned with the undiscriminating "extension of life" to its abnormal fringes (an aim of modern art) than with the quality of the life led by the mass of people. Another witness makes this pronouncement: "The humanism that purports to defend classical and Judeo-Christian values by cherishing the texts in which those values supposedly reside is indeed jeopardized by extraliterary knowledge, but such a humanism amounts to little more than the confusion of a book list with an education, and its practical results are hardly worth preserving."[4] Thus, with Olympian or Podsnappian finality, the critic waves aside most Western literature. A true humanism, he tells us, would start from scratch, "a comparison of man to the nearest primates," and move up to psychoanalysis, which seems to provide the only valid approach to literature. Such "scientific" sophistication may quicken the impulse to reread Arnold, a great humanist who had authentic roots and who, knowing what literature had meant to man through so many ages, would not have approached it with the cut-and-dried formula, "the astonishing sameness of the repressed unconscious across all recorded eras and civilizations." Pondering on this last, vast, and quite unverifiable datum, on the substance and tone of other parts of the discourse, and on more or less fantastic misinterpretations that psychoanalytical criticism has produced, we may think that Arnold (who has been one of its victims) was overoptimistic when, apropos of Bishop Colenso and others, he said: "But let us in the meanwhile rather endeavour that in twenty years' time it may, in English literature, be an objection to a proposition that it is absurd" (Super, 3, 282).

---

[4] Quoted by permission from Frederick Crews, "Anaesthetic Criticism: II," *New York Review of Books*, March 12, 1970, p. 49; and from pp. 11–12 of the essay as reprinted in F. Crews *et al.*, *Psychoanalysis & Literary Process*, quoted by permission of Winthrop Publishers, Inc., Cambridge, Mass., © 1970.

To end this prelude on a more positive note, I may borrow compendious judgments from two of Arnold's best interpreters:

He possessed a profound intuition of the historical irrevocability of the disruptive, atomizing forces of modern life, and a keen instinct for the problems and perils these forces were bringing and would continue to bring into being.[5]

But Arnold's peculiar distinction as a literary critic is founded on the strong sensitivity of his response to the modern situation. He uniquely understood what Hegel had told the world, that the French Revolution marked an absolute change in the condition of man. For the first time in history, Hegel said, Reason—or Idea, or Theory, or Creative Imagination—had become decisive in human destiny. Arnold's argument in "Literature and Science" was the affirmation of the French Revolution; he was speaking on behalf of the illumination and refinement of that Reason by which man might shape the conditions of his own existence. This is the whole purport of his famous statement, "Literature is the criticism of life."

That saying used to have a rough time of it. . . . But less and less, I think, will anyone find ground on which to quarrel with it. Whatever else we also take literature to be, it must always, for us now, be the criticism of life.[6]

Finally, we may touch on the assessment of Arnold's critical relevance given by his current successor in the Oxford Professorship of Poetry, Roy Fuller, in his inaugural lecture in the centennial year of *Culture and Anarchy* (*The Times Literary Supplement,* February 20, 1969). Mr. Fuller affirmed the urgent need of criticism that would, with something of Arnold's clarity and power, bring his standards and ideals of literature and culture to bear on the various kinds of Philistinism now prevalent on all levels from the intellectual to the merely crude. Arnold's

[5] Leon Gottfried, *Matthew Arnold and the Romantics* (Lincoln: University of Nebraska Press; London: Routledge & Kegan Paul, 1963), 1-2.

[6] Lionel Trilling, "The Leavis–Snow Controversy," *Beyond Culture: Essays on Literature and Learning* (New York: Viking Press, 1965), 159. This essay first appeared in *Commentary,* June 1962.

One proof-text might be Arnold's assertion that "it is the great glory of the French Revolution . . . passionately to have embraced the idea: the work of making human life, hampered by a past which it has outgrown, natural and rational." (*My Countrymen,* Super, 5, 14–15)

efforts toward a classless equality on a high level, "the humanisation of man in society," Mr. Fuller sees—if brevity does not too
much blunt or distort his reflections—as defeated by a classless
vulgarization or repudiation of literary, ethical, and social values
and disciplines. But if this many-sided Philistinism is much more
powerful and pernicious than the kind Arnold fought against,
his conception of culture—in its true meaning, not in the traditional misrepresentation—must still be man's goal.

# I: *Life*

A SKETCH OF Matthew Arnold's life must begin with a reminder of the life and work of his father. Thomas Arnold (1795–1842) would hold a prominent place among the minor Victorians even if he had not been the father of a major one. He was the son of a Collector of Customs for the Isle of Wight. After achieving distinction at Oxford he decided against holy orders and during 1819–24 was his brother-in-law's partner in a school at Laleham, on the Thames near Staines; later he took in private pupils. In 1820 he had married Mary Penrose, the sister of an Oxford friend. His appointment as Headmaster of Rugby (1828) inaugurated a career that was to bring national repute to the school and to himself. Through his personality and his program Arnold did a great deal to rouse English public schools out of moral, religious, and intellectual lethargy, brutality, and what Sydney Smith in 1810 had called "a system of premature debauchery." His aims and methods drew some criticism, then and since, mainly because of his imposing premature moral responsibility upon his boys, in particular those seniors who were given a share of disciplinary power; but the many-sided revolution he brought about was almost wholly good and it was widely emulated.

To classical scholarship Arnold contributed an edition of Thucydides and a *History of Rome* (he had learned German in order to read the great Niebuhr). His large and vital historical sense (a quality that was to win his son's special praise) was combined with a liberal—and strongly Coleridgean—view of religion and the Church of England. The Church, like the public schools, had been sunk in worldly lethargy and was in urgent need of intellectual and spiritual renewal if it was to cope with the problems of modern society. The question was what form that renewal should take, and several ecclesiastical-political incidents sharpened the issue between conservatives and liberals, High and Low Churchmen. At Oxford in July 1833 John Keble— a friend of Dr. Arnold and Matthew's godfather—had delivered the sermon on "National Apostasy" which was looked back upon as the beginning of the Oxford or Tractarian Movement, the first shot fired in the campaign against political encroachments upon the Church that would, it was feared, bring disestablishment, doctrinal laxity, and disaster. Since then, Oxford and the country at large had been increasingly and emotionally divided. Thomas Arnold, though by no means an Evangelical or antiritualist, vigorously opposed the sacerdotal and dogmatic Anglo-Catholicism and the social indifference of the Tractarians —"The Oxford Malignants and Dr Hampden" was one of his articles (the title was not his). He was a forceful pioneer in the Broad Church movement: he envisaged a "society of Christians" that would include Nonconformist bodies and would be in a real and full sense the Church of England. In 1841, to his great joy, Arnold was appointed Regius Professor of Modern History at Oxford. But on June 12, 1842, just before his forty-seventh birthday—when Matthew was nineteen—he died from a heart attack (the weakness which had caused his father's death and was to cause Matthew's).

Matthew Arnold was born at Laleham on December 24, 1822. He was the eldest son in a family of five sons and four daughters. The young Arnolds grew up in a happy atmosphere of books, piety, games, charades and play-acting, exploratory walks, the editing of a family magazine—an atmosphere much like that of the large brood of Tennysons, except that Dr. Arnold, unlike the embittered father of the Tennysons, was a lively companion of his children. Thanks to his father's love of travel, Matthew in his youth saw a good deal of the Continent. Attachment to the Lake country led Dr. Arnold in 1833–34 to build a house at Fox How, near Ambleside. Thus the Arnolds became summer neighbors and friends of the Wordsworths, and the young Matthew's personal acquaintance with the elderly poet in his proper setting initiated the special regard that he was to feel throughout his life. When Dr. Arnold died his widow—who survived until 1873—lived on at Fox How, and Matthew enjoyed spending holidays there.

Matthew received elementary instruction under his uncle at Laleham, where he did not apply himself, and had private tutoring. At the age of nine, reading Virgil's fourth *Eclogue*, he said, he first realized the beauty of poetry. He had a year (1836–37) at Winchester, his father's old school, and in 1837 he was shifted to Rugby. The main material of education was of course Greek and Latin literature, studied in its literary, ethical, philosophical, and historical bearings; these terms describe the impetus given by Dr. Arnold, who was a leader in reviving the humanistic tradition in its old breadth and depth. To be one of the boys in a school governed by one's father would have been difficult for the ordinary son of an ordinary father, and neither Arnold was ordinary; Dr. Arnold worried about Matthew, who was too gregarious and whose studies lacked fixity of purpose.[1] Apparently Matthew's way of establishing his own identity was the adoption of both the elegant attire and the airy flippancy of a man of the world, a pose which developed more fully at Oxford. Meanwhile, self-assertion could take more boyish form, as in the schoolroom incident, so often cited, of his last year at Rugby: having displeased Dr. Arnold, he was told to stand behind his father's chair, a vantage point from which he made faces at his classmates. Although he seemed to have no great scholastic zeal, indeed little zeal of any kind except for dress and fishing, he wrote a quantity of verse, and in 1840 he gained a Rugby prize for a longish and highly respectable poem, *Alaric at Rome*. In the same year the supposed idler won a classical scholarship to

[1] Norman Wymer, *Dr. Arnold of Rugby* (London, 1953), 186. *Cf.* Lord Coleridge, pp. 112–13 of his "Matthew Arnold," *The New Review*, 1889, No. 2 (111–24), No. 3 (217–32).

Balliol, which in 1841 was supplemented by an award from Rugby.

Arnold's residence at Balliol began with the autumn term of 1841. The Oxford Movement had reached one crisis with Tract 90 (February 1841) and was to reach another in 1845 when W. G. Ward and Newman seceded to Rome. The young Arnold was moved aesthetically (not otherwise, according to his brother) by Newman's preaching at St. Mary's—which, many years later in his lecture on Emerson (1883), he recalled in phrases of unwonted visionary glow; but the son of Dr. Arnold stood on guard against seduction by the siren voice (the theme, perhaps, of the early poem, *The Voice*). Initially, at least, he would talk of the disruptive effects of religious authoritarianism upon churches, nations, and families; he had, however, more fundamental and positive concerns, both religious and poetical. It is clear that his loss of orthodox religious faith, if not a painful experience, left a painful void. We know that he was strongly drawn to such emancipated idealists as George Sand, Carlyle, Emerson, and Goethe; and a conscious and earnest effort to find new standing-ground is suggested by his heavy philosophical reading in the 1840's (presumably the studies with which, he wrote to Clough in 1853, he had "choked" himself). While we have little direct knowledge of Arnold's early state of mind, we have a good deal about the racking anxieties of his closest friend.

Arthur Hugh Clough (1819–61) has long been recognized as the embodiment *par excellence* of the spiritual distresses of the age. In 1837 he had come from Rugby with a Balliol scholarship and he remained at Oxford for eleven years, more than a quarter of his short life. He was almost a foster son of Dr. Arnold (his family being in the United States), and to many people he has stood as the most unhappy case of Dr. Arnold's influence. His extreme intellectual, moral, and religious conscientiousness has been held to have blighted his dazzling promise and resulted in ineffectual drifting—though he did, after all, become a poet of distinctive individuality, very modern in his psychological probing and his skeptical, astringent irony, a poet more fully known and appreciated in our time than in his own. At Oxford one

compelling and disturbing influence was the intransigent Tractarian, W. G. Ward. Although Clough's most concrete difficulty
was to be with resubscription to the Thirty-Nine Articles (required for the M.A.), his skepticism (in the literal sense) had already taken in the whole of life. Inward turmoil, along with Oxford's dull repetition of reading he had done at Rugby and his
father's financial troubles, was evidently the main cause of his
getting only a Second Class—a ranking that bewildered and dis-
mayed his admiring contemporaries. But, after an unsuccessful
attempt at Balliol, in the spring of 1842 Clough was elected a
fellow of Oriel; his examination, by the way, was the last in
which Newman took part. Arnold's brother Tom, who came up
to University College in 1842, had a similarly disturbed if more
flexible religious conscience ("my misguided Relation," in Matthew's phrase); later he was twice converted to Roman Catholicism. Arnold's early poems, some of them written before he left
Oxford, make it clear that he had his own questionings, not so
much about the Thirty-Nine Articles or the Church of Rome but
—like Clough's—about the total and personal meaning of life.
This subterranean current, however, was quite unsuspected by
his intimates and even his family.

In the later recollections of the German scholar, F. Max
Müller, Arnold

was beautiful as a young man, strong and manly, yet full of dreams
and schemes. His Olympian manners began even at Oxford; there was
no harm in them, they were natural, not put on. The very sound of his
voice and the wave of his arm were Jovelike. He grappled with the
same problems as Clough, but they never got the better of him, or
rather he never got the worse of them.

Unlike the ascetic Clough, he—according to Tom—"read a little
with the reading men, hunted a little with the fast men, and
dressed a little with the dressy men." His buoyant lighthearted-
ness and genial charm made him highly popular, though his
friends could already feel something of that ironical aloofness
which protected his inward self and which in later years was to
infuriate many readers of his prose. His closest associates, along
with Clough, were Theodore Walrond, one of Clough's first pu-

pils, who later was Secretary to the Civil Service Commission, and Tom Arnold, who in 1847 emigrated to New Zealand in quest of an ideal society and, as we say nowadays, of his own identity. These four were a Rugbeian coterie who talked and walked and boated together ("I can talk tremendous," said Clough) and had Sunday breakfasts in Clough's rooms; on such occasions Clough may have relaxed his rule of leaving his rooms in their natural frigidity to discourage callers (and perhaps to save money). This quartet, and another close friend of Arnold's, John Duke Coleridge (who was to become Lord Chief Justice), belonged to the Decade, a small discussion club (like the Cambridge "Apostles") which during its limited life included—to anticipate their subsequent destinies—Arthur Stanley, pupil and biographer of Dr. Arnold, Dean of Westminster, a leading Broad Churchman, and the subject of Arnold's late elegy, *Westminster Abbey*; Benjamin Jowett, Balliol's most famous Master; R. W. Church, Dean of St. Paul's and historian of the Oxford Movement; J. C. Shairp, man of letters and Principal of United College, St. Andrews; Frederick Temple, contributor (like Jowett) to the notorious *Essays and Reviews* of 1860 and Archbishop of Canterbury; and other eminent figures.

For Arnold, the sophisticated worldling, academic obligations were not unduly heavy, and his insouciance could worry Clough. He was studious enough to be runner-up for a Latin scholarship (1842), but when in the summer of 1844, to cram for his final examinations, he repaired with Clough to Fox How, he could put aside work for walking and fishing. He got a Second Class in "Greats," as Clough had predicted he would (saying that it was above his deserts). Arnold had, however, won the Newdigate prize in 1843 with his poem *Cromwell*; and, while he was teaching briefly at Rugby (February–April, 1845), he was—like Clough and Dr. Arnold—elected to a fellowship at Oriel (March 28, 1845). This, according to Clough, pleased "the Venble Poet at Rydal, who had taken Matt under his special protection as a 2d classman." Arnold held the fellowship until his marriage in 1851.

He was required to spend a probationary year of residence at Oriel (probably from April 1845 till March 1846). Thereafter he enjoyed comparative freedom. In the summer he made a pilgrimage to George Sand in France. In 1876 he recorded her telling Renan of their one interview: "Je lui faisais l'effet d'un Milton jeune et voyageant" (Russell, 2, 151); and—though in 1859 he was disinclined to journey from Paris (quoting a Frenchman) "to see such a fat old Muse" (*ibid.*, 1, 123)—in later years he paid her full tribute. Another object of fervent admiration was the actress Élisa Félix Rachel, whom Arnold perhaps first saw in London in the summer of 1846; now, in Paris for six weeks (December 29–February 11, 1846–47), he "never missed one of her representations." When he came back to Oriel in February 1847, Clough reported to their friend Shairp:

Matt is full of Parisianism; theatres in general, and Rachel in special: he enters the room with a chanson of Beranger's on his lips—for the sake of French words almost conscious of tune: his carriage shows him in fancy parading the rue de Rivoli;—and his hair is guiltless of English scissors: he breakfasts at twelve, and never dines in Hall, and in the week or 8 days rather (for 2 Sundays must be included) he has been to Chapel *once*. (*Correspondence of Arthur Hugh Clough*, ed. F. L. Mulhauser, Oxford, 1957, 1, 178)

Arnold did not linger in the academic fold. In April 1847 he became private secretary to Lord Lansdowne, President of the Council in Lord John Russell's ministry and a strong admirer of Dr. Arnold. His removal to the great world of London and politics occasioned misgivings in Clough and his brother Tom, and perhaps in other friends and relations—though a few years later his mother at least was reassured by his wholly unspoiled family affection. Arnold held this post for four years, until April 1851. While his official work was insignificant, these were important years in his life and also in Clough's. The latter, because of his prolonged religious disquiet (which soon became avowed disbelief) and because of his leftist social ideas and general dissatisfaction with Oxford, gave up first his tutorship and then his fellowship (October 1848); he now renewed his efforts— with some practical suggestions from Arnold—to gain subsistence elsewhere. His first position (October 1849–December 1851), which ended with his forced resignation, was the headship of University Hall, a residence for students in the nonsectarian University of London; in 1850 the professorship of English was added. These two years of course brought Arnold and Clough together again. In November 1848 Clough had published his "Long-Vacation Pastoral," *The Bothie of Tober-na-Vuolich* (to use the later and familiar title), a more than delightful poem, which Arnold at this time strangely disliked. Clough's second volume, containing his earlier Oxford poems (and those of a mediocre friend), and Arnold's first came out in close succession, *Ambarvalia* in January 1849, *The Strayed Reveller* in February. These several volumes announced two important poets, though the very best work of both was just ahead of them.

Of their correspondence (1845–61) we have—except for one letter—only Arnold's side. His letters range from the impenetrable mystery of Shakespeare (the theme of his sonnet) to the *Bhagavad Gita*, from the Chartist demonstration of April 10, 1848, to the "enormous obverse" of the singer Jenny Lind. The most valuable parts—to be reviewed later—are Arnold's many, candid, and revealing comments on Clough's and his own poetry and poetic aims and his thoughts and feelings about the poetic life and life in general in "these . . . damned times." Comments on the French revolution of 1848 suggest the lifelong character of Arnold's liberalism: strong, rational, forward-looking conviction tinged or edged with skepticism about the cant of politics and progress. He praises the *"wide and deepspread intelligence"* that distinguishes France from the rest of Europe, although by midsummer of 1848 he was temporarily disenchanted. Carlyle's article on Louis Philippe elicits a tribute to a prophet whose influence Arnold and his generation had absorbed (and whose once "puissant voice" he recalled in his lecture on Emerson) but whom he was soon to class with "moral desperadoes" (Lowry, 72, 75, 111); we might remember Clough's saying, when he bade farewell to Emerson in 1848, that "Carlyle has led us all out into the desert, and he has left us there."

The chief personal experience of these years was Arnold's falling in love with "Marguerite" in Switzerland (1848–49) and then, during 1850, with a less mysterious young woman, Frances Lucy Wightman, daughter of Sir William Wightman, a judge of the Court of Queen's Bench. The enigma of Marguerite must be left for discussion of the poems. Lucy Wightman—who also received a poetical garland—was, before she became his wife, the determinant of Arnold's occupation for the next thirty-five years: her father would not permit an engagement with a young man whose livelihood was so scanty and uncertain, and, thanks mainly to Lord Lansdowne, Arnold's way was cleared by his appointment to an inspectorship of schools (April 15, 1851). The pair were married on June 10. In the early autumn they had a delayed honeymoon tour in France, Italy, and Switzerland; it included a visit to the Grande Chartreuse. In 1851 Arnold said to an Oxford friend: "You'll like my Lucy; she has all my sweetness and none of my airs." To Clough, who in these unhappy London years had been breakfasting with Arnold twice a week, the prospective bride appeared as "a sort of natural enemy." To Tom Arnold in the Antipodes he described her as

small with aquiline nose, and very pleasing eyes, fair in complexion —I have only seen her, however, in her bonnet. I think she will suit well enough; she seems amiable, has seen lots of company and can't be stupid.

Tom remarked that "It is very difficult to fancy the 'Emperor' married!" (*Correspondence of . . . Clough*, 1, 290).

In October Arnold entered upon what was to be a busy, migratory, and wearing life. To supplement his salary, he managed for a time to attend as Marshal upon Judge Wightman when he went on circuit. In the earlier years Mrs. Arnold lived with her parents or traveled with her husband or joined him at one of his stopping-places or for holidays. In a speech on his retirement in 1886 Arnold recalled their early "wandering life"; "We had no home; one of our children was born in a lodging at Derby, with a workhouse, if I recollect right, behind and a penitentiary in front" (Neiman, 308). In February 1858, when he took a small house in London, Arnold wrote that "it will be something to unpack one's portmanteau for the first time since I was married, now nearly seven years ago" (Russell, 1, 71). In 1866 they moved to Dorking and in 1868 to Harrow; from 1873 until Arnold's death they lived at Cobham in Surrey, not far from Laleham.

Although his immediate motive in seeking an inspectorship was matrimonial bread and butter, in his later literary, social, and religious criticism Arnold was, in the fullest sense of the words, a very conscious educator, and his official work was the direct and practical beginning of the larger effort. On October 15, 1851, a few days after he commenced his duties (and eighteen years before *Culture and Anarchy*), he wrote to his wife (Russell, 1, 20):

I think I shall get interested in the schools after a little time; their effects on the children are so immense, and their future effects in civilising the next generation of the lower classes, who, as things are going, will have most of the political power of the country in their hands, may be so important. It is really a fine sight in Manchester to see the anxiety felt about them, and the time and money the heads of their cotton-manufacturing population are willing to give to them. In arithmetic, geography, and history the excellence of the schools I have seen is quite wonderful, and almost all the children have an equal amount of information; it is not confined, as in schools of the richer classes, to the one or two cleverest boys.

In spite of incessant traveling, interviews, oral examinations, the reading of examination papers, and writing of reports, and much discouraging experience, Arnold put his heart and his mind into his work, and he had his moments of feeling rewarded. One of his more cheerful comments was made in 1863: "All this is a busy life, but I am very well, and enjoy it. Inspecting is a *little* too much as the business half of one's life in contradistinction to the inward and spiritual half of it, or I should be quite satisfied" (Russell, 1, 223). He could finish a long day with a hundred lines of the *Odyssey* or another classic "to keep myself from putrefaction."

Arnold's educational activity was not limited to the daily grind. In 1862 he published in *Fraser's Magazine* a vigorous attack on the new scheme of the Vice-President of the Committee of Council on Education, Robert Lowe, for allocating government grants on the basis of "payment by results"; but he was not made to suffer for his boldness. As his statesmanlike competence was increasingly recognized, Arnold was sent abroad on educational missions which led to the publication of substantial reports; these combined ideas with masses of concrete detail. The first visit (March–August 1859) yielded *The Popular Education of France* (1861) and *A French Eton* (1864), the second (April–November 1865) *Schools and Universities on the Continent* (1868), his longest book. The third and fourth official visits were made in 1885 and 1886. The preface to the first of these reports was reprinted as *Democracy* in Arnold's *Mixed Essays* (1879), which included *Porro Unum Est Necessarium* (1878), on the need of public secondary schools. A similar plea was made in *Ecce, Convertimur ad Gentes* (1879), an address to the Ipswich Working Men's College.

However much he may have chafed against prolonged bondage and drudgery, Arnold made little complaint in his letters. Writing to his wife from Cambridge in July 1863, he remarked: "I have made up my mind that I should like the post of Master of Trinity"; whether or not this was only a momentary and jesting fancy, we may wish it had been gratified. In the later 1860's Arnold applied for three posts less arduous or better paid than his own: a Charity Commissionership, the librarianship of the House of Commons, and a Commissionership under the Endowed Schools Act (this the work of his brother-in-law, W. E. Forster); all three applications were unsuccessful, the first two at least for reasons unconnected with Arnold, the third obstructed by Gladstone.

In December 1863 the sudden death of Arnold's father-in-law, followed in a fortnight by the likewise sudden death of Thackeray (whom he did not "thoroughly" like as a man and did not regard as "a great writer"), moved him to take stock of himself on his birthday (Russell, 1, 247–48):

To-day I am forty-one, the middle of life, in any case, and for me, perhaps, much more than the middle. I have ripened, and am ripening so slowly that I should be glad of as much time as possible, yet I can feel, I rejoice to say, an inward spring which seems more and more to gain strength, and to promise to resist outward shocks, if they must come, however rough. But of this inward spring one must not talk, for it does not like being talked about, and threatens to depart if one will not leave it in mystery.

In June 1870 Arnold could tell his mother that he is "glad to find—what I find more and more—that I *have* influence." Six months later he reported another side of the picture (Russell, 2, 54):

My interview with the Income Tax Commissioners at Edgware the other day, who had assessed my profits at £1000 a year, on the plea that I was a most distinguished literary man, my works were mentioned everywhere and must have a wide circulation, would have amused you. "You see before you, gentlemen," I said, "what you have often heard of, *an unpopular author.* . . ." The assessment was finally cut down to £200 a year, and I told them I should have to write more articles to prevent my being a loser by submitting to even that assessment, upon which the Chairman politely said, "Then the public will have reason to be much obliged to us."

Arnold's later life—apart from his official labors, travels, social engagements, and domestic events—is mainly a record of his publications and growing fame. His second volume, *Empedocles on Etna, and Other Poems* (1852) he withdrew, for the reasons explained in the Preface to *Poems: A New Edition* (1853), reasons which attest the rigor of his artistic and ethical conscience and his embracing of a classical view of poetry signalized by *Sohrab and Rustum.* There followed *Poems: Second Series* (1854: dated 1855), which included Arnold's second epic narrative, *Balder Dead; Merope* (1857: dated 1858), that dubious drama on the Greek model; and *New Poems* (1867), in which Arnold restored his chief work, *Empedocles,* and added *Thyrsis* and other pieces. But by this time he had for a decade given himself mainly to prose (though he cherished the hope of returning to poetry). Nearly all his best poems had—like Clough's—been born of inward conflict and distress, and that pressure had been largely if not wholly surmounted. The introspective and troubled poet had achieved a working philosophy, a positive and increasingly religious stability and direction, which enabled him to set about the important task of stirring and enlightening his inert or wrongheaded countrymen on several fronts.

Circumstances also combined to push him into prose: his

election in May 1857 as Professor of Poetry at Oxford (and re-election in 1862); the urge to write a pamphlet, *England and the Italian Question* (1859); and his first educational mission to the Continent and subsequent report (1859–61). Arnold's best-known early prose was the fruit of the Oxford post. He very sensibly abandoned the tradition of lecturing in Latin and thereby enlarged the number of his auditors and, far more, of his readers. His inaugural discourse, *On the Modern Element in Literature*, might be called both a sequel to the Preface of 1853 and a preface to all his later writings, since it was an exposition of the critical spirit of genuine, timeless classicism. Of the professorial lectures of 1858 and 1859 very little is known. A series of three lectures (1860–61) made up *On Translating Homer* (published in 1861); in 1861 came a fourth (published in 1862), a more or less urbane reply to Francis Newman's defense of his uncouth version of Homer, which Arnold had tossed and gored. *Essays in Criticism* (1865) contained, along with a notable preface, lectures and studies of 1862–64 (one was added in 1875). The collection set a new model for English criticism because of its European and chronological range and especially because of its method and its seminal ideas, which remain active in modern minds. One indication of the fame Arnold had achieved by 1863 is the fact that his essay on Marcus Aurelius was announced on placards all over London and by a sandwich-man parading Regent Street (Russell, 1, 237)—a phenomenon highly creditable to Victorian culture, for all its Philistinism, and inconceivable nowadays. Besides the *Homer*, Arnold delivered in 1865–66 another consecutive series of lectures (published in 1867), this time on Celtic literature, a subject in which he was far less at home; but he did much to stir public interest and his critical intuitions—which were to affect the Irish renaissance—retain some general and particular value.

On June 7, 1867, Arnold gave his last professorial lecture, *Culture and its Enemies*; one admiring auditor, a Mrs. Drummond, sent him a keg of whiskey. The theme and title led on to his central work in political and social criticism, *Culture and Anarchy* (1869). In 1867 the second Reform Act (Disraeli's) had greatly enlarged popular power and responsibility and hence, as Arnold had long before anticipated, the need for wider and better education for the middle and lower classes. The breadth and depth of meaning that he gave to "culture" was made plain to all who were not prejudiced or perverse; but many people were, even some who should have known better, and Arnold was quickly tagged as a dilettantish dispenser of literary pills for the cure of serious diseases in the body of society. *Culture and Anarchy* was in fact a penetrating diagnosis of fundamental defects in the English mentality and outlook and a prescription for long-range remedies. It was also the first sustained display of Arnold's genius for phrase-making, a quality present even in his poems and far more in his modern, half-journalistic prose. Many of his phrases, such as the "Sweetness and Light" taken over from Swift, have been doing duty ever since, though generally vulgarized and cheapened. In 1870, when Arnold was given an honorary D.C.L. at Oxford, Lord Salisbury, the Chancellor, said that he should have addressed the recipient as *Vir dulcissime et lucidissime*. During 1866–70 Arnold's satirical and ironical wit had still livelier expression in the letters to the *Pall Mall Gazette* which became *Friendship's Garland* (1871), a half-comic, half-serious parallel or pendant to *Culture and Anarchy*.

The son of Dr. Arnold had long been personally and deeply concerned with the problem of religion in the modern world, as his poems so insistently show. Continuing concern inspired various discourses on religious and philosophic spirits from Marcus Aurelius to Spinoza, from St. Francis and Dante to Joubert and the Guérins, and it runs through *Culture and Anarchy*. As Arnold achieved religious standing ground for himself, he felt strongly moved to share it with others (an impulse he praised in his father), to salvage what was precious and irreplaceable before that was swept away along with what could not and should not be retained. To this effort he gave a series of books, *St. Paul and Protestantism* (1870), the central *Literature and Dogma* (1873), *God and the Bible* (1875), and *Last Essays on Church and Religion* (1877). *Literature and Dogma* sold far more widely, in various editions, than any other book of Arnold's; it met with both favor and, on different levels, hostility, from shocked fundamentalism up to sophisticated complaints against Arnold's reducing religion to "morality touched with emotion" and his replacing what had been religious realities with nebulous ideas and phrases. Modern readers and critics have been given to dismissing these books as a waste of effort or worse, but in their own age and later a multitude of people were soberly grateful for Arnold's endeavor to "guard the fire within" from being smothered by what now seemed impossible beliefs.

In the next few years Arnold's lectures and essays were devoted mainly to politics and literature. Two collections were *Mixed Essays* (1879) and *Irish Essays and Others* (1882). Among the more important things of this period were *Equality* (1878), *Ecce, Convertimur ad Gentes* (1879), an address which also stressed social reform, and *The Future of Liberalism* (1880); *The Study of Poetry* and essays on Gray and Keats, Wordsworth and Byron (written for anthologies), which, with pieces on Milton, Shelley, Amiel, and Tolstoy, were collected in the second series of *Essays in Criticism*, published posthumously in 1888. *Literature and Science*, the Rede lecture at Cambridge (1882), Arnold was to use in America. He twice declined renomination for the Oxford Professorship of Poetry (1877, 1885); the second invitation to stand was supported by two memorials, one from heads of colleges and tutors, the other from four hundred undergraduates. In 1882 the author of *Literature and Dogma* felt that he would receive no more official advancement from Gladstone and that he had better think of retiring; but in 1883, to his surprise, Gladstone offered him a Civil List pension of £250 "as a public recognition of service to the poetry and literature of England," an offer which, after some thought, the not overprosperous author accepted. Arnold had long been a prominent figure in the intellectual, political, and social world of London, the world of the higher ranks of the establishment, but he had remained a lowly inspector of schools. He revealed perhaps only one trace of something like resentment: in the letter to John Morley just cited (October 24, 1882), about retirement, Gladstone, and *Literature and Dogma*, Arnold said: ". . . my life is drawing to an end, and I have no wish to execute the

Dance of Death in an elementary school." In 1884 he was made Chief Inspector.

Arnold had postponed retirement until 1886, and he was apparently granted leave of absence for a tour in the United States. He sailed in October 1883, with his wife, their daughter Lucy, and the completed manuscripts of two lectures, *Numbers: or The Majority and the Remnant* and a slightly revised version of *Literature and Science* (which proved to be in special demand); a third, on Emerson, Arnold worked at on the ship and in New York. The American tour gave birth to countless anecdotes, true and false, but mostly amusing; some publicized items were malicious inventions. Reporters of course played up any hint of Arnold's levity of speech or oddity of appearance (notably a monocle). His first remark—made to a fellow passenger when their ship was off Staten Island—got into the newspapers and was not auspicious: "Just like Richmond, and not a single Mohican running about!" The first lecture, in New York, was disastrous because of the lecturer's not being audible (which he thought exaggerated). General Grant's comment to his wife is well known: that, since they had paid to see the British lion and could not hear him roar, they had better go home. In Boston a professor of elocution gave Arnold a couple of lessons and cured him of dropping his voice at the end of a sentence. Two brief Bostonian items (derived from Professor Samuel E. Morison) may be added: being driven about by President Eliot to view the colors of autumn foliage, Arnold asked "Do your trees have a disease?"; and, at table, opening a sort of fishcake, he exclaimed, "I say, something has died in my bun." A Detroit newspaper compared him, when he stooped to look at his manuscript, to "an elderly bird pecking at grapes on a trellis." One man affirmed to a bishop that "Denver was not ripe for Mr. Arnold." A former president of Indiana University, Dr. William L. Bryan, told me that he, the head of an undergraduate committee, had wanted to bring Arnold to the Indiana campus, but his fee was $150 and the majority feared a deficit. The story of Arnold's first encounter with pancakes seems to be attached to as many places as claimed the birth of Homer. One tale, heard from a professor at Oberlin College, it may be hoped is authentic: after a reception and before his lecture there Arnold was asked by his hostess, the president's wife, what he would like, and he said "Whiskey"; whereupon, after anxious consultation with her husband (these were days of academic dryness), she appeared at her guest's door with a tray, a bottle, and a spoon.[2]

Although Arnold's writings had contained uningratiating references to American as well as English vulgarity (which were now confirmed), he was generally and cordially welcomed, at least by the cultivated; he had good audiences, he was interested in people and new scenes, and in the main, with all the wear-and-tear of travel and being always on exhibit, he enjoyed himself. The "Matthew Arnold troupe" (the label printed on railway tickets) covered a good deal of ground—less in the South than Arnold wished. He was happy to find that his books, notably *Literature and Dogma*, were well known and valued, and was probably happier still to find that his father's memory was a "living power" at Dartmouth College and throughout New England. Lucy, by the way, had spent most of the time with friends in New York and became engaged to Frederick W. Whitridge. The Arnolds returned to England in March 1884, with about $6000, then a substantial sum—which was not, as we might have expected, to be stored against old age, but to repay a loan incurred for their son Richard's Oxford debts. The three lectures were published in 1885 as *Discourses in America*. According to George Russell (who later edited his letters), Arnold said that this was the volume of his prose by which he wished chiefly to be remembered.

In the summer of 1886 Arnold made another visit to the United States, to join his wife in visiting their married daughter. Since 1885, at least, he had suffered from heart trouble, and—like his father and grandfather—he died suddenly, on April 15, 1888. He and his wife had gone to Liverpool to meet the ship that was

---

[2] My hope of launching this tale in print has just been foiled by Professor Super, in the opening of his substantial lectures, *The Time-Spirit of Matthew Arnold* (Ann Arbor, 1970).

The purpose of the American tour, referred to in the next paragraph of the text, was made clear by R. L. Lowe (*American Literature* 23, 1951–52, 250–52, and 30, 1958–59, 530–33) and R. L. Brooks (*ibid.*, 31, 1959–60, 336–38).

bringing Lucy and their son Richard and his wife from New York.[3] He was nearly four months past sixty-five. He was buried at Laleham, beside his three sons who had died young.

A paragraph or two may round out the family history. Arnold's admiration and reverence for his father—distilled in *Rugby Chapel*—grew deeper with his own efforts to preach a liberal Christianity (though of course he went well beyond Dr. Arnold's limits). For his mother he not only retained grateful affection, expressed or implied in many letters, but was especially moved by the spirit that showed itself in a letter she sent him after reading *Literature and Dogma*. On her death in 1873 he wrote to his friend Lady de Rothschild: "I can think of no woman in the prime of life, brought up and surrounded as my mother was, and with my mother's sincere personal convictions, who could have written it; and in a woman past eighty it was something astonishing" (Russell, 2, 124–25). Arnold was attached to all his brothers and sisters, but his life long favorite seems to have been his slightly older sister Jane (1821–99), whom we meet in his letters as "K" and as "Fausta" in *Resignation*; in 1850 she had married W. E. Forster, a statesman of ability and character whom Arnold admired and who died in 1886. His brother Tom, whose early career was touched upon above, wound up as Professor of English at University College, Dublin, where he had Gerard Manley Hopkins as a classical colleague: he lived until 1900. Arnold's brother William died at Gibraltar in 1859 at the age of thirty-one; he was on his way home on leave after short but valuable service in establishing native education in the Punjab. He was memorialized in two poems, *Stanzas from Carnac* and *A Southern Night*. The sister and

[3] The legendary circumstances of his death, often repeated in slightly variant forms, were reexamined in the light of contemporary evidence by R. H. Ronson, J. P. Curgenven, K. Allott, and S. Jeffery in the *Times Literary Supplement* (October 10, 17, 24, 1968). The main facts seem to be as follows. Arnold and his brother-in-law and Liverpool host, T. W. Cropper, set off for an evening walk and—apparently recalling easy feats of his youth—Arnold jumped over a low railing near the house (he did not at first succeed). The next day he and Mrs. Arnold walked to a tram stop to go to the docks; just as they reached the stop, he collapsed and died instantly. This version was confirmed by the evidence given by W. S. Peterson (*ibid.*, August 28, 1969).

the two brothers combined much of their father's earnestness with attractive independence of their own. William's novel, *Oakfield* (1853), might be called an ancestor of *A Passage to India.*

Arnold and his wife (who died in 1901) remained devoted to each other and to their children. In 1866 he wrote to his mother: "This is our wedding day. We have been fifteen years married, and it seems as if it was only last week." They had six children, three less than Arnold's parents but enough to make a stirring household and to require all the money the father could earn. There were three sons (born in 1852, 1853, and 1855), two daughters (1859, 1861), and another son (1866). Like his own father, Arnold delighted in playing with his children. But three of the sons died early: Basil, the youngest, and the delicate Thomas, the eldest, in 1868; the second son, Trevenen William, known in the family as Budge, in 1872, at the age of eighteen. Of this last loss Arnold's old friend, J. D. Coleridge, wrote to his father:

I enclose you dear Matt's letter. . . . It is a most bitter and heavy blow. Forster told me he was terribly cut up by it, but that his behaviour was admirable. He had to be at an examination of pupil-teachers, and Mr. Forster found him there with his poor eyes full of tears, yet keeping order and doing his duty till he could be relieved.

We have Arnold's own letters about the deaths of the three boys (Russell, 1, 443–46, 464–66, 2, 92–95). The only surviving son, Richard (the "Dicky" of affectionate references in the letters), who attended Harrow and Oxford, became something of a problem, as we noted in regard to the proceeds of Arnold's American tour; Richard married in Australia, returned to England to become a factory inspector, and died in 1908. The latest survivors of the immediate Arnold family were Lucy (Mrs. Whitridge, mother of Professor Arnold Whitridge), who died in February 1934, and her sister, Viscountess Sandhurst, who died in December of the same year.

# II : *Poetry*

◊❀◊❀◊❀◊❀◊❀◊❀◊❀◊❀◊❀◊❀◊❀◊❀◊❀◊❀◊❀◊❀◊❀◊❀◊❀◊❀◊❀◊❀

## 1. *Arnold's Early Critical Theories*

MOST OF Arnold's important poems were written in the decade 1843–53 and published in volumes of 1849–54. The
best introduction to them is provided by his letters to his fellow
poet and closest friend, Arthur Hugh Clough. These informal
letters give us the views of the world held by a young man who
has lately entered it and of the kind of poetry that should or can
be written in such a world. We have only Arnold's side of the
correspondence, but we can infer Clough's responses from that
and from Clough's other writings, especially his rather sour review of Arnold's poems in the *North American Review* of 1853.
The best work of both thoughtful poets grew out of their own
experience, mainly inward; in Clough's case this was exacer-
bated by the atmosphere of Oxford and London University.

Clough would have qualified or perhaps denied what may be
called Arnold's major negative premise, a recurrent one (February 1849: Lowry, 99):

Reflect too, as I cannot but do here more and more, in spite of all
the nonsense some people talk, how deeply *unpoetical* the age and
all one's surroundings are. Not unprofound, not ungrand, not
unmoving:—but *unpoetical*.

A little later Arnold wrote (September 23: Lowry, 111):

My dearest Clough these are damned times—everything is against
one—the height to which knowledge is come, the spread of luxury,

our physical enervation, the absence of great *natures,* the unavoidable contact with millions of small ones, newspapers, cities, light profligate friends, moral desperadoes like Carlyle, our own selves, and the sickening consciousness of our difficulties. . . .

In January 1851, writing from London to his sister Jane, Arnold gives a picture of himself which does not suggest a man of twenty-eight who is secretary to a cabinet minister (Russell, 1, 18):

I read his [Goethe's] letters, Bacon, Pindar, Sophocles, Milton, Th. à Kempis, and Ecclesiasticus, and retire more and more from the modern world and modern literature, which is all only what has been before and what will be again, and not bracing or edifying in the least.

Two years later he ejaculates to Clough: "Only let us pray all the time—God keep us both from aridity! *Arid*—that is what the times are" (Lowry, 131). The word was to be repeated in the little poem *The Progress of Poesy* (1864-67?).

A major positive premise is that poetry has two offices,

one to add to one's store of thoughts and feelings—another to compose and elevate the mind by a sustained tone, numerous allusions, and a grand style. What other process is Milton's than this last, in Comus for instance. There is no fruitful analysis of character: but a great effect is produced. What is Keats? A style and form seeker, and this with an impetuosity that heightens the effect of his style almost painfully. (*c.* March 1, 1849: Lowry, 100–01)

The great thing, even in Sophocles, is

the grand moral effects produced by *style.* For the style is the expression of the nobility of the poet's character, as the matter is the expression of the richness of his mind: but on men character produces as great an effect as mind.

Although the complexity of modern thought and feeling now makes heavier demands upon poets, as compared with the ancients or with Shakespeare and Milton, Arnold says, like T. S. Eliot—and this is his main quarrel with Clough—that it is not a poet's business to *think,* to be a philosopher: "For in a *man* style is the saying in the best way *what you have to say.* The *what you have to say* depends on your age." (1847–48: Lowry, 65)

Arnold had a jaundiced view of Clough's relatively light-hearted *Bothie* (Lowry, 95, 147), though in his lectures *On Translating Homer* (1861) he was to praise its Homeric rapidity and plain directness of style. In Clough's more fully serious Oxford poems Arnold found less to praise than to complain of, and he could not respond to such an ironic picture of indecisiveness as *Amours de Voyage* (written in 1849). While he acknowledges the invigorating effect of Clough's sincere effort "to get breast to breast with reality" (July 20, 1848: Lowry, 86), Arnold protests against his excessive anxiety to find answers to ultimate questions:

Yet to *solve* the Universe as you try to do is as irritating as Tennyson's dawdling with its painted shell is fatiguing to me to witness. . . . (December 1847: Lowry, 63)

A growing sense of the deficiency of the *beautiful* in your poems, and of this alone being properly *poetical* as distinguished from rhetorical, devotional or metaphysical, made me speak as I did. But your line is a line. . . . I doubt your being an *artist*. . . . (*c.* February 24, 1848: Lowry, 66)

. . . but you know you are a mere d—d depth hunter in poetry. . . . (May 24, 1848: Lowry, 81)

Naturalness, "i.e.—an absolute propriety—of form" is "the sole *necessary* of Poetry as such: whereas the greatest wealth and depth of matter is merely a superfluity in the Poet *as such*" (February 1849: Lowry, 98–99); and Arnold quotes his own *Resignation* (line 214): "Not deep the poet sees, but wide." Hence Clough's overintellectual poems, not attaining "the *beautiful*," excite "curiosity and reflexion" instead of giving "pleasure."

You certainly do not seem to me sufficiently to desire and earnestly strive towards—assured knowledge—activity—happiness. You are too content to *fluctuate*—to be ever learning, never coming to the knowledge of the truth. This is why, with you, I feel it necessary to stiffen myself—and hold fast my rudder.

My poems, however, viewed *absolutely*, are certainly little or nothing. (November 30, 1853: Lowry, 146)

A year before these last remarks Arnold had moved so far from his earlier emphasis on style that he anticipated in part his Preface of 1853 and *The Study of Poetry* of 1880. After deploring Keats's and Shelley's revival of the Elizabethans' prodigality of sensuous images, he declared:

. . . modern poetry can only subsist by its *contents*: by becoming a complete magister vitae as the poetry of the ancients did: by including, as theirs did, religion with poetry, instead of existing as poetry only, and leaving religious wants to be supplied by the Christian religion, as a power existing independent of the poetical power. But the language, style and general proceedings of a poetry which has such an immense task to perform, must be very plain direct and severe: and it must not lose itself in parts and episodes and ornamental work, but must press forwards to the whole. (October 28, 1852: Lowry, 124)

A. H. Warren affirms that "this quasi-religious function of poetry . . . ultimately determines all the elements of Arnold's poetics"; but "all" seems excessive, in view of Arnold's late as well as early insistence on artistic power. Indeed Warren himself, speaking of the Preface, says that "Arnold is virtually the only critic in the Early Victorian period who was seriously concerned with the problem of form in poetry, and who gave anything like an adequate weight to it in his theory."[1]

Clearly Arnold's theorizing in these years is not consistent in itself, in its relation to his own poetry, or in its censures of Clough's. At first style is the one thing needful; later it is contents. Although Arnold exalts style and form and charges Clough with an excess of thought and lack of beauty, he condemns Keats as "A style and form seeker" and Keats and Shelley together for reviving Elizabethan richness; yet throughout his poetical life Arnold himself was not always "plain direct and severe" but could indulge in sensuous imagery—sometimes with Keatsian echoes—that was not strictly functional. Further, he sees Keats, with a very high gift, and Browning, with a moderate one, as alike achieving only "a confused multitudinousness" (1848–49?: Lowry, 97):

[1] Alba H. Warren, *English Poetic Theory 1825–1865* (Princeton: Princeton University Press, 1950), 160, 169.

They will not be patient neither understand that they must begin with an Idea of the world in order not to be prevailed over by the world's multitudinousness: or if they cannot get that, at least with isolated ideas: and all other things shall (perhaps) be added unto them.

Thus Arnold criticizes Clough for grappling with philosophical ideas and Keats and Browning for not doing so. But all these opinions are understandable, and even radical changes of attitude and emphasis are natural enough in the course of a young poet's evolution. And in part he is, as critics observe, reprobating in Clough weaknesses he finds in himself.

Walter Houghton[2] in particular has defined the nature of the gap in understanding and appreciation that separated the two young poets, in spite of their warm affection and mutual respect and dependence. Houghton sees Clough as a subtle continuator of Augustan satire, a realistic, ironic analyst of his own and the contemporary mind, an avant-garde modernist in aims, material, and technique, whereas Arnold is in theory a half-romantic, half-classical upholder of poetry that is, in the conventional sense, poetical, beautiful, and edifying. But in exalting the undervalued Clough this contrast seems less than fair to Arnold, at least if we modify his theory by appeal to his practice.

It is true that Arnold was so much in the Romantic tradition that, although he was to become a master of irony in prose, he rarely approached it in verse. However, a good deal of his disquiet—and of his poetical force—came from his recognition that the Romantic sensibility and vision, whatever his own instinctive affinities, were no longer adequate, and he was preoccupied with finding a modern equivalent. Also, he was not in technique a mere conformist. *Sohrab and Rustum* was not the first model he offered in opposition to contemporary poetry. After the publication of his first volume he wrote to his sister Jane (Whitridge, 15–16):

At Oxford particularly many complain that the subjects treated do not interest them. But as I feel rather as a reformer in poetical matters, I am glad of this opposition. If I have health & opportunity to go

[2] *The Poetry of Clough: An Essay in Revaluation* (New Haven and London, 1963), 5 f.

on, I will shake the present methods until they go down, see if I don't. More and more I feel bent against the modern English habit (too much encouraged by Wordsworth) of using poetry as a channel for thinking aloud, instead of making anything.

While many of Arnold's poems, however well shaped and phrased, may approach "thinking aloud," a considerable number, beginning with *The Strayed Reveller*, are decidedly made objects of marked originality.

Secondly, the most commonplace fact about Arnold's poetry is that he was an impressive analyst of his own and the modern mind, in that respect admittedly the most significant of Victorian poets. In 1852 he could say of his own work what he had said against Clough's (Lowry, 126):

As for my poems they have weight, I think, but little or no charm. . . . But woe was upon me if I analysed not my situation: and Werter[,] Réné[,] and such like[,] none of them analyse the modern situation in its true *blankness* and *barrenness,* and *unpoetrylessness.*

Moreover, if Arnold's explorations of modern spiritual and ethical problems are less subtle than Clough's (which is perhaps a question), they are less special, more readily available to the generality of readers. Arnold tries to see the modern situation in a large perspective and normally avoids Clough's novelistic contemporaneity and topicality. At one moment in 1848, at Oxford, Arnold reacted strongly against local enthusiasm for Clough's new *Bothie,* not from jealousy but because he could not allow himself to

be sucked for an hour even into the Time Stream in which they and he [Clough] plunge and bellow. I became calm in spirit, but uncompromising, almost stern. More English than European, I said finally, more American than English: and took up Obermann, and refuged myself with him in his forest against your [Clough's] Zeit Geist. (Lowry, 95)

Later, reassuring Clough—now in America—of his unalterable attachment, Arnold apologized for this moment of hostility as a flash in the pan (February 12, 1853: Lowry, 129); but he had been defending his own poetic sanctuary.

It was in keeping with his general attitude that Arnold's most elaborate analysis of his own and the modern malaise should have as its protagonist a Greek philosopher of the fifth century B.C. What concerns us at this point is the famous Preface to Arnold's *Poems* of 1853 in which he explained the reasons for his withdrawing the poem published in 1852 (an act which attests the sacrificial severity of his artistic and ethical conscience, even though in 1867, at Browning's solicitation, he restored it to its place). Those reasons broaden into a challenge to current taste, particularly the demand that modern poets should deal with modern subjects and leave "the exhausted past." Arnold alludes to some such voices, and there were many others, in and outside his own circle: for example, John Sterling, in a review of Tennyson which was largely a modernist plea (*Quarterly Review*, 1842); Mrs. Browning (though she was a fervent Hellenist); reviews of Arnold's poems by Charles Kingsley (1849) and, in 1853–54, by his friends Clough (who favored the modernism of the "Spasmodic" poet Alexander Smith over the cultivated Arnold's classical and Oriental themes), J. D. Coleridge, and J. A. Froude; his friends J. C. Shairp and Edward Quillinan, Wordsworth's son-in-law, in letters; and the *Economist* (13, 1855, 148), which bluntly denounced Arnold's "stories of gods, charms, and old sayings" as poetry "worse than meaningless and worthless; it is false and disgusting."

The Preface, Arnold's first published piece of prose (and one that gave him trouble), was a manifesto of the modern classicism he had now arrived at; we have seen hints, and more than hints, of such an attitude in his letters to Clough. His intention in *Empedocles*, he said, was "to delineate the feelings of one of the last of the Greek religious philosophers," who has lived into the uncongenial age of the Sophists. His predicament is a fitting theme for modern poetry because in him "the dialogue of the mind with itself has commenced; modern problems have presented themselves; we hear already the doubts, we witness the discouragement, of Hamlet and of Faust." But, however interesting a subject, its poetical treatment should "inspirit and rejoice the reader" (here Arnold, while citing Hesiod and Schiller, is nearer contemporary orthodoxy than he is in regard to ancient

vehicles), and *Empedocles* does not yield the true tragic enjoy-
ment because the situation is one of "those in which the suffering finds no vent in action; in which a continuous state of
mental distress is prolonged, unrelieved by incident, hope, or resistance; in which there is everything to be endured, nothing to
be done"; these situations "are painful, not tragic."

Against the demand for fresh modern subjects, individual responses to life, Arnold argues that the eternal subjects of poetry
are human actions, those "which most powerfully appeal to the
great primary human affections: to those elementary feelings
which subsist permanently in the race, and which are independent of time." "The description," says A. H. Warren, "suggests
Aristotle's universals in Wordsworthian phrase." The date of an
action, ancient or modern, has nothing to do with its fitness for
poetry. The stories of Achilles, Prometheus, Clytemnestra, and
Dido have far stronger and more enduring interest than such inventions of Romantic subjectivity as Goethe's *Hermann and
Dorothea*, Byron's *Childe Harold*, Lamartine's *Jocelyn*, and
Wordsworth's *Excursion*. These "leave the reader cold," whereas
in the last books of the *Iliad*, in the *Oresteia*, and the episode of
Dido "the action is greater, the personages nobler, the situations
more intense: and this is the true basis of the interest in a poetical work, and this alone." It is clear enough throughout that the
Aristotelian Arnold is discussing epic and drama, that he is not—
as he acknowledged in a short preface to his *Poems* of 1854—
applying his principles to lyric poetry.

The rest of the Preface sets classical—and Goethean—concern with the structure of a whole against modern concern with
unintegrated parts, incidental beauties. Even Shakespeare has
been a dubious influence because, while he chose great actions
and created great situations and characters, his gift of expression
—sometimes tortured expression—could run away with him.
(Arnold remarked to Clough, on September 6, 1853: "Certainly
Goethe had all the *negative* recommendations for a perfect artist, but he wanted the *positive*—Shakespeare had the positive
and wanted the negative.") A later example is Keats's *Isabella*.
This poem, Arnold finds it possible to say, "contains, perhaps, a
greater number of happy single expressions which one could

quote than all the extant tragedies of Sophocles," but the action, excellent in itself, is so feebly conceived and constructed that its effect "is absolutely null." It is from the ancients that the modern writer can best learn "three things which it is vitally important for him to know:—the all-importance of the choice of a subject; the necessity of accurate construction; and the subordinate character of expression." "As he penetrates into the spirit of the great classical works, as he becomes gradually aware of their intense significance, their noble simplicity, and their calm pathos, he will be convinced that it is this effect, unity and profoundness of moral impression, at which the ancient poets aimed"; and, if he learns such lessons, he will "escape the danger of producing poetical works conceived in the spirit of the passing time . . ."—a danger not escaped by Clough. Along with poets, men in general who live with the ancients tend to acquire a respect for facts, a steadiness of judgment, a perspective, which preserve them from extreme views, optimistic or pessimistic, of their own age.

Arnold ends with modest deprecation of his poems—which now in 1853 include *Sohrab and Rustum* in place of *Empedocles* —as representing only a "sincere endeavour to learn and practise, amid the bewildering confusion of our times, what is sound and true in poetical art," an endeavor in which he finds "the only sure guidance, the only solid footing, among the ancients."

This Preface was an assertion of classical principles aimed at critics, readers, and poets committed to the kind of Romantic poetry represented by Keats and, by implication, Tennyson and the new meteor, Alexander Smith; more immediately, of course, it was a defense of the conception of poetry implicit in *Sohrab and Rustum.* (Most of T. S. Eliot's earlier criticism had parallel purposes.) At the same time, however, Arnold's strictures upon *Empedocles* might be applied to the similar sins in his shorter poems, since they too displayed (not without resistance and gleams of hope) a state of prolonged "mental distress . . . in which there is everything to be endured, nothing to be done." His critical admissions and affirmations grew primarily out of his independent and evolving thought (which we have followed in outline), but his arrival at such a positive creed may have been somewhat quickened by reviewers' complaints about his depressing and debilitating skepticism as well as his antique themes' remoteness from actual life.

It has been argued[3] that the classicism of Arnold's Preface did not adequately present the conception of tragedy embodied in *Empedocles* (and, far less successfully, in *Balder Dead* and *Merope*): that is, the defeat and despair of a high-minded individual caught between opposing historical forces in a revolutionary age. This view of tragedy, which originated in the nineteenth century (partly in Arnold's Senancour) and is common in the twentieth, was embodied in a late historical essay, Arnold's moving eulogy of Lord Falkland (1877: *Mixed Essays*, 1879), the "martyr of sweetness and light, of lucidity of mind and largeness of temper," who could not give full support to the absolutism of either side in the Civil War and who, espousing royalism as the better of the two, welcomed death on the battlefield.

It may be added that Arnold's objections to *Empedocles* might be taken as a prophetic definition of a good deal of later literature, especially and increasingly in our own period, but the climate has so greatly changed that those objections would now seem strange. (Yeats, who saw in them the proof of a great critic, incurred general obloquy by excluding Wilfred Owen, on similar though weaker grounds, from his *Oxford Book of Modern Verse*.) The most modern modernists, rejecting traditional ideas of the heroic and tragic, take it for granted—not without some smugness over modern honesty and sensibility—that the literature of a sick world should be sick, the sicker the better. Both the greatness of *Empedocles* and its author's censure of it belong to a healthier age. And we may remember that Arnold, though seldom very hopeful of the future, did recover from despair, that in *Culture and Anarchy* and the religious books he did affirm a moral order and process in the world, a neo-Stoic, almost metaphysical conception of the *Zeitgeist* much larger and more positive than his early one.

The letters to Clough and the Preface show two forces at work,

---

[3] John P. Farrell, "Matthew Arnold's Tragic Vision," *Publications of the Modern Language Association* 85 (1970), 107–17.

sometimes in harmony, sometimes not. Classical and especially Greek literature, not merely an educational deposit but assimilated into his being, was one large part of Arnold's poetical and critical heritage; the other large part was modern Romantic literature, in which German and French counted rather more than English; and both classical and modern forces had their aesthetic, ethical, and technical components. Besides, for a poet whose formative years covered the transition from the Romantic to the Victorian age, there were all the problems, personal, English, and European, that weighed upon a sensitive spirit.

While Arnold did not and could not instantly abandon all subjective poetry for epic episodes and a Greek tragedy, there is a further clue to his altered course which starts from but is not confined to artistic difficulties. In a letter to his sister Jane of September 6, 1858 (wrongly dated August 6 in Russell, 1, 72), he defended his drama *Merope* (which has left its readers as cold as the works of Romantic subjectivity he named in the Preface of 1853) and spoke of the strong temptation,

if you cannot bear anything not *very good*, to transfer your operations to a region where form is everything. Perfection of a certain kind may there be attained, or at least approached, without knocking yourself to pieces, but to attain or approach perfection in the region of thought and feeling, and to unite this with perfection of form, demands not merely an effort and a labour, but an actual tearing of oneself to pieces, which one does not readily consent to (although one is sometimes forced to it) unless one can devote one's whole life to poetry.

Thus Arnold's espousal of classical objectivity was in part an endeavor to escape from himself and to surmount the wearing conflicts analyzed not only in *Empedocles* but in his short reflective poems.

R. H. Super, in the first of the lectures mentioned earlier, controverts the usual view of Arnold's poems "as self-expression, as personal": "they are representative, not individual, in the emotion they express." While Mr. Super speaks on Arnold with special authority, one may venture to question the posing of such alternatives as if they were mutually exclusive. We have met a good many revealing phrases in Arnold's letters: for instance, "But woe was upon me if I analysed not my situation"; "an actual tearing of oneself to pieces"; and such evidence supplements what the reflective poems surely proclaim, that they begin in personal experience, as self-expression. Some may remain little more than that; others, the more important ones, become generalized and representative. If Arnold had not been disturbed by his subjective instincts, by poems which he saw as fragments produced by a fragmented self, would he have made such conscious efforts to achieve objectivity?

## 2. Themes and Ideas

Its main theme has already been alluded to . . .—that distractedness, that dividedness of mind, which prevents us from performing our proper task on earth, or, what is the same thing, from surrendering ourselves to those unseen forces whose instruments we are, and only in fulfilling whose purposes we can give a meaning to our lives.

We lack the infallible instinct and the undivided consciousness of the animals. . . . Our perpetual awareness of our transitoriness as a limitation prevents us from trying to accept it as a condition. After some fleeting perception of eternity we fall back into the flux of time, and flounder there in a kind of desperate dividedness. No sooner have we concentrated upon one thing than we think of some other thing, to which it is to be a means, or which is to follow it, or which we might have chosen instead. We are perpetually oscillating between what we are doing and what we might be doing, between what we have chosen and what we might have chosen, between what is immediately before us and what is, or may be, just round the corner. We are 'half-filled masks', only half-heartedly and half-attentively playing the parts allotted to us. . . .

But . . . could we retain or regain the open and undivided consciousness of the child, distracted neither by past nor future, surrendering itself entirely to the eternal present, we should be able to play our parts.

We might suppose these remarks—whatever qualifications we might make—to be a summary of Arnold's central themes; actually, they come from a commentary on Rilke.[4] The fact is surely

---

[4] *Rainer Maria Rilke: Duino Elegies: The German Text, with an English Translation, Introduction and Commentary by J. B. Leishman & Stephen Spender* (London: Hogarth Press, 1939), 116–17.

striking evidence of Arnold's essential modernity or enduring relevance. The commentary would also help to explain reviewers' reception of his first volume: the melancholy questionings as well as the antique themes of *The Strayed Reveller* were clearly out of touch with the actual life and the taste of the mass of readers.

The intellectual and ethical pressure of most of Arnold's significant poems is not necessarily at odds with his lectures to Clough against oversubtle wrestling with insoluble problems. However uneven in quality, his poems fulfill the requirement later made by Arnold the critic, that literature and poetry in particular should be "a criticism of life," should be seriously concerned with ideas. A less familiar dictum (uttered apropos of Tennyson, whom Arnold in his letters consistently disparaged) is that "no modern poet can make very much of his business unless he is pre-eminently strong" in "intellectual power" (1860: Russell, 1, 147; *cf.* 241–42). Arnold, more than any major poet or critic of his time, was an heir of the long tradition of classical humanism, and it was in keeping with critical opinions cited above that he should uphold the doctrine that poetry should teach and delight—a doctrine which, for good poets, never meant prosy or palpable didacticism. T. S. Eliot complained that Arnold the critic was concerned with what poetry is *for*, rather than with what it is. He did, as we have seen already, reflect much on what poetry is, but he was concerned also with a question of prime importance for readers, who are—or used to be—more numerous than poets. It is true that many of his own best poems neither teach nor delight in the obvious sense; but the most gloomy ones—"Yes! in the sea of life enisled" and *Dover Beach*, for instance—accomplish both ends by giving the reader the inspiriting sense of a serious, authentic idea or experience powerfully rendered. Arnold, however, who felt the need of warring against low spirits, wanted something more positive. "I am glad you like the Gipsy Scholar," he wrote to Clough on November 30, 1853,

but what does it *do* for you? Homer *animates*—Shakespeare *animates* —in its poor way I think Sohrab and Rustum *animates*—the Gipsy Scholar at best awakens a pleasing melancholy. But this is not what we want. [Here he quotes his *Youth of Nature*]

> The complaining millions of men
> Darken in labour and pain—

what they want is something to *animate* and *ennoble* them—not merely to add zest to their melancholy or grace to their dreams. —I believe a feeling of this kind is the basis of my nature—and of my poetics. (Lowry, 146)

It is perhaps not naive to go along with the essence of these remarks. And, if we have the misfortune to think of Arnold as only a poetic moralist, we should not make him narrower than he was: in his late essay on Wordsworth he says, quoting "For ever wilt thou love, and she be fair," that Keats here "utters a moral idea."

Most of Arnold's poems are more or less related to one another in theme, a fact which, while it indicates a range far more limited than that of Tennyson and Browning, indicates also a remarkably coherent body of poetry—although in 1849 he could tell his sister Jane not to fret about his inconsistencies because "my poems are fragments—*i.e.* . . . . I am fragments, while you are a whole; the whole effect of my poems is quite vague & indeterminate—this is their weakness. . . ." (Whitridge, 18). On the other hand, a network of more or less unresolved conflicts has a power of its own, especially when the poet is not content with negations but is always seeking unity and totality. Arnold's late and different judgment has also been often quoted:

My poems represent, on the whole, the main movement of mind of the last quarter of a century, and thus they will probably have their day as people become conscious to themselves of what that movement of mind is, and interested in the literary productions which reflect it. It might be fairly urged that I have less poetical sentiment than Tennyson, and less intellectual vigour and abundance than Browning; yet, because I have perhaps more of a fusion of the two than either of them, and have more regularly applied that fusion to the main line of modern development, I am likely enough to have my turn, as they have had theirs. (June 5, 1859: Russell, 2, 10)

The headings used hereafter are only partial hints, because so many poems might with equal reason appear under two or three. Since most of the poems deal with problems of an intellectual, they apply to a poet; but, after a glance at some explicit presentations of the poetic character, the rest may be roughly grouped in accordance with their larger focus.

## POETRY AND THE POET

The sonnet *Shakespeare* (1844) is, though the dubious logic of the images has been diversely interpreted, a monumental statement of the impenetrable impersonality of the supreme explorer of human pains, weakness, and griefs. The plain citizen who walked about among his fellows remains for us an imagination of infinite range and a uniquely expressive voice. Arnold touched the idea again in the letter of 1847 in which he warned Clough against "individuality" and against trying "to *solve* the Universe" (Lowry, 63).

In *The Strayed Reveller* (1847–48?) Arnold uses a recast Homeric setting with a maternal Circe, Ulysses the man of action, and a follower of Dionysus who has drunk Circe's here innocuous potion. In his intoxication the young man describes various scenes as beheld by the gods: Tiresias, the Centaurs, Scythian nomads, and so on; then he rehearses all these—the characters being now pictured in painful situations—with the sympathetic insight of a human being. The point is that, whereas the observing of earthly experience does not ruffle the remote serenity of the gods, the bards who depict such scenes understand (like the Shakespeare of the sonnet) the suffering each involves, because the price the gods exact for song is "To become what we sing." This is, we might say, a semilyrical and pictorial treatment of the theme of Keats's two *Hyperions*, though Arnold could not have known the unpublished second and may not have thought of the first. It has indeed been suggested that his young Dionysian embodies his early view of Keats (witness the citations above) and a misunderstanding of "negative capability" as surrender to sensation. But the young man, though a strayed reveller and though eager for painless visions, recognizes the sterner demands made upon the poet. The elaborate series of vignettes tends, however, as in Tennyson's *Palace of Art*, to submerge the serious theme. (*The Palace of Art*, we are reminded, was Tennyson's most overt statement—a compromise—on the poet's problem of aesthetic detachment versus social responsibility, a problem he treated in such poems as *Timbuctoo, The Poet, The Poet's Mind, The Hesperides, The Lady of Shalott, The Lotos-Eaters*; most of these pieces were more or less on the side of detachment, imaginative seclusion—a phase that gave way to social consciousness.)

*The Strayed Reveller*, with relatively cool and unphilosophic picture-making, objectifies an idea of involvement quite different from the view of the poet presented in *Resignation* (1843–48?). Among the apparent influences operating here were some works Arnold especially prized in this period, Lucretius' *De Rerum Natura*, Goethe's *Wilhelm Meister* (ii.2), Senancour's *Obermann*, and perhaps Spinoza and the *Bhagavad Gita*. *Resignation* was inspired by the retracing in 1843 of a long walk in the Lake country taken in 1833. In 1843 Arnold and his sister Jane (the Fausta of the poem) not only were grown up but had lost their father (1842); and Jane's engagement to a Rugby master had been broken off shortly before the wedding. The repetition of the walk does not bring the spiritual rebirth of *Tintern Abbey*, to which, indeed, *Resignation* has been called "a conscious reply," an expression of Arnold's inability to accept the Wordsworthian religion of nature.

For all its fine scene-painting (and symbolic detail), the poem is a moral essay, an essay for men in general; "the poet" is only a special representative of one of the two main types of mind and life described, the half-Stoic, half-Oriental quietist. The other type, the impatient activist, is represented by Fausta, here Arnold's *alter ego*. (To quote the first *Obermann* poem,

> Ah! two desires toss about
> The poet's feverish blood.
> One drives him to the world without,
> And one to solitude.)

The historical prelude sets both in a large and long perspective, the quietist accepting time, the activist presuming to command it. At the foot of the scale are the gipsies the walkers had met; these thoughtlessly rub through the succession of their days. At the top is the contemplative poet, who is said to scan, "Not his own course, but that of man"; his gaze takes in public affairs, love, nature, the passage of time:

> Before him he sees life unroll,
> A placid and continuous whole—
> That general life, which does not cease,
> Whose secret is not joy, but peace;
> That life, whose dumb wish is not missed
> If birth proceeds, if things subsist;
> The life of plants, and stones, and rain,
> The life he craves—if not in vain
> Fate gave, what chance shall not control,
> His sad lucidity of soul.

These famous lines may somewhat surprise us: although Arnold has his own strain of primitivism, and although the phrase "general life" sounds a Stoic note, the poet here seems to crave participation, not in the cosmic order, but in mere nonsentient being well below even the gipsy level.

Fausta, he thinks, would rate the gipsies as less, the poet as more, than man: the poet is not a prisoner of time but "flees the common life of men." Then comes the line Arnold quoted to Clough the "depth hunter": "Not deep the poet sees, but wide" (Lowry, 99)—the last word is applied to Goethe in Arnold's *Stanzas in Memory of the Author of 'Obermann'* and marks a quality of "Hellenism." For the poet, action and the quest of power are vain; he has his armor against fate, a wisdom supplied by the things of nature, which "Seem to bear rather than rejoice." That wisdom, for not only the poet but other men, is more passive, disengaged, and joyless than what Arnold later said Goethe had found in Spinoza: "And a moral lesson not of mere resigned acquiescence, not of melancholy quietism, but of joyful activity within the limits of man's true sphere" (Super, 3, 177)—the lesson to be preached by Empedocles to Pausanias and enforced in various short poems. Man must recognize his dependence upon himself, the necessity of accepting limits (as Romantics like Fausta are unwilling to do), and of tempering action with disinterested contemplation. We may take as footnotes to *Resignation* three poems of about March 1848, *The*

*World and the Quietist* and two sonnets called *To a Republican Friend,* these two certainly and the first probably written for Clough (whose ardent espousal of the French revolution of 1848 moved Arnold to address a letter to "Citizen Clough").

Several late poems have to do with poetry, but in the less urgent and more detached manner of a critic looking back at old problems and agitations. We have observed the lack of irony in Arnold's verse, in contrast with his abundant use of it in prose, and one possible clue appears in *Heine's Grave* (1858–63?). Apart from the well-known lines on England—"The weary Titan," "Staggering on to her goal," bearing the Atlantean load "Of the too vast orb of her fate"—this poem is less memorable than Arnold's Oxford lecture on Heine (1863), in which he praised the wit that had been the weapon of a soldier in the liberation war of humanity; and it was that Heine he probably remembered in *The Last Word* (1864–67). But in *Heine's Grave* Arnold is too much in the main Romantic tradition (despite his high estimate of Byron) to approve, in serious poetry, of Heine's bitter wit and scorn and lack of the uniquely poetic virtue of "charm" (Arnold had remarked in 1852 that his own poems had weight but little or no charm). The idea goes deeper than we might expect, because "Love is the fountain of charm," and here we touch a principle of Arnold's poetics. The "secret unrest," the "harsh and malign" ferment in Heine kept him below the great spirits, Virgil, Dante, Shakespeare ("loveliest of souls"), and Goethe, who had a comprehensive sympathy with life.

Beauty merges with wit and scorn in *Bacchanalia; or, The New Age* (1860–67?), a mixture of quiet pastoralism and journalistic satire on the noisy vogue of supposed novelty and genius in all areas of life—a vision equally far removed from that of the Strayed Reveller and the ending of *Obermann Once More*:

> Raphaels in shoals,
> Poets like Shakespeare—
> Beautiful souls!

The moral is that "The world but feels the present's spell,/The poet feels the past as well."

The *Epilogue to Lessing's Laocoön* (1864–65?) is a kind of

essayish urban pastoral which, while originating in the famous treatise on the confusion of poetry and painting, becomes a debate on the relative power and completeness of music, painting, and poetry. It touches ideas Arnold had treated more firmly in earlier verse. The palm is here given to poetry because the poet must tell of "life's *movement*," "Its pain and pleasure, rest and strife." With empathic intensity and joy he must grasp and penetrate, in all its breadth and depth, the complex, shifting maze of the world, the outward and inward lives of the heterogeneous multitude of individuals:

> Beethoven, Raphael, cannot reach
> The charm which Homer, Shakespeare, teach.

If "charm" seems strangely inadequate, we must turn back to *Heine's Grave* for the profound meaning Arnold gave it.

## The Loss of Christian Faith

The broad scope of *Resignation* brings us into the main stream of Arnold's poems of ideas. They are all more or less conditioned by one large premise, usually implicit but sometimes explicit: that Christianity no longer serves to establish man in an ordered providential universe with assured religious and moral guidance. (It may seem odd that Arnold does not, like Tennyson, cite the large share of science in creating the dark void; perhaps—like such contemporaries as his friend J. A. Froude, Francis Newman, and Mary Ann Evans (George Eliot)—he was initially alienated by the ethical implications of evangelical doctrines.)[5] Cut off from such external and internal support, modern man and life have no apparent meaning or direction, and one who abhors surrender to either unthinking passion or unthinking busyness is thrown back on his own resources, his capacity to order his own nature and chart his course, if he can, in obedience to his own best ideals and in the face of obstacles

[5] H. R. Murphy, "The Ethical Revolt against Christian Orthodoxy in Early Victorian England," *American Historical Review* 60 (1955), 800–17; D. J. DeLaura, *Hebrew and Hellene in Victorian England: Newman, Arnold, and Pater* (Austin and London: University of Texas Press, 1969), 13.

without and within. Such a summary may sound like a tissue of faded clichés, but this is still the general problem of modern life, and we may think that modern questions and answers have not markedly surpassed Arnold's in weight and insight and power of presentation.

The troubled introspectiveness of his first volume, *The Strayed Reveller, and Other Poems* (February 1849), surprised even his relatives and friends, who knew the dandy of pose and persiflage and had hardly suspected the inner life going on behind the protective mask (which he evidently enjoyed wearing);[6] in his late sonnet, *The Austerity of Poetry* (1864?), the Muse has a robe of sackcloth under her gay attire. Arnold's mature feelings of loneliness and uncertainty we might, if we wished, trace back to verses written when he was only thirteen and had just left home for Winchester School (Allott, 567). His Rugby and Oxford prize poems (1840, 1843), on the assigned subjects of Alaric and Cromwell, were in a vein of reflective melancholy, historical and personal. The earlier—and, as Arnold thought, better—piece was an obvious imitation of *Childe Harold; Cromwell*, written in the Tractarian Oxford that revered the martyr and saint, King Charles, was in line with Carlyle's conception of Cromwell the Hero, though most of it was a nostalgic and somewhat Wordsworthian evocation of youth.

Within months or a year after *Cromwell*, competent rhetoric modulated into something much closer to Arnold's own voice, in perhaps the earliest poem included in *The Strayed Reveller* (though it was revised before publication), that is, *To a Gipsy Child by the Sea-shore* (1843?). The poem is composed of speculations on the reasons for the infant's seeming to feel already the "clouds of doom" that envelop life, "the vanity of hope" and the sureness of pain. This child does not belong with the happy-go-lucky gipsies of *Resignation*. Repudiating Wordsworth's exalted vision of the infant soul "trailing clouds of glory" from the Pla-

---

[6] " 'Hide thy life,' said Epicurus, and the exquisite zest there is in doing so can only be appreciated by those who, desiring to introduce some method into their lives, have suffered from the malicious pleasure the world takes in trying to distract them till they are as shatter-brained and empty-hearted as the world itself" (Russell, 1, 62–63: December 6, 1856).

tonic heaven of its origin, the poet finds support, support more stoic than Stoic, only in the "majesty of grief." The substance of the poem, if not the manner, may remind us of Leopardi or Hardy or Rilke; Arnold was to write many finer poems, but not to give a darker view of life than he presents here. His second volume, *Empedocles on Etna, and Other Poems* (1852), was a more intense revelation of inward turmoil than his first, yet such poems of that first one as the *Gipsy Child, Stagirius, Mycerinus, The Sick King in Bokhara, The New Sirens, Resignation,* and others would hardly seem to warrant the label "Parnassian calm" given by one of Arnold's best critics (Culler, 116).

Although the two poems that deal most explicitly with the loss of religious faith come eight or nine years later than the *Gipsy Child,* we may look at them now because, it may be repeated, they describe the situation that conditions other poems; and we may then go on to a lesser but very real loss, the Romantic or at least Wordsworthian "religion of nature" and the corresponding sense of unity and inward power in the human self.

*Dover Beach* (June 1851?) stands at the head of Arnold's shorter poems as his most perfect work of art. As a presentation of ideas it is one of the simplest, because, although the archetypal image of the sea is rich in suggestion, there is almost none of Arnold's usual discursive analysis: he only turns away from a dark world emptied of religious meaning to cling to human love. The poem may at first seem strange as the product of a brief wedding trip, which it appears to have been, but it is after all a distillation, an extreme one, of Arnold's grimmest and gloomiest thoughts and feelings of earlier years, and marriage would reinforce the idea of love as an anchorage in a Godless, chaotic, hostile world.[7] Here, as in other poems, salvation, a very limited salvation, comes through feeling, not reason, although love is

[7] We might note a few diverse examples of the advance in critical sophistication since Arnold's day. Stanley Kauffmann refers to "Victorian pessimism of the *Dover Beach* kind, which to me always suggests that there is a comforting cup of tea waiting somewhere in the cosmic void" (*New Republic,* June 22, 1968, p. 34). Norman Holland, in a weird Freudian explication, finds "a well-nigh universal sexual symbolism in this heard-but-not-seen, naked fighting by night. This is one way Arnold's poem turns our experience of disillusionment or despair into satisfaction, namely, through

only a desperate refuge; it does not, as in *The Buried Life,* bring profound self-knowledge and intimations, however dim, of a reality beyond the self. But of course it is the negative theme that matters most, and "We are here as on a darkling plain" may be taken as "the central statement which Arnold makes about the human condition," a statement that no Romantic poet ever made and that no Victorian poet before Hardy made "with such uncompromising severity" (Culler, 41).

In the impressive but much less felicitous *Stanzas from the Grande Chartreuse* (1852?), a honeymoon visit to the Carthusian monastery—combined probably with thoughts of the Oxford Movement—quickens the poet's painful sense of the gulf between the cloistered perpetuation of medieval faith and a skeptical though sympathetic man of good will immersed in the stream of modernism. While the Gipsy Child had suggested the "majesty of grief," now "The nobleness of grief is gone"; modern man only chafes and frets and finds no light or support. "The kings of modern thought are dumb"; Byron's reverberating groans and Shelley's lovely wail and Senancour's escapism are alike of no help; and the spiritually disinherited, like the monks, cannot join the world of either triumphant progress or mindless action and pleasure.

In a letter to Clough of September 6, 1853, Arnold, speaking from the artist's standpoint, declared: "If one loved what was beautiful and interesting in itself *passionately* enough, one would produce what was excellent without troubling oneself with religious dogmas at all" (Lowry, 143). He went on to say (with apparent unawareness of some difficulty in his prescription):

As it is, we are *warm* only when dealing with these last—and what is frigid is always bad. I would have others—most others stick to the old religious dogmas because I sincerely feel that this *warmth* is the

---

the covert gratification we get from this final primal scene fantasy." (*The Dynamics of Literary Response,* New York: Oxford University Press, 1968, p. 121; this analysis was first printed in *Victorian Studies* 9, 1965–66, Supp. 5–28, and occasioned debate, *ibid.,* 10, 70–82). Two parodies are Anthony Hecht's *The Dover Bitch* (*A Criticism of Life*) (*Transatlantic Review,* Winter 1959–60, pp. 57–58; *The Hard Hours,* New York, 1968), which, while registering the modern substitution of sex for love, seems to end up on Arnold's side; and M. L. Rosenthal's *Homage to Matthew Arnold or Splash* (*Beyond Power,* New York, 1969, p. 44).

great blessing, and this frigidity the great curse—and on the old religious road they have still the best chance of getting the one and avoiding the other.

In perhaps the same year as the *Grande Chartreuse* (1852?) Arnold earnestly pleaded for undogmatic warmth in *Progress*, which is more of a sermon than a poem and anticipates his religious books of twenty years later. The poet of the *Grande Chartreuse* feels like a sophisticated Greek standing "Before some fallen Runic stone"; in *Progress* he exhorts: "Leave then the Cross as ye have left carved gods,/But guard the fire within!" And while in the best-known lines of the *Grande Chartreuse* he pictured himself—echoing Carlyle's *Characteristics*—as "Wandering between two worlds, one dead,/The other powerless to be born," in *Progress* he urges, as he says all religions have urged, *"Thou must be born again!"* The most elaborate statement of Arnold's reborn hope for mankind is *Obermann Once More* (1865–67?), but that may be postponed.

## NATURE

Another major premise, in part bound up with the religious one, is also mainly negative: nature's indifference to man. The traditional Christian view of nature is not available, and, as John Dewey said (in an essay of 1891 on Arnold and Browning), nature, in ceasing to be divine, ceased to be human. Arnold offers a metaphysical approach to the question in *In Utrumque Paratus* (1846?), a compressed, abstract, and—as the title implies—inconclusive poem. In brief, it poses alternative conceptions of the origin and growth of the world and of man's consequent status: the Plotinian conception of downward emanations from "the silent mind of One all-pure" and evolutionary ascent from "the wild unfathered mass." The first alternative would allow man to rise to lonely exaltation above the world of appearances. If the second is true, man's pride in his attaining consciousness must bow to recognition of his being a part of nature —a lonely, indeed an alien, part. Arnold's temperamental idealism is inevitably kept in check by modern rationalism; and his attitudes toward nature—or Nature—are variable, within or sometimes outside the major premise. Of course such a lover of streams and flowers is fully open to the healing power of the beauties of earth, but that is limited and occasional and only mitigates the "ground-tone/Of human agony."

In *Philomela* (1852–53?) such healing power is found quite inadequate. The main theme could be the human lot in general, but "What triumph! hark!—what pain!" seems to echo *The Strayed Reveller* ("But oh, what labour!/O prince, what pain!") and suggests "the triumph and pain of poetic creation" (Allott, 348). The nightingale's song, heard by an English poet on a moonlit English lawn, prompts the allusive retelling of the ugly myth, and time and space are bridged, with emotional intensity, by the thought of "Eternal passion!/Eternal pain!"—the thought to which Keats was involuntarily driven in the climactic stanza of his *Ode to a Nightingale.* As a parable of un-Romantic or anti-Romantic disenchantment Arnold's poem has its fitting place between Keats and Eliot. (Aldous Huxley, in his *Literature and Science*, chided all three poets for falsifying the song of a bird which sings only to claim time and space for the consumption of caterpillars.)

Even a direct heir of Wordsworth, and a poet who in his cradle "Was breathed on by the rural Pan," can now seldom feel himself wedded to a goodly universe, as a part of a total unity and harmony that nourishes life with "joy," a word which for Wordsworth and Coleridge had the special and profound sense of oneness with the cosmic whole. (One of the Wordsworthian words is recalled in the late and sardonic poem, *A Wish,* perhaps of 1865: the poet wishes, when he comes to die, to be freed from the usual "ceremonious air of gloom" and to gaze from the window at the wide landscape, so that he may feel his soul "wed" to "the universe my home," "The pure eternal course of life.") In the vehement sonnet *To an Independent Preacher* (1844–47?), later called *In Harmony with Nature*, Arnold denounced rhapsodic sentimentalism, listing the vital differences between Nature and man. Nature is strong, cool, cruel, stubborn, fickle, unforgiving: "Man must begin, know this, where Nature

ends." And in the sonnet *Religious Isolation*, addressed to Clough
—presumably in 1848 when Clough, about to resign his Oriel
fellowship, was agonizing over "unanswerable questions" instead
of simply following his convictions—Arnold urged upon him the
Emersonian and traditionally humanistic doctrine of law for
man and law for thing: "Nature's great law, and law of all men's
minds . . ./Live by thy light, and earth will live by hers!"

Arnold's revulsion from the sick hurry of contemporary life led
to his feeling a strong affinity with Étienne Pivert de Senancour,
the minor French Romantic who had fled from civilization to
Alpine solitude and had analyzed his experience in *Obermann*
(1804). The attachment waned as Arnold found firmer standing-
ground for himself, although Senancour was echoed in the positive "Wish" recorded in the preceding paragraph (Allott, 516–
17) and of course was the supposed speaker in *Obermann Once
More* (1865–67?). In *Stanzas in Memory of the Author of 'Obermann'* (1849) Arnold praises three modern spirits, Senancour,
Wordsworth, and Goethe. Senancour has the appeal of one fully
involved in "The hopeless tangle of our age." Goethe, the Olympian sage, few can emulate. The prominence given to Wordsworth is undercut by the admission that his "eyes avert their
ken/From half of human fate." Wordsworth's "sweet calm" was
insecurely founded; as Arnold was to say in his lecture on Heine
(1863), Wordsworth "plunged himself in the inward life, he voluntarily cut himself off from the modern spirit." After Wordsworth's death the same kind of admission was made in *Memorial Verses* (1850) and *The Youth of Nature* (1850–52), although
then it was naturally submerged in a positive, elegiac eulogy of
the "priest to us all/Of the wonder and bloom of the world."
There may be another Titanic rebel like Byron, or another philosophical diagnostician like Goethe, but not another poet of
Wordsworth's "healing power," because such pure simplicity of
feeling cannot be recaptured in the modern world, where man
is bruised and baffled by complex pressures and where "The
complaining millions of men/Darken in labour and pain." Yet,
as such references show, Wordsworth is one source and symbol
of what is perhaps Arnold's most central antinomy, between feeling and reason, which involves the further antinomy between

"The freshness of the early world" and a sick civilization, "this iron time"; in general, Wordsworth (like Goethe and others) seems to be given a character and role more in accord with Arnold's personal and emotional needs than with objective views. At times, to be sure, Arnold can endow Nature with transcendental life, as in several poems of about 1852, *The Youth of Nature, The Youth of Man, Lines Written in Kensington Gardens*, and even in *Morality*, where the conscientious inspector of schools hears Nature's voice contrasting man's "struggling, tasked morality" with the effortless motion of her spheres, yet acknowledging a common divine origin for both. But such moments seem rather to reveal the poet's transcendental longings than to give Nature a benign Wordsworthian reality.

As *Morality* reminds us, Arnold can make rational and exemplary use, not so much of changing terrestrial nature, for all its beauty, but of the planetary order ("The army of unalterable law," as T. S. Eliot mockingly said, recalling "Matthew and Waldo" and Meredith's sonnet *Lucifer in Starlight*). His most familiar statement is the sonnet *Quiet Work* (1848?), which in nearly all his editions stood first as an introductory poem. Here he appeals from "Man's fitful uproar" to the ceaseless, regular movements of the stars, silently working—a blend, apparently, of Goethe, Carlyle, and Plotinus. So too in *Self-Dependence* (1849–50?), written probably soon after Arnold's parting with Marguerite, the stars are invoked as sublime models, serene self-poised agents, undistracted by the fevers of human egoism and discontent; and the same counsel, of self-knowledge, is given by the poet's own heart.[8] In *A Summer Night* (1849–52) the quiet heavens give a similar rebuke and more hopeful inspiration to divided and unquiet man. Clough, in his review of 1853, saw no reason to suppose, because "the heavenly bodies describe ellipses," that "human souls do something analogous in the spiritual spaces," but we may feel that Arnold's images are not altogether vain.

[8] One may wonder, by the way, if the unexpected idea, "And with joy the stars perform their shining," was derived from Wordsworth's "The Moon doth with delight/Look round her" or from Richard Hooker's angels, whose functions are "performed with joy" (*Ecclesiastical Polity*, I.iv.2).

### FEELING AND REASON: YOUTH AND AGE

The four terms of the heading gain a special Arnoldian significance and prominence as we read many more or less personal poems; but before we come to them we may look at three impersonal pieces (of about 1847–48) which involve the same four terms or ideas, though in a broad general sense.

*The Sick King in Bokhara* developed an anecdote which in Arnold's source, Alexander Burnes's *Travels into Bokhara* (1834), exemplified "the rigour of the Mohammedan law" in telling of the fate of one who was either "a bigot or a madman"; the poet saw another interpretation. The story is told in dramatic dialogue of Oriental coloring. A "Moollah" (mullah) had persistently confronted the young king, demanding the death penalty for himself because, in a time of drought, he had concealed a pitcher of water and had cursed his mother and brethren who had found and drained it. Finally tried and condemned by the priests, he is stoned, in spite of the king's efforts to save him, and he dies joyfully praising Allah. The young king's humanitarian sympathy is rebuked by his old Vizier because he allows pity for an individual, a stranger, to soften his respect for law: one man cannot pity all who suffer. The young king, made sick by his failure, can only give the martyr rich burial in the tomb prepared for himself. Many readers may share Burnes's attitude rather than the poet's—as the same readers would give undivided sympathy to Milton's Adam when, unmindful of loyalty to God and law, he sides with Eve, or might fail to comprehend how the innocent Socrates, awaiting death, could reject his friends' plan of escape. The poem dramatizes, as A. D. Culler says, "the conflict between redemptive and sociological justice," between absolute and relativistic ethics, and also the conflict between reason and feeling, age and youth.

We may think that the large principle behind the conflict is somewhat blurred by the Vizier's emphasis on permissible degrees of sympathy, which, he affirms, must lessen or vanish as it moves out from family to strangers and all mankind. However, this idea appears also in the *Fragment of an 'Antigone'*, in the praise of him who, instead of seizing happiness, "dares/To self-selected good/Prefer obedience to the primal law,/Which consecrates the ties of blood"; and Haemon, who here opposes Antigone, not (as in Sophocles) his father, corresponds in feeling to the sick king of Bokhara. But the essential theme of both poems is the exaltation of primal law over self-selected good, and the *Fragment of Chorus of a 'Dejaneira'* likewise rebukes self-assertion, the human pride which in prosperity neglects, in adversity misinterprets, the wisdom of the gods. These Greek poems were not mere formal exercises: witness Arnold's somewhat cryptic remark to Clough, "But my Antigone supports me and in some degree subjugates destiny" (Lowry, 101; *cf.* 103), and especially his citing the last stanza of the *Dejaneira*—on the happiness of dying in the prime of life, with a soul "Unworn, undebased, undecayed"—in 1872, when he was deeply shaken by the death of his eighteen-year-old son (Russell, 2, 93).

To come to more directly personal poems, Arnold's central effort—given the loss of religious faith—is to achieve balanced wholeness and unity in the face of the disruptive pressures and complexities of the self and the world. Ideas that are expounded in positive terms in the later prose appear in variable and partial form in the poems: man's will seems to be free, but his divided impulses, outward circumstance, and "Fate" or "some unknown Power" set narrow bounds upon liberty and harmonious, fruitful integration is very difficult. The Duke of Wellington, in the early sonnet, was great because he "saw one clue to life, and followed it"; the Scholar-Gipsy was happy at least in having "*one* aim, *one* business, *one* desire." In another early sonnet, *Written in Butler's Sermons* (1844?), Arnold rejects the bishop's mechanical parcelling out of the self into "Affections, Instincts, Principles, and Powers," and—in a too intricately rhetorical metaphor—he insists upon "man's one nature." The sonnet *To a Friend* (probably Clough, in 1848?), which begins with the worst line in all of Arnold's verse, names, as his chief props in these bad days, Homer, Epictetus, and Sophocles; the last elicits his most famous line, "Who saw life steadily, and saw it whole"—not that Sophocles or anyone could grasp all of life but that he had an integrated view of it.

The eulogy of Sophocles is cast in what was to be a characteristic Arnoldian mold: his "even-balanced soul/. . . Business
could not make dull, nor passion wild." Most of Arnold's poems
of ideas range themselves into related antitheses or polarities:
religious faith and skepticism; man and nature; freedom and necessity; feeling and reason; youth and age; contemplation and action; integration and fragmentariness; the inward lonely self
and the busy distracting world; ideal past and ugly present
(partly reflected in country and city). . . . A fairly comprehensive label for some of these would be "Dionysian" and "Apollonian." If Arnold's Dionysian strain stopped well short of the
sensual and violent, it was none the less genuine. In 1865 he
wrote to his mother (Russell, 1, 289–90):

No one has a stronger and more abiding sense than I have of the
'dæmonic' element—as Goethe called it—which underlies and en-
compasses our life; but I think, as Goethe thought, that the right
thing is, while conscious of this element, and of all that there is in-
explicable round one, to keep pushing on one's posts into the darkness,
and to establish no post that is not perfectly in light and firm. One
gains nothing on the darkness by being, like Shelley, as incoherent
as the darkness itself.

Many years earlier, in September 1849, when in Switzerland he
was breaking with Marguerite, Arnold made a confession to
Clough which, coming from a man usually identified with conscious self-discipline, may startle us:

What I must tell you is that I have never yet succeeded in any one
great occasion in consciously mastering myself: I can go thro: the
imaginary process of mastering myself and see the whole affair as it
would then stand, but at the critical point I am too apt to hoist up
the mainsail to the wind and let her drive. (Lowry, 110)

The last metaphor reappears, in extreme form, in *A Summer
Night*, in the picture of those who are swept away by passion.
In the letter Arnold went on, using of himself a plain phrase
which in his poem on *Obermann* is used of the three great modern spirits who have "attained . . . to see their way": his "one
natural craving is not for profound thoughts, mighty spiritual

workings etc. etc. but a distinct seeing of my way as far as my own nature is concerned. . . ."

One persistent manifestation of the Apollonian-Dionysian antinomy takes the form of weighing the rational self-discipline of maturity against the emotional spontaneity of youth: is earnest dedication to the Apollonian and half-Stoic ideal so certainly the better guide to true happiness? On the one side we remember the tributes to Epictetus and Sophocles, Empedocles' last proud declaration that he has never been the slave of sense, and such lines as these, from *Mycerinus*:

> rapt in reverential awe,
> I sate obedient, in the fiery prime
> Of youth, self-governed, at the feet of Law;

or the personal statement in the *Grande Chartreuse*:

> For rigorous teachers seized my youth,
> And purged its faith, and trimmed its fire,
> Showed me the high, white star of Truth,
> There bade me gaze, and there aspire.

(Among the "rigorous teachers" would be the philosophers Arnold was studying in the 1840's and especially, no doubt, Lucretius, Epictetus, Spinoza, Senancour, Carlyle, Emerson, and Goethe; some critics include Dr. Arnold.) But there are many rebellious or nostalgic testimonies on the other side. The most openly personal regrets for lost youth are in Arnold's letters:

The aimless and unsettled, but also open and liberal state of our youth we *must* perhaps all leave and take refuge in our morality and character; but with most of us it is a melancholy passage from which we emerge shorn of so many beams that we are almost tempted to quarrel with the law of nature which imposes it on us. (To Jane, January 25, 1851: Russell, 1, 17)

what a difference there is between reading in poetry and morals of the loss of youth, and experiencing it! And after all there is so much to be done, if one could but do it. (To Clough, October 28, 1852: Lowry, 125)

I am past thirty, and three parts iced over. (To Clough, February 12, 1853: Lowry, 128)

I feel immensely—more and more clearly—what I *want*—what I have (I believe) lost and choked by my treatment of myself and the studies to which I have addicted myself. But what ought I to have done in preference to what I have done? there is the question. (To Clough, May 1, 1853: Lowry, 136)

Some direct reflections on youth and age appear in verse. In *Youth's Agitations* (1849–50?) the poet, when "some ten years" short of full maturity, looks forward to being rid of the ebb and flow of youthful passions; yet age, he knows, will bring a nostalgic longing for youth's generous fire. There is similar discontent in *Youth and Calm* (1849–51?):

> Ah no, the bliss youth dreams is one
> For daylight, for the cheerful sun,
> For feeling nerves and living breath—
> Youth dreams a bliss on this side death. . . .

> It hears a voice within it tell:
> *Calm's not life's crown, though calm is well.*
> 'Tis all perhaps which man acquires,
> But 'tis not what our youth desires.

In Arnold's later years of relative equanimity, a last lament for vanished youth was *Growing Old* (1864–67), a bleak reply, conscious or unconscious, to Browning's *Rabbi Ben Ezra*. Worse than physical decay is "to spend long days/And not once feel that we were ever young," or to be feebly aware that passionate dreams have given place to incapacity for feeling. The lines describing the final stage have long been a familiar quotation: "To hear the world applaud the hollow ghost/Which blamed the living man."

Two poems, both written before Arnold's encounter with Marguerite, deal, in totally different ways, with the senses as agents of solace or fulfillment—not that that is the real theme of *Mycerinus* (1843 f.). Here he transformed a tale of Eastern ingenuity (Herodotus, ii.133) into a small variation on the problem of Job. The exemplary young king, whose father had flourished long in iniquity, is doomed by the oracle to an early death. He reviews in turn the classical philosophies, finds them all wanting, and gives his six remaining years to sensual revelry; but the deliberately indirect conclusion seems to imply that his noble nature was not thus satisfied, that he has learned something of what Empedocles was to teach Pausanias about the meaning of true virtue and acceptance of life's conditions. It has been suggested that Mycerinus' bitter dismissal of religion and philosophy was deepened by Dr. Arnold's premature death (1842)—perhaps particularly recalled in lines 29–30, on the "unjust" end of "the strenuous just man"—and by Matthew's being warned that his own heart had a similar defect.

Some critics, quite logically, link *The New Sirens* (1843–45?) with *The Strayed Reveller*, since the poet-speaker is dealing with the conditions of poetic creativity; but it may also be linked with *Mycerinus* in its broadly human application. It is a diffusely descriptive but significant poem which Clough called "a mumble"; in accepting the label Arnold provided a prose summary of the piece (Lowry, 105–07; Allott, 34–35). The speaker, "one of a band of poets," is tempted by an emotional view of life and art. In contrast with the Homeric Sirens, "the fierce sensual lovers of antiquity" (to quote the un-Homeric item from the summary), the New Sirens promise the high experience of romantic passion; but that, the wavering poet knows, means only momentary ecstasies followed by ennui—as he was to say again in *Tristram and Iseult* (iii.133 f.). Thus he discounts in advance the young Swinburne's celebration of raptures and languors. (Arnold, by the way, dropped *The New Sirens* from later editions but was persuaded by the admiring Swinburne to restore it.) What is of more interest is that he anticipates the central theme of *Empedocles* and other poems of his own: however delusive the New Sirens are, they define an Arnoldian conflict: "the brain is seeking,/While the sovran heart is dead"; "Only, what we feel, we know." Allott plausibly suggests that the germ of the poem was the debate in chapters 33–38 of George Sand's *Lélia*; but the theme was thoroughly Arnoldian.

The most personal revelation of Arnold's "Dionysian" youth— if the last word may be used of a man of 25–26—is his involvement in 1848–49 with a young Frenchwoman, "Marguerite." With one signal exception, the poems written to or about her cannot be called poems of ideas (indeed, they have less interest as poetry than as documents of a poet-lover's self-consciousness), but the prolonged episode must be registered in the present context. The one firm fact we have is in Arnold's letter to Clough of September 29, 1848, in which he says he is going to linger one day at the Hotel Bellevue in Thun "for the sake of the blue eyes of one of its inmates" (Lowry, 91; a year later, at Thun, he was in "a curious and not altogether comfortable state": *ibid.*, 110). An odd related fact in the letter of 1848 is that he had only two books with him, Béranger and Epictetus!—and he was, when tired, not much drawn to the latter and was getting tired of the former. We cannot go into the guesses about Marguerite's character and status and the reasons for Arnold's withdrawal; the most that can be said (and some would say less) is that the author of *The New Sirens* fell passionately in love and then felt obliged to sever relations. He was to leave behind "Once-longed-for storms of love" (*Absence*, 1849–50) for the secure though still exciting haven of Miss Wightman. Yet the depth of first love makes Marguerite a symbol of Arnold's youth and his capacity for being swept away by feeling. As late as 1863 the memory was strong enough to inspire—if the poem permits that word—*The Terrace at Berne*.

Among the poems to Marguerite, the signal exception to mediocrity that was mentioned above is the swift, impassioned outburst, "Yes! in the sea of life enisled," which some critics have thought Arnold's finest achievement.[9] Through the closely coherent working out of the one simple metaphor of separated islands, once perhaps united as a continent, the theme of love is submerged in the larger idea that all human beings—once perhaps united in the "mind of One all-pure" (to quote *In Utrumque Paratus*)—are inevitably isolated from one another in "The unplumbed, salt, estranging sea" of life.

[9] The latest is Alan Roper (*Arnold's Poetic Landscapes*, Baltimore: Johns Hopkins Press, 1969, p. 155). John Fowles, calling it "perhaps the noblest short poem of the whole Victorian era," quoted it in full in his "Victorian" novel, *The French Lieutenant's Woman* (Boston, 1969, pp. 426–27). Kathleen Tillotson's valuable article on the lyric and its sources (*Review of English Studies* 3, 1952) is reprinted in her and Geoffrey Tillotson's *Mid-Victorian Studies* (London, 1965).

Whether or not *The Forsaken Merman* (1847–49?) has any connection with Arnold's love for Marguerite (and the poetic situation hardly fits the facts), it belongs to the general theme and to this period. The poem has been a popular favorite from the first—though some critics found it rather too Tennysonian and T. S. Eliot dismissed it, and *Tristram and Iseult*, as "charades." Arnold re-created George Borrow's prose version of a Danish ballad with unexpected command of speed, melody, grace, pathos, and something of the "natural magic" he was to find in Celtic literature. The picture of loneliness links itself with his other poems of love—and with *The Raven* and *The Blessed Damozel*. Readers may be contentedly carried away by the obvious attractions of sentiment, sound, and imagery, but, along with the overt theme, there is a richly significant contrast between the pious, busy round of human life on land and the deep sea with its mermen and mermaids and huge beasts, a primitive world of vitality, freedom, and mystery—an idea perhaps suggested by Tennyson's *The Mermaid* and *The Kraken* and suggestive of the early Eliot, notably *Prufrock*.

Arnold was avowedly interested in some aspects of the Middle Ages, as *Balder Dead* and a number of short legendary pieces testify, and among modern English-speaking poets he was the pioneer in treating the tragic romance of Tristram and Iseult. He had never met it until at Thun, presumably in September 1849, he read what became his formative source, an article in the *Revue de Paris*, "and it fastened upon me." He worked on the poem during 1849–52. We can readily imagine how the story of the two Iseults would affect the young poet who parted from Marguerite and married Frances Wightman.[10]

Instead of telling a consecutive story, Arnold chose to begin just before the crisis and to bring in the past by way of flashbacks: in the opening scene the delirious Tristram, near death and watched over by his silent wife, is longing for his first love,

[10] To mention one tiny possible link, the arrival of Iseult of Ireland is heralded by the lines: "What voices are these on the clear night-air?/ What lights in the court—what steps on the stair?" (I.372–73). The lover in *Parting* (September 1849) asks: "But on the stairs what voice is this I hear,/Buoyant as morning, and as morning clear?"

Iseult of Ireland. One early complaint, about lack of clarity in the story line, might not be made by modern readers, who are familiar with the plot and accustomed to flashbacks and ellipses. But we may still be disconcerted by shifts in point of view (the three persons and the narrator) and by shifts (however Arnoldian) between past and present, passion and reason, action and withdrawal, youth and age, because these various elements seem to reveal some uncertainty of direction and sympathy or at any rate are not worked into a coherent dramatic whole. Arnold is at once attracted and repelled by romantic passion. Even if, in the stanzaic exchanges between Tristram and Iseult of Ireland in Part II, the high-pitched operatic unreality is the poet's intentional exposure of violent passion, the result is only falsetto or fiasco. The narrator is closer to the antiromantic than to the romantic Arnold, and he takes over entirely in Part III, the best part, the quiet account of the widowed Iseult playing with her children and telling them the tale of Merlin and Vivian (who, like Marguerite—and others—has blue eyes), a tale of passion now viewed from a distance as a fairy-tale she loved in childhood. The whole section is the most elaborate example (perhaps too elaborate, Arnold later admitted) of his conscious effort, at the end of a poem, to provide relief, especially through enlarging the vertical or the horizontal perspective. However familiar we are with the recurrence of ideas in Arnold, we may be surprised, in this context, to come upon lines (119–26) which might have appeared in *Empedocles*, about the furnace of the world drying up the youthful capacity for feeling and joy; yet the idea is relevant to the monotonous round of Iseult's later life.

A farewell to another phase of romantic youth—written just after the parting with Marguerite—is *Stanzas in Memory of the Author of 'Obermann'* (1849). We have noticed Arnold's linking in this poem of the three modern spirits who could "see their way"; but, he says, in the present hurried and harassed age, we turn from the calm and wisdom of Wordsworth and Goethe to the nearer voice of feverish unrest and despair that speaks to our condition. Senancour had renounced the world of action to seek contemplative solitude in the Alps, where he could share in the "general life" craved by the poet of *Resignation*; he had become one of "The Children of the Second Birth,/Whom the world could not tame." For all its sympathy, however, the poem reveals decisive if regretful disenchantment with the "sad guide" of earlier years, a man of agonized sincerity but "unstrung will." Yet the poet, fated as he is to live in the world and fortify his own strength of will, can confess: "but I leave/Half of my life with you."

*A Summer Night* (1849–52) presents another quarrel with, and final acceptance of, the active life, and here more immediate personal agitation and discontent broaden out to take in all men. The speaker, torn between the two poles of passion and the world, has the further pain of being not quite possessed by the one or quite benumbed by the other. Most men toil unhappily until death in the brazen prison of the world's routine; a few, the passionate, escape, but only to sail wildly on a stormy sea (we remember Arnold's confession that he himself was "too apt to hoist up the mainsail to the wind and let her drive"):

> Is there no life, but these alone?
> Madman or slave, must man be one?

The conclusion returns to the bleak physical scene of the opening; but now the vast quiet heavens declare that man's soul still has boundless possibilities of serene and fruitful freedom—a hope hardly validated by what has gone before.

In *The Buried Life* (1849–52) it is pure feeling that answers questions beyond the reason, that can rescue the individual from the noisy world of action, that can plumb the gulf between the quotidian and the true, buried self. The question starts from the difficulties of full understanding and communication even between lovers and expands to describe man's compulsive craving to get below the unreal flux of worldly existence and trace the underground stream of his own real self and real life, to comprehend the mystery of his deep and wildly beating heart—his Dionysian self, one might say. That mystery eludes conscious search, though at times vague intimations float up from "the soul's subterranean depth" and convey "A melancholy into all our day." But the greatly desired revelation may come to

a man in those rare moments of togetherness when love is seen
and felt in all its penetrating reality and clarity—a quieter
situation than the end of *Dover Beach*. And the Arnoldian Prufrock is not left entirely baffled.

The final wisdom of Empedocles is that we should "at last be
true/To our own only true, deep-buried selves," which has a
more than Polonian meaning. Arnold's dramatic poem (1849–
52) brings together most of the ideas and conflicts we have so
far encountered. The design—including the *dramatis personae*,
the mountain setting, and the time scheme—is partly modeled
on Byron's "Gothic" *Manfred*, though Arnold's philosopher is a
more complex being than Manfred, has no burden of guilt, and
does not traffic with supernatural powers (notwithstanding the
popular label of "wizard" gained through his medical skill).
The physical and dramatic scenes carry a plain, symmetrical,
and impressive symbolism: Empedocles, the lonely, despairing
thinker, who mounts from the hot, crowded city of Catana to
the desolate peak of Etna; Pausanias, his well-meaning, half-
enlightened physician-friend, the Greek Hamlet's Horatio (as
critics have called him), who reaches the upper slopes and is
kindly dismissed to return to normal life in the city; and Callicles, the harper and singer, the embodiment of youthful feeling, who remains in the shady valley. The time scheme extends
from early morning to evening.

In the first scene Callicles and Pausanias exchange opinions
about the cause of the dark mood that has taken possession of
their admired and beloved master: Pausanias ascribes it to his
being supplanted by the Sophists and banished, Callicles dis-
cerns "some root of suffering in himself," and, though neither
understands fully, Callicles is closer to the truth. In the second
scene Empedocles, brushing off Pausanias' curiosity about his
recent medical "miracle," declares that "Mind is the spell which
governs earth and heaven"; but Pausanias' reply approximates
Empedocles' own later conviction: "Mind is a light which the
Gods mock us with/To lead those false who trust it." From below the voice of Callicles breaks in, contrasting his lush valley
with the bare, hot slopes of the upper mountain. That picture
of the simple realities of nature is followed by the first of his
mythological lyrics: he sings of the young Achilles' learning from

Chiron the Centaur of the simple life and creed of the heroic age.

Empedocles then launches, with his harp, upon a 350-line "lyric," a sermon to Pausanias and all men on the problems of life and belief in the modern world. It might be called a large development of Mycerinus' survey of current philosophies. Arnold put into this drama material he had hoped to use in a tragedy on Lucretius, and Empedocles starts from the partly Lucretian image of man's soul as a mirror blown about by the wind (*De Rerum Natura* iv, *passim*; Allott quotes *Obermann*): it gets confused glimpses but "never sees a whole." From this very Arnoldian text Empedocles goes on to preach, with gnomic plainness, the possibility of grasping a limited whole through knowledge of one's self:

> Once read thy own breast right,
> And thou hast done with fears;
> Man gets no other light,
> Search he a thousand years.

Empedocles' sermon draws wisdom from many sources which had become more or less parts of Arnold's being: the ancient Stoics, the *Bhagavad Gita*, Spinoza, Goethe, Senancour, Carlyle, Emerson, and others. Man, a stranger and afraid in a world he never made (to echo a poet whose pessimism was more *fin de siècle* than Arnold's), must recognize that he has "no *right* to bliss"; he must accept the conditions of life, knowing that Nature is indifferent, that appeals to supernatural powers are weak evasions of reality. Youth's claim to raptures of the senses and age's dreams of heavenly rewards are equally vain: self-assertion is worth no more than self-delusion. In the spirit of *Resignation*, Empedocles recites the positive satisfactions that life affords, the sun, the spring, love, thought, achievement. The great imperative is to moderate desires:

> I say: Fear not! Life still
> Leaves human effort scope.
> But, since life teems with ill,
> Nurse no extravagant hope;
> Because thou must not dream, thou need'st not then despair!

Thus Empedocles sums up and expands what Arnold had said piecemeal in many short poems—and what had been said by various masters, from his favorite Pindar (*e.g.*, *Pyth.* 3.59–62) to Carlyle. But the sage's astringent exhortation is addressed to others, not himself, since his questing mind has been driven beyond his own precepts. Fifteen years later Arnold would not recognize the voice of his former self.

The stanza quoted is followed by another song from Callicles, a beautiful and appropriate fusion of Ovid and Pindar: Cadmus and Harmonia knew supreme mundane felicity, then billows of calamity, and finally, through metamorphosis, attained another felicity, as "two bright and aged snakes" straying "For ever through the glens, placid and dumb." They have become, on that level, part of the "general life."[10a]

In Act II Empedocles, having sent Pausanias away, is alone in the evening on the summit of Etna: what follows is "the dialogue of the mind with itself." He can no longer live with men or in solitude, because his spirit's "self-sufficing fount of joy" is dried up: he can only return to the elements before he has lost all hold upon reality. As he moves to the edge of the smoking crater, Callicles sings of Typho, the rebel whom Zeus had imprisoned beneath Etna. Empedocles draws from the myth the lesson that the world has no place for the brave heart, that "littleness united/Is become invincible." (On June 7, 1852, Arnold wrote to Clough of his conviction that "a great career is hardly possible any longer," "that the world tends to become more comfortable for the mass, and more uncomfortable for those of any natural gift or distinction"; but, he added, "it is as well perhaps that it should be so," since the gifted have "not trained or inspired or in any real way changed" the world.) Like Aeschylus' Cassandra just before her death, Empedocles throws aside his golden circlet and purple robe, the "fool's-armoury of magic" which had impressed the childish populace.

[10a] In 1934, when a married daughter was hovering between life and death, Robert Frost, a man who had many troubles, wrote to Louis Untermeyer: "My favorite poem long before I knew what it was going to mean to us was Arnold's 'Cadmus and Harmonia.'" *The Letters of Robert Frost to Louis Untermeyer* (New York: Holt, Rinehart and Winston, 1963), 240; Lawrance Thompson, *Robert Frost: The Years of Triumph* (New York: Holt, Rinehart and Winston, 1970), 407, 662, nn. 34, 35.

Callicles sings again, this time of the musical contest in which Marsyas was vanquished by Apollo, and flayed, as the vengeful god looked serenely on and Marsyas' young attendant—like Callicles—wept for his master's fate. Empedocles, the poetical and medical servant and victim of Apollo, lays down his laurel bough, and returns to his problem of unbearable society and unbearable solitude: only death can "Bring him to poise." He recalls his happy youth, when—here, as Swinburne noted, speaks the voice of Wordsworth—"we received the shock of mighty thoughts/On simple minds with a pure natural joy." In those days slavery to thought had not killed feeling, response to the "general life" of nature and man. But he no longer has, like Arnold's Sophocles, an "even-balanced soul."

As darkness deepens, Empedocles addresses the stars, which in the old world of myth and faith were agents of a mightier order (witness earlier poems of Arnold's), but are now "lonely, cold-shining lights . . ./In the heavenly wilderness." Yet the stars and all nature still live; Empedocles alone is "dead to life and joy." He has become "Nothing but a devouring flame of thought." The body can return to its elements, but where will mind and thought "find their parent element?" They will

> keep us prisoners of our consciousness,
> And never let us clasp and feel the All. . . .

> And we shall feel the agony of thirst,
> The ineffable longing for the life of life
> Baffled for ever. . . .

Pushed hither and thither among the alien elements,

> we shall unwillingly return
> Back to this meadow of calamity,
> This uncongenial place, this human life;
> And in our individual human state
> Go through the sad probation all again,
> To see if we will poise our life at last,
> To see if we will now at last be true
> To our own only true, deep-buried selves,
> Being one with which we are one with the whole world;

> Or whether we will once more fall away
> Into some bondage of the flesh or mind,
> Some slough of sense, or some fantastic maze
> Forged by the imperious lonely thinking-power. . . .

And, as external and internal conflicts become more intense,

> we shall fly for refuge to past times,
> Their soul of unworn youth, their breath of greatness;
> And the reality will pluck us back,
> Knead us in its hot hand, and change our nature.
> And we shall feel our powers of effort flag,
> And rally them for one last fight—and fail;
> And we shall sink in the impossible strife,
> And be astray for ever.

Probably no part of Arnold's poetry equals this long passage in penetrating psychological insight and in dramatically rendering the process of intense thought and emotion. Just before he leaps into the crater, Empedocles cheers himself with the recollection that he has never been the slave of sense or betrayed his intellectual integrity: and he had earlier declared his search for poise and balance. Yet, in its culminating effect, the long speech is a vehement affirmation of faith in feeling rather than reason. And that is supported by Arnold's *alter ego*, the young Callicles, whose concluding lyric is one of the poet's finest achievements, a swift evocation first of the "general life" of nature and man, then of Apollo and the Muses. If—to echo Frank Kermode[11]— Callicles may be called (in later Arnoldian terms) a Romantic poet who does not know enough, Empedocles knows too much; and we have seen how Arnold could prize the saving vitality, and lament the conquest or decay, of youthful feeling and vision. If both are out of balance, both wrong, the philosopher seems to be more wrong than the singer; yet it is too late in history to be Callicles, just as the world may have another Byron or Goethe but not another Wordsworth—though we may remember that John Stuart Mill, in an Empedoclean crisis, found salvation in Wordsworth's world of feeling.

Callicles' last lyric has been taken by A. D. Culler (176–77)

[11] *Romantic Image* (London: Routledge & Kegan Paul, 1957), 13.

as an anticipation of the Preface in which Arnold condemned
*Empedocles,* as an announcement of a new type of poet who
will "appeal to the great primary human affections; to those elementary feelings which subsist permanently in the race, and
which are independent of time." But surely the theme of the
lyric is not independent of time; it celebrates a vanished world.
Apollo and the Muses sing of the heroic age of gods and men,
of the code of life and natural piety which, in Callicles' first
lyric, Chiron had taught the young Achilles:

> First hymn they the Father
> Of all things; and then,
> The rest of immortals,
> The action of men.
>
> The day in his hotness,
> The strife with the palm;
> The night in her silence,
> The stars in their calm.

The whole lyric is a jet of that mythic primitivism which inspired so much of Arnold's most felicitous writing; and it links
itself with Empedocles' memories of the simple rhythms and
rituals of nature and life his youth had rejoiced in (II.250–57).
One may think that Arnold's public argument against the tragic
validity of *Empedocles* (which was summarized in the first section above) was not the only one; he might well have had some
vague qualms for having made the youthful life of feeling no
less and perhaps more needful than the skeptical intellect. He
had also shown the apparent impossibility of balanced, harmonious coexistence; one faculty could live only in the absence or
with the extinction of the other. Critics have been able to take
Empedocles' suicide as a moral victory and also as a moral failure; certainly it solves no problem, though it has its symbolic
significance. In the letter of early 1853 in which Arnold lec-
tured Clough on his morbidly inquiring indecisiveness (and con-
fessed that he himself was "past thirty, and three parts iced
over"), he said: "yes—*congestion of the brain* is what we suffer
from—I always feel it and say it—and cry for air like my own

Empedocles" (Lowry, 130). In some private reflections recorded apparently between 1849 and 1853, the period of *Empedocles,* Arnold wrote:

> I cannot conceal from myself the objection which really wounds & perplexes me from the religious side is that the service of reason is freezing to feeling, chilling to the religious moods.

> & feeling & the religious mood are eternally the deepest being of man, the ground of all joy & greatness for him.[12]

As I once remarked, it is no reflection on the poet's spiritual integrity that he himself did not jump into the Thames; if the subject was to yield its full value, Empedocles must be presented *in extremis.* More important is Arnold's remark, which followed what was quoted above from his letter to Clough of June 7, 1852: there, speaking of the leveling of distinction in the deteriorating modern world, he wound up: "Still nothing can absolve us from the duty of doing all we can to keep alive our courage and activity" (Lowry, 123). R. H. Hutton, perhaps the best of Arnold's Victorian critics, thought the suicide contrived and inadequately motivated, but said truly, of *Empedocles* and the poems in general, that Arnold

> cannot paint the restlessness of the soul—though he paints it vividly and well—without painting also the attitude of resistance to it, without giving the impression of a head held high above it, a nature that fixes the limits beyond which the corrosion of distrust and doubt shall not go, a deep speculative melancholy kept at bay, *not* by faith, but by a kind of imperious temperance of nature.

We may, postponing *Sohrab and Rustum,* touch briefly on Arnold's two other long works of tragic vision, the epic narrative *Balder Dead* (1853–54?) and the drama *Merope* (1856–57?), which go largely unread because of their reputation as solid, competent, dignified, and dull. One reason for neglect of *Balder*

---

[12] Quoted from the Yale Manuscript by C. B. Tinker and H. F. Lowry, *The Poetry of Matthew Arnold: A Commentary* (New York and London: Oxford University Press, 1940), 270; and by K. Allott, "A Background for 'Empedocles on Etna,'" *Essays and Studies 1968* (London, 1968), 96; cf. *Poems,* 147. Among discussions of the poem, apart from those in the critical books, is Walter Houghton's in *Victorian Studies* 1 (1958), 311–36.

is simply our common lack of familiarity with Scandinavian myth. Sir Edmund Chambers thus summed up conventional opinion: "Here is no excellent human action, where the shadowy figures of a priestly mythology are impelled by unintelligible motives to inconclusive ends."[13] Among more sympathetic critics, some have seen an affinity between Balder and Lord Falkland, the doomed, high-minded victim of the Civil War portrayed in Arnold's later essay.

*Merope*, which was provided with a long and scholarly preface, was intended to give Greekless readers "a specimen of the world created by the Greek imagination" (Russell, 1, 68) and perhaps, as a modern and original work, a more vital sense of Greek tragedy than translations commonly yielded. Arnold hoped that *Merope* might arouse, if not pity and terror, at any rate commiseration and awe; he also thought and hoped that it would "have what Buddha called the 'character of *Fixity*, that true sign of the Law' " (Russell, 1, 66). But this aim and hope were hardly fulfilled; most readers have found less "*Fixity*" than *rigor mortis*. The theme does involve a serious conflict of ethical values. Many years earlier, Polyphontes had gained power by murdering the king, Merope's husband, and two of their three sons; he has vainly urged marriage, but she has counted on the return of her surviving son to exact vengeance. He does return, secretly, and is almost killed, in error, by his mother; but he kills Polyphontes and becomes king, with popular support. Merope's problem is choosing between Polyphontes' "liberal, pragmatic ethic of compromise" and "the older ethic of absolute values," in this case the primitive right of revenge or justice (Culler, 223–24). The drama's failure is rather in execution than in conception; we are chilled by what seems a plaster reproduction of the antique. One chorus—"Much is there which the sea" (622 f.)—has been justly singled out; it recalls Arnold's other reflections on the buried, inaccessible self.

The conflict between past and present in *Empedocles*, *Balder*, and *Merope*, especially in the first, brings us back to the shorter poems. The nostalgic and painful contrast between youth and

[13] "Matthew Arnold," *Proceedings of the British Academy* 18 (1932), 32.

age in the individual life has large parallels in the contrast between the infancy or youth of the world and the race and modern complexity and disintegration—the same kind of contrast, however different the technique, that is used in the early poems of Eliot. This idea is the matrix of Arnold's mythological and biblical and Wordsworthian allusions. His most explicit fable of the history of man, *The Future* (1852?), utilizing his favorite image of a river, here the river of Time, traces its descent from the purity of its mountain source down to the cities of the plain that crowd its edge "In a blacker, incessanter line" (a passage that seems to echo Tennyson's Cambridge poem, *Timbuctoo*, on the extinction of myth by scientific progress—a poem Arnold knew). In keeping with that descent is the state of the modern soul, which, as a victim of historical process, the *Zeitgeist*, cannot recover the truth of simple feeling that guided Rebekah and Moses. The concluding image of the river joining "the infinite sea," perhaps attaining at last "a solemn peace of its own," may embody a vague hope for the race or for the individual's discovery or recovery of his "best self." No such hope lightens the contrast in *Dover Beach* between the age of faith and the empty darkness of the modern world.

The most elaborate examples of Arnold's contrasting of past and present are—apart from *Empedocles—The Scholar-Gipsy* (1852–53) and *Thyrsis* (1864–66), and these poems, like *Empedocles*, gather in other Arnoldian antinomies. In both, the desire for stability encounters the fact of continual change, in the outer world and in the self. In the one the old tale of the frustrated scholar who left Oxford to learn the gipsies' magical lore (mesmerism)—a tale which had long been in Arnold's mind—becomes a parable of the modern spirit's vain, lonely quest of unity and totality; and the seventeenth century—which had its fill of change, commotion, and war—is seen as a time

> when wits were fresh and clear,
> And life ran gaily as the sparkling Thames;
> Before this strange disease of modern life,
> With its sick hurry, its divided aims,
> Its heads o'ertaxed, its palsied hearts, was rife. . . .

The Scholar-Gipsy's *"one* aim, *one* business, *one* desire," which Arnold craves, is decidedly not, except in its unity, the "one clue" seen and followed by the Duke of Wellington. Although Arnold is wistfully celebrating the contemplative freedom of the dedicated spirit, especially no doubt the poet, and although pastoralism throughout its long history was, on a serious plane, conceived as a criticism of urban civilization, the appearance of escapist dreaming may seem in danger (as the poet recognizes at line 131) of attenuating the seriousness of the "quest"; we may feel that such nostalgic beauty does not approach "imaginative reason." We remember Arnold's own complaint about the poem (it was quoted above near the beginning of section II), and such Arnoldian critics as Stuart Sherman and F. R. Leavis[14] have spoken in similar or stronger terms. Alan Roper's reply to Arnold is more sympathetic: "As often as it is read, the poem confirms the possibility of good dreams in bad times; and if the poem also questions the validity of such dreams, it never quite commits itself against them: that, after all, is what the Gipsy Scholar does for you" (*Arnold's Poetic Landscapes*, 224).

So too in the less vividly memorable *Thyrsis* the Oxford days of Clough and Arnold are linked with pastoral and mythic Greece as a world of untroubled unity of soul and harmony with nature; Clough, unlike the Scholar-Gipsy, had left Oxford and lost his peace of mind. Arnold had long wanted "to connect Clough with that Cumner country" (Russell, 1, 380), and in the poem the "idyllic" almost submerged the elegiac; as a structural figure Clough became more shadowy than the Scholar-Gipsy. Arnold recognized—with some embarrassment in regard to Mrs. Clough—that he had composed less of a rounded elegy on his old friend than another commemoration of his beloved Oxford and its countryside, another lament for vanished youth; he presumably did not realize that the history of Clough's development got distorted in the process. In neither poem, not even in *The Scholar-Gipsy*, written soon after *Empedocles*, does the pres-

[14] Sherman, *Matthew Arnold: How to Know Him* (Indianapolis, 1917, pp. 76–77), a book which, despite the title of the series it belonged to, remains a good introduction; Leavis, *Revaluation* (ed. New York, 1963), 190–91, *The Common Pursuit* (London, 1952), 29–31.

sure of spiritual crisis have the anguished immediacy of the philosopher's last speeches. Now, or at least in these two poems, that experience has receded far enough into the past to become largely "mythic," to be beautifully overlaid with pastoral and Keatsian imagery, and, if we agree with Arnold's opinion of the earlier one, to awaken only a pleasing melancholy. In *Thyrsis* he could not, being Arnold, even try to emulate the exalted intensity of Milton's Christian or Shelley's "Platonic" resolution. But if he cannot get much beyond the "false surmise" of idyllic pastoralism, he knows that this is not wholly false; and at the same time he reminds himself repeatedly of "the signal-tree," "the throne of Truth," which cannot be reached but still is there. We should not be grudging in the face of two poems—or one poem in two parts—which are unique not only in the Arnoldian canon but in English poetry and which cast such a spell. With all their richness of phrase and image, they record the melancholy transition from sanguine youth to disenchanted age, a changed self in a changed world, and nostalgia is not necessarily debilitated or evasive.

## POEMS OF AFFIRMATION

It would appear that Arnold's inward conflicts and negations were pretty much exorcised if not resolved by *Empedocles*. As we have just seen, those conflicts did receive famous expression in *The Scholar-Gipsy* and *Thyrsis*, but there they were recollected in comparative tranquility; in a similar vein is a well-known stanza (69–72) in Arnold's elegy on his brother William, *A Southern Night* (1859). While, like other poets, he had at all times his variable moods, some of his chief later poems, in keeping with the prose he was beginning to write, show an increasingly affirmative and at times religious outlook, much less preoccupation with the internal problems of the individual and much more with social possibilities. This does not link Arnold with what is called "Victorian optimism," an attitude that almost no Victorian writer held.

We took earlier account of the positive literary stance of the

Preface of 1853. The poem that exemplified it, *Sohrab and Rustum* (1852–53?), is a far more attractive specimen than *Balder Dead* (1853–54) of epic objectivity, of "a very noble and excellent" story displaying in action "the great primary human affections . . . which are independent of time." (It is also a version of the Arnoldian antinomy between youth and age.) The story, told by the Persian poet Firdausi, had been retold by Sainte-Beuve (*Causeries du Lundi*, 1, 1850) and, with background details that Arnold used, in Sir John Malcolm's *History of Persia* (1815: 1, 31–54). Arnold, who ranked Homer above all other poets, set out to make his epic episode as Homeric as possible in narrative method and texture, and the poem is full of echoes and imitations. At the same time he evidently had in mind Aristotelian principles of structure (so prominent in the Preface of 1853) and the example of Sophoclean tragedy, which involves full use of dramatic irony. Such irony was of course implicit in the story itself, in a father's killing his son in combat, each being ignorant of the other's identity; but Arnold consciously and effectively worked up that irony in many details, from the first moment we hear of Sohrab's quest of his famous father and his hope of greeting him on some well-fought field.

Irony becomes more poignant as the combatants confront each other. The renowned warrior, in pity, urges the young man to forgo battle and be as a son to him, and Sohrab, rushing to embrace his knees, asks if he is not Rustum. When Rustum's club misses its stroke and drops from his hand, Sohrab chivalrously spares his unarmed opponent, and, touched again by a filial feeling, he urges a truce. It seems as if heaven and nature took part in "that unnatural conflict": sudden darkness, wind, and sand envelop the two. In accordance with Aristotle's ideal pattern of tragedy, the "recognition" and the "peripeteia" (change of fortune) are simultaneous: Rustum at last shouts "Rustum" and Sohrab, unnerved, as he later says, by that beloved name, recoils, lets fall his shield, and receives a wound that is soon fatal. Rustum is finally convinced of Sohrab's identity by the seal pricked on his arm (Sohrab had needed no tokens to recognize his father), and the dying son tries to lighten his grief. Night comes on, the two armies start their fires and have their meal, while Rustum, his cloak over his face, sits in the plain beside the body of his son. Then comes that quite un-Homeric but greatly Arnoldian coda: the description of the Oxus river as a complex symbol of the timeless continuity of life in which individual lives and noble souls make only momentary ripples; it might also be called a brief parallel to *The Future*. The conclusion, if not the poem as a whole, "conducts us" (to quote the preface to *Merope*) "to a state of feeling which it is the highest aim of tragedy to produce, to *a sentiment of sublime acquiescence in the course of fate, and in the dispensations of human life*."

This is such a finely written and really moving poem that one is reluctant to admit that it falls short of its author's high aims. For one thing, although the two figures, especially Sohrab, are so noble and embody universal feelings, the basic situation is not brought about by character. The story is not tragic in the full sense of involving such a moral choice as Oedipus and Antigone make; it is a pathetic accident, an ironic stroke of fate.

In the second place, Arnold, in opposition to Romantic subjectivity and his own *Empedocles*, was offering an objective treatment of a great action as a model for misguided poets. Clearly the poem cannot fulfill that function, since Arnold withdraws from the troubled world of modern experience into a primitive heroic age. Homer himself of course remains animating and ennobling for modern readers, but modern poets cannot reach such readers or be true to themselves by ignoring their own world and trying to be literally Homeric. The most insistent element of artifice in *Sohrab and Rustum* is the continual use— or imposition, one might say—of elaborate Homeric similes, nearly two dozen in 892 lines. However functional these are in providing (as in Homer) a recurrent contrast between the worlds of peace and conflict, each one comes in as a conscious *tour de force* and gives us a shock of unreality from which it is not easy to recover. And yet, though we might not crave another poem like this, we may be truly glad to have the one.

*Balder Dead* (1853–54?), which is such another and which was briefly noticed before, may count also as a poem of affirmation, especially by virtue of its moving conclusion. This prophesies a new dawn of good, whose agents, in the words of a recent critic,

J. P. Farrell, are "the 'saving remnant' or the 'Children of the Second Birth.' They regenerate the world by preserving from the vicissitudes of the *Zeitgeist* their integrity and their humanity."

Since Freudian formulas are exempt from the usual need for evidence, it has been said by numerous critics that *Sohrab and Rustum* owes much of its power to Arnold's unconscious releasing of early antagonism to his father. Dr. Arnold, to be sure, had been more religious and scholarly than poetical, and he had felt prolonged anxiety about his son's lack of studious zeal, but we know of no "antagonism";[15] and Sohrab feels nothing but devotion to Rustum. As Arnold the critic became more and more engaged in enlightening his countrymen, he paid continual tributes in his letters to his father's rare qualities of mind and leadership. *Rugby Chapel* (1857–60)—animated partly by Sir James Stephen's hostile account of Dr. Arnold—was a heart-felt eulogy of his character and career, shaped, appropriately, in terms of a mountain climb (a quest was one of Arnold's archetypal images), and emphasizing—as he had done in a letter to his mother of 1855—the active friend and helper of mankind, the guide to "the City of God."[16] The whole poem seems to echo themes of Dr. Arnold's Rugby sermons, remembered or read, and in the latter half the religious tone and the character of the man are heightened by parallels with Moses' leading the Israelites through the wilderness. And the foe of religious delusions can hardly resist the feeling that such a strong and beneficent spirit must still be somewhere at work.

A short and generalized celebration of the heroic, a poem as

---

[15] In a letter of 1840 to a clerical friend Dr. Arnold, expressing his concern about Matthew's unstudious ways, spoke of his being "so loving to me" that a father should be hopeful and very patient (E. K. Brown, *Matthew Arnold: A Study in Conflict*, Chicago: University of Chicago Press; London: Cambridge University Press, 1948, pp. 176–77; *cf.* 216–17, n. 104). *Cf.* above, Ch. I, n. 1.

[16] This last phrase, says David Daiches, "is employed here as little more than an obeisance to the public school code of carrying on," and he cites Kipling and Newbolt (*Some Late Victorian Attitudes*, London: André Deutsch, 1969, p. 37). This idea seems unworthy of Arnold's understanding of his father's religious and social aims and of his own constant vision of "perfection" as man's ultimate goal.

simply didactic as a pulpit anecdote but one of Arnold's best, is
*Palladium* (1864–65?). Here morality is touched with emotion.
The statue of Pallas, on which the safety of Troy depended
and which stood high above the city, is the soul (our "best self,"
as Arnold would say in prose), the power that sustains man in
his struggle through life as he fluctuates " 'twixt blind hopes and
blind despairs." ("Blind hopes" is a grim phrase in *Prometheus
Bound* 252.) Critics cite a private jotting of Arnold's: "Our re-
motest self must abide in its remoteness awful & unchanged,
presiding at the tumult of the rest [?] of our being, changing
thoughts contending desires &c as the moon over the agitations
of the Sea." The poem seems to include suggestions from Lucretius and the French critic, Edmond Scherer, but the main inspiration for the idea of Everyman's perpetual Trojan war is
surely the saying of Goethe that Arnold quoted in his first
Homeric lecture: "From Homer and Polygnotus I every day
learn more clearly that in our life here above ground we have,
properly speaking, to enact Hell." In *Palladium* the battle, unlike that at the end of *Dover Beach*, is not hopeless.

We noticed before the positive religious spirit of *Progress*,
though it was apparently written soon after *Dover Beach* and
about the time of the *Grande Chartreuse*. A decade later, in
1863, Arnold was moved to write a cluster of sonnets, such as
*East London*, on Christian humanitarianism, and *The Better
Part* and *Immortality*, on the imitation of Christ and the true
heaven of righteousness. These sonnets, however inferior as
poetry, are, as Stuart Sherman said, much closer than the idyllic
stanzas of *The Scholar-Gipsy* to the center of Arnold's mature
thought and feeling. The most elaborate poetical exposition of his
later outlook is *Obermann Once More* (1865–67?), a rapid historical essay which varies in texture from poetry to prose: it
embodies a religious hope of a general rebirth of spiritual energy and social commitment.

The opening Alpine scene, which suggests the enduring life
of nature, brings a vision of Senancour in person, the long-
abandoned master of the poet's wandering youth, and most of
the poem is spoken by that ineffectual but earnest seeker of
harmony and order. Senancour first develops the parallel—a

parallel very present to both Dr. Arnold and his son—between the modern world and the Roman empire, and he exemplifies (from Lucretius, iii.1060–67) the restless ennui that fell on "that hard Pagan world" (93–104). One sample of Arnold's generalizing imagination is this (in quoting Senancour's discourse we may omit the regular quotation marks):

> The East bowed low before the blast
> In patient, deep disdain;
> She let the legions thunder past,
> And plunged in thought again.

Then come the birth of Christianity and its effect on Rome, an ascetic revolt against paganism—a flat but forceful picture which Yeats may have remembered in the first of his *Two Songs from a Play*:

> She veiled her eagles, snapped her sword,
> And laid her sceptre down;
> Her stately purple she abhorred,
> And her imperial crown. . . .

Christ's gospel of love was an inspiring reality, and "He lived while we believed." But, as in *Dover Beach*, the tide of faith receded:

> *Unduped of fancy, henceforth man*
> *Must labour!—must resign*
> *His all too human creeds, and scan*
> *Simply the way divine!*

This is the argument of the earlier *Progress* and of the later religious books and of the present poem.

The next great renewal was the French Revolution, but it lost its unifying fire and disintegrated.

> The millions suffer still, and grieve,
> And what can helpers heal
> With old-world cures men half believe
> For woes they wholly feel?

As in the *Grande Chartreuse*, the old world is out of date, the new not yet born; but here—as in *Rugby Chapel*—there is no sympathy with seclusion:

And who can be *alone* elate,
While the world lies forlorn?

Senancour describes his own retreat and his "frustrate life," the consuming Romantic thirst for a new hope which had been an "Immedicable pain" (the adjective may be remembered from parallel contexts, *Childe Harold* iv.126 or *Prometheus Unbound* II.iv.101). But now he feels the stirrings of a world being reborn:

> One common wave of thought and joy
> Lifting mankind again!

In *Empedocles* thought had been the destroyer of joy; here they are united. And while Empedocles' sermon to Pausanias had concerned individual salvation or survival through acceptance of limits, Senancour's speech proclaims a new social vision fortified by a valid faith—in which we need not discern "a counterfeit ring" (Allott). The simple last line, "I saw the morning break," is more confident and less vaguely hopeful than the conclusions of *A Summer Night* and *The Future*. If it marks the death of Arnold the poet, it marks the birth of Arnold the critic; disillusioned post-Romantic introspection and pessimism have given place to the positive creed of *Essays in Criticism* and *Culture and Anarchy*.

### 3. Poetic Craftsmanship

While the separation of ideas and artistry is artificial and awkward, it would be still more awkward to offer rounded discussions of several dozen poems one by one. We may therefore look now at some of the artistic virtues and defects of poetry considered earlier mainly as a body of ideas.

It is obvious that Arnold had only a modest share of the creative imagination, versatility, and artistic power that Tennyson and Browning so abundantly display. Indeed a reader may rather often feel that he himself could improve on Arnold's phrasing or rhythm or even his handling of an idea, whereas Tennyson and Browning, on their lower levels, are still too distinctively artists to invite such presumption. Of course Arnold, in both his gifts and his shortcomings, differs widely from them, as they differ from each other. And, apart from the fact of different gifts, we may remember that Arnold was not able to give a long life solely to poetry but wrote in the intervals of more or less harassing official duties and in his later decades produced many volumes of prose. He did, to be sure, find time for a good deal of revision, though his capacity for self-criticism was less alert than it might have been. From the start critics complained of a gap between the critical theory of his Preface of 1853 and his practice, in regard to both structural coherence and style.

Arnold's better poems plainly embody much more of reflective commentary on life than of imaginative or dramatic creation.  The actual or potential critic is often visible, not merely in such an essay as *Memorial Verses* or in the very conception of such an objective poem as *Sohrab and Rustum* but in his more typical dialogues of the mind with itself. It is not surprising that he expresses his ideas and feelings very directly and seldom leaves interpretation to the reader; even in *Dover Beach* and *Palladium* an image is openly applied and expounded. We noted before that, in spite of his early resolve to upset a partly Wordsworthian tradition, in many of his poems he is "thinking aloud, instead of making anything." What saves the numerous more or less good ones is their intelligence, urgency, and sincerity, along with, to be sure, considerable artistic competence and sometimes far more than that. On the other hand, it seems safe to say that, of the poems or passages where Arnold writes with something like inspired felicity, many are those in which he is escaping from his own age and spiritual struggles into a dream-world of primitive unity and simplicity of feeling; here if anywhere he enjoys "A pleasure in creating." The most sustained examples are *The Scholar-Gipsy* and *Thyrsis*. Such escapism is not necessarily weak evasion; it may be, like the pastoral tradition as a whole, an integral element in the criticism of life. And escapism might, in a sense, include *Sohrab and Rustum*, which Arnold thought the best thing he had yet done, and which he had "the greatest pleasure in composing," "a rare thing with me, and, as I think, a good test of the pleasure what you write is likely to afford to others" (Russell, 1, 34–35); this last opinion has not been unanimously endorsed.

The ethical and psychological conflicts that Arnold feels with intensity he can describe with intensity and with analytical precision that is not only direct but often subtle; and under the stress of the experience we may hardly notice the style. In general, and in keeping with his dominant principles and characteristic themes, Arnold uses the plain language of speech and prose; in this respect his verse is closer to Wordsworth and to modern modes than the more "poetical" vein of most of his contemporaries. (In his letters he takes anything Tennysonian as *ipso facto* bad, although Tennyson had a variety of great styles as well as some weak ones.) But while Arnold's diction tends to be acceptably ordinary, it can be flat or inflated, and word-order and syntax and rhythm are often awkwardly angular; in manner as in matter we are sometimes reminded of Hardy. We may be put off by the recurrence of "Ah" and of italics; by archaisms ("thou," "ye," "hath"); by periphrases which, unlike Milton's, seem pointless: "the son of Thetis" (*Stanzas . . . Obermann* 89), "thou son of Anchitus" (*Empedocles* I.ii.111); by inept words such as "wight" and "elf" (*Empedocles* I.ii.129, 306) thrown in for the sake of meter or rhyme; by bathetic fillers like "Glion, but not the same!" (*Obermann Once More* 4). This last item is a reminder that Arnold can be weak in starting, before a theme has taken hold of him. That finely penetrating poem, *The Buried Self*, begins with stilted rhetoric:

> Light flows our war of mocking words, and yet,
> Behold, with tears mine eyes are wet!
> I feel a nameless sadness o'er me roll.

Such things, however small, are so frequent that Arnold's best poems seldom attain entire perfection. Even the conclusion of Callicles' superb last lyric is not flawless: in "Whose praise do they mention?" the misused verb is jarring. In the likewise superb "Yeş! in the sea of life enisled" the phrases "enclasping flow" and "endless bounds" (lines 5 and 6) suggest "uniting sea" and "spacious freedom" rather than the evidently intended sense of "separating sea" and "everlasting confinement."

Arnold's most felicitous images may be charged with emotion—"The unplumbed, salt, estranging sea"—or be directly and freshly pictorial: "In the hedge straggling to the stream,/Pale, dew-drenched, half-shut roses gleam" (*Resignation* 178–79); "some wet bird-haunted English lawn" (*Parting*). Equally clear-cut are the whole series of vignettes in *The Strayed Reveller*, the descriptions of both the persons and the young man's visions; the poem—if it did not embody an idea—might be called pure Imagism. Here and elsewhere, it may be observed, Arnold's mythological and classical scenes and figures have an outdoor mythic actuality quite different from Tennyson's beautifully composed re-creations, in which antique décor and atmosphere tend to be submerged by the modern theme. Wholly Imagist are these lines from *Mycerinus*:

> While the deep-burnished foliage overhead
> Splintered the silver arrows of the moon.

A similar image in Tennyson (*In Memoriam* ci) has a shade more of studied contrivance:

> Or into silver arrows break
> The sailing moon in creek and cove.

A good many of Arnold's friends and critics, as Sidney Coulling[17] has noted, saw the strong influence of Tennyson in his poems—such as *Mycerinus, The New Sirens, The Forsaken Merman, Sohrab and Rustum*—an idea that would and did vex Arnold (who admitted that Tennyson was so much in one's head that echoes were inevitable) but that to us now may not seem over-discriminating.

Like Tennyson (and many other poets), Arnold arranged scenes for symbolic suggestiveness; we have observed already a large-scale example, the setting of *Empedocles* and the placing of its three figures. Indeed the method of description and application is almost an Arnoldian formula. In *Resignation* the long walk, the mountain, the noisy town, all have their place in the pattern of meaning; even "the bells of foam" that wash away "from this bank, their home," suggest Fausta's self-assertive disposition. *A Summer Night* opens on "the deserted moon-blanched street" and the lonely echo of the speaker's feet; the white, silent

[17] "Matthew Arnold's 1853 Preface: Its Origin and Aftermath," *Victorian Studies* 7 (1963–64), 233–63.

windows are "Repellent as the world." At the same time "A break between the housetops shows/The moon" and behind it the darkness of "a whole tract of heaven"—a latent image of hope and fulfillment picked up at the end of the poem.

The opening of *Dover Beach* is a more subtle blend of assurance and disquiet:

> The sea is calm to-night.
> The tide is full, the moon lies fair
> Upon the straits.

But the word "to-night" reminds us that the sea is not always calm, the tide not always full, the moon not always fair. The poem proceeds:

> on the French coast the light
> Gleams and is gone; the cliffs of England stand,
> Glimmering and vast, out in the tranquil bay.

Against apparent peace and stability are the facts of the vanishing of the light and the glimmering of the cliffs. There seems to be untroubled serenity in "Come to the window, sweet is the night-air!" But then we meet the ominous "Only," the hint of alien coldness in "the moon-blanched land," and the full recognition of the sinister in "the grating roar" of the pebbles drawn back and flung up on the strand, the endlessly repeated process which brings "The eternal note of sadness in." What follows confirms the hint that men are like the pebbles, for ever swept back and forth by circumstances and forces beyond their control.

If Sophocles' likening of human calamities to the stormy sea (*Trachiniae* 112 f., *Antigone* 583 f., etc.) is not strictly relevant, Arnold's allusion to his favorite Greek dramatist has the effect— like the myth in *Philomela*—of joining past and present in one long chain of suffering. His association of the tide with "the turbid ebb and flow/Of human misery" is wholly logical, though it must be granted that his transfer of the impressive image to "The Sea of Faith" is not, since it does not perpetually ebb and flow but has ebbed once for all; however, we need not be upset by that any more than we are by Keats's making the mortal nightingale immortal. The image, by the way, may have come from Sainte-Beuve.[18]

The conclusion is unexpected—if one may speak thus of so familiar a poem and may quote such familiar lines:

> Ah, love, let us be true
> To one another! for the world, which seems
> To lie before us like a land of dreams,
> So various, so beautiful, so new,
> Hath really neither joy, nor love, nor light,
> Nor certitude, nor peace, nor help for pain;
> And we are here as on a darkling plain
> Swept with confused alarms of struggle and flight,
> Where ignorant armies clash by night.

This conclusion was apparently written before the preceding lines 1–28. The final picture of ignorant armies clashing by night was taken from Thucydides' account (vii.43–44) of a disastrous night battle in Sicily—which Clough had already referred to in the Bothie (ix.50–54). The image breaks away from that of the sea, which has hitherto been massively dominant; yet the conclusion depends for its full meaning and impact on what has preceded, and there are particular links in the fact of darkness and in the lines "for the world . . . pain," which return to and reject the delusive beauty and security described in the opening lines. But "that we have no sea in the last section is the very point of the poem" (Culler, 40) may be thought an over-subtle forcing of the metaphor.

The Scholar-Gipsy and Thyrsis, linked together in everything except dates of composition, stand apart in manner from all of Arnold's other poems. Both are at the furthest extreme from the "plain direct and severe" style required (he had said in October 1852) for the serious themes of modern poetry. Along with the semi-Keatsian stanza, many verbal echoes in The Scholar-Gipsy attest Arnold's responsiveness to Keatsian imag-

---

[18] One may query the recent opinion (Culler, 40; Roper, 179–80) that Arnold was thinking of the "Sea of Faith" as the "Ocean Stream" that girdled the Homeric world. The theme, the ebbing of Christian faith, would surely be confused by an image from primitive Greek cosmology; and could the Ocean Stream be described in terms of tides?

ery[19] (which he had censured not long before); and the main body of the poem, in which he imagines the Scholar-Gipsy appearing in various Oxford settings, has been cited as an expansive—and probably unconscious—imitation of the various guises and settings of Keats's spirit of Autumn (and of the "Youth" in Gray's *Elegy*). Keats's nightingale is recalled too by the "immortal lot" of Arnold's wanderer, a shadowy figure of history now become a mythic symbol. Although the poet willingly indulges in such imaginings, he pulls himself up with the acknowledgment that they are an escapist dream, and turns to the disease and dividedness of the modern soul. After an analysis of this condition in abstract terms, the poem resumes the pastoral and decorative mode of the first part, and it ends with the most elaborate image in all of Arnold (what in the same letter of October 1852 he might have classified as flagrant "ornamental work"), the much-discussed symbolic picture of the Tyrian trader fleeing from Greek intruders. The image (apparently suggested by Herodotus, iv.196) is an epitome of the whole poem, and yet its functional relevance and coherence are rather obscured than strengthened by the elaborate descriptive detail, so that—except by the more fanciful reinterpreters—the stanzas may be felt as little more than a concluding purple patch.

The cherished idea of linking Clough with the Oxford countryside seemed to prescribe the same idyllic manner for *Thyrsis*. Arnold recognized that it was too late to revive the formal and thematic conventions of the pastoral elegy (which had inspired the least successful parts of *Adonais*), though he did contrast the "unawakening sleep" of death with the reawakening life of nature. He could, however, make full use of Greek pastoralism and mythology in conjuring up an age of primitive happiness and of harmony between the world—the world of nature—and man; the pastoralism of *The Scholar-Gipsy* had been modern and realistic—"Nor let thy bawling fellows rack their throats." Thus in the elegy the semi-Keatsian vein of *The Scholar-Gipsy* has an infusion of Theocritus, Bion, and Moschus—and of Arnold's very knowledgeable love of flowers. It is all very beautiful,

---

[19] George H. Ford, *Keats and the Victorians: A Study of His Influence and Rise to Fame 1821–1895* (New Haven, 1944).

though the beauty perhaps blurs and softens the austere quest
of Truth symbolized by the tree that "yet crowns the hill."

Arnold's recurring ideas and antinomies develop the nucleus
of an individual and unifying vocabulary, which is in the main
a help to the reader: "age," "alone," "business," "calm," "feel,"
"joy," "pain," "passion," "youth," and so on. Some key words, variable in traditional usage, retain special ambiguities in Arnold.
Thus "the world" may refer to the Stoic world-process or, more
commonly, to the everyday world of action and distraction as
opposed to contemplation. "Nature" (a word full of pitfalls, as
Arnold said in *Literature and Dogma*: Super, 6, 388), may
have such diverse meanings as the order of the universe, the
mythic "Mighty Mother," a set of blind evolutionary or destructive forces, or the beauties of the visible scene. But such ambiguities are generally made clear by their contexts; they are not
the ambiguities of conscious irony.

Arnold's favorite symbolic images, such as the mountain, the
plain, the sequestered glade, light (notably moonlight) and
darkness, contribute far more than abstract words to the coherence of his poems.[20] Two of the most conspicuous are those
of the river and the sea, which may vary (especially the sea)
but as a rule have a generic import. Arnold had a deeply instinctive liking for water and the fresh vitality it implies: witness the
allusions, cited above, to dew-drenched roses and a "wet bird-
haunted English lawn" (where "wet" does not have its usual depressing connotation), and Callicles' cool watery valley at the
beginning of *Empedocles*. "Papa loves rivers" was a saying of
Arnold's son Dicky (Russell, 1, 328; *cf.* 323, 352). In the letter
of September 29, 1848, the one in which he referred to Marguerite, Arnold exclaimed: "And the curse of the dirty water—
the real pain it occasions to one who looks upon water as the
Mediator between the inanimate and man is not to be described"
(Lowry, 92). In his simple but effective uses a river's continuous

[20] These symbols, expounded by Alan Roper in *Publications of the Modern Language Association* 77 (1962), are elaborately treated in the books,
already cited, by Culler (1966) and Roper (1969). Of course Arnold's
critics in general have taken more or less account of so manifest an element
in his poetry.

flow may be a parallel to, or a timeless contrast with, human life
and human troubles. Symbolic images range from the brook in
*Resignation* to the majestic Oxus that sweeps past the dead
Sohrab and the stricken Rustum. Even in the early prize poem,
Cromwell's "inward light" "Bound all his being with a silver
chain—/Like a swift river through a silent plain!" At the end
of *Mycerinus* the noise of the doomed young king's revelry is
"Mixed with the murmur of the moving Nile," the river taken
earlier in the poem as a symbol of the irresistible cosmic process
of Stoicism. *The River* (1850) is a love poem, its scene a boat on
the Thames. The "river of Life" separates lovers in *A Dream*
(1849–53). In *In Utrumque Paratus* man is imagined as ascend-
ing toward the pure source of "life's stream"; in *The Future* the
"river of Time" flows down from its pure source to the ugly plain
of history. True feeling is the unregarded subterranean river in
*The Buried Life*. At the end of *Obermann Once More*, "only the
torrent broke/The silence," the torrent Senancour had identified
with *la fuite de nos années*. There is an actual river in *The
Scholar-Gipsy* and *Thyrsis*, but it is "the stripling Thames,"
"the youthful Thames," a symbolic part of well-remembered
scenes.

Images of the sea are hardly less frequent, and, like those of a
river, are at their best no less effective than obvious. The most
familiar—and very different—examples are the "Sea of Faith"
in *Dover Beach*, the mysterious depths inhabited by the "Forsaken Merman" and the primitive sea-beasts, and, in "Yes! in
the sea of life enisled," the hostile element that separates islands
once united, the force that condemns the "mortal millions" of
human beings to "live *alone*." *Human Life* (1849–50?) describes
the impossibility of steering a course "As, chartered by some
unknown Powers,/We stem across the sea of life by night." In
*A Summer Night* the few bold spirits who escape from the prison
of everyday routine become storm-tossed victims of passion, "Still
standing for some false, impossible shore." In the *Grande Chartreuse* the word "watered" creates as unhappy a metaphor as
poet ever made: "Our fathers watered with their tears/This
sea of time whereon we sail."

On the other hand, the sea may be viewed as the great body

of water into which rivers flow. (The world-weary young Swinburne, in 1866, could thank whatever gods may be "That even
the weariest river/Winds somewhere safe to sea.") For Arnold
this image may suggest individual attainment of true self-knowledge and identity, of fruitful unity, or a parallel movement in the
evolution of the race, or it may be a symbol of a neutral or
benign "Platonic" infinity (I will not say of the return to the
womb), derived partly no doubt from "that immortal sea" of
*Intimations of Immortality.* We remember the conclusion of
*Sohrab and Rustum,* the Oxus river—"A foiled circuitous wanderer"—joining the bright and tranquil Aral Sea. In *The Youth
of Man* (1852) the now aged and ignoble pair, who in youth
had denied the reality of Nature, the "Soul of the world," look
with clearer vision at "the imperial stream" flowing "On, to the
plains, to the sea." In *The Future* "the river of Time," which lost
its primal purity as it descended to the plain of human life and
cities, may in the end bring peace to the soul of man, "Murmurs
and scents of the infinite sea." So too at the end of *The Buried
Life,* in rare moments a man's insight may be illuminated by love,

> And then he thinks he knows
> The hills where his life rose,
> And the sea where it goes.

There is a hint of the same kind in *Resignation* (84–85), where,
after the long and dusty walk, "We bathed our hands with
speechless glee,/That night, in the wide-glimmering sea."

Arnold has often been charged with a defective ear, and some
of his rhythmical and other sins are especially conspicuous in
his sonnets, whatever their substantive value. The required compression and rhyme-scheme tend to produce cramped, ungainly
rhythms and oracular rhetoric, even obscurity; one would not
like to think that he thought he was being Miltonic. It would
seem hardly possible that anyone could ever write, much less
print, that notorious opening line: "Who prop, thou ask'st, in
these bad days, my mind?" In reading Arnold, to be sure, we
must try to distinguish between mere awkwardness and a degree
of "unpoetical" roughness appropriate to what he is saying—as
in Empedocles' sermon (which, we are surprised to find, is

written in the stanza of Shelley's *To a Skylark*, though Shelley's trochaics become iambics). But if cacophonies are intended to reflect the discords of the theme and the age, they can sometimes misfire. Arnold did not lack a metrical conscience. Anticipating some disrelish for the meter of *Haworth Churchyard*, he explained: ". . . but I could not manage to say what I wished *as* I wished in any other metre"; it is hard to understand the necessity of chopped prose. Similar jerky effects may appear in the short lines of such other poems as *Consolation, Rugby Chapel*, and *Heine's Grave*. One occasional fault is the use of a clipped meter that fights against the reflective and exploratory substance and tone. In the opening of the *Grande Chartreuse* it is said that "slow we ride," but the meter and the pouncing rhymes of each stanza's final couplet suggest a smart canter. The beginning of *Memorial Verses* sounds like an elegiac clog-dance (and could there be more inept phrasing than that of the third line?):

> Goethe in Weimar sleeps, and Greece,
> Long since, saw Byron's struggle cease.
> But one such death remained to come;
> The last poetic voice is dumb—
> We stand to-day by Wordsworth's tomb.

Arnold could use conventional meters with expressive skill and grace, as in the slow quatrains of *Lines Written in Kensington Gardens* and *Palladium* or the swift ones of Callicles' last lyric:

> Through the black, rushing smoke-bursts,
> Thick breaks the red flame;
> All Etna heaves fiercely
> Her forest-clothed frame.
>
> Not here, O Apollo!
> Are haunts meet for thee.
> But, where Helicon breaks down
> In cliff to the sea,
>
> Where the moon-silvered inlets
> Send far their light voice
> Up the still vale of Thisbe,
> O speed, and rejoice! . . .

At the other end of the spectrum are the elaborate stanzas of the two Oxford poems, derived from the stanza of Keats's *Ode to a Nightingale*. A critic of Keats, M. R. Ridley, thinks Arnold's stanza "curiously invertebrate," because the sestet precedes and overweights the quatrain, so that it drifts uneasily to a standstill; but readers of less technical expertise may, with due regard to purposes quite different from Keats's, find Arnold's swaying stanzas not only adequate but admirable. And among successes we must not forget the muscular and finely expressive blank verse of the concluding third of *Mycerinus* and Empedocles' last speeches.

Arnold's most distinctively original achievements, however, were in free verse, or what R. H. Hutton called "pieces of un-rhymed *recitative*," for which his models seem to have been both Greek lyrics and poems of Goethe and Heine. Naturally he was not always fortunate. He had misgivings about his most direct attempt to reproduce the effects of Greek choric rhythms, in the choruses of *Merope*, and an early reader unkindly likened them to the sound of a boy's drawing a stick along area railings. Of very different rhythmical quality are such poems as *The Strayed Reveller*, *Dover Beach*, *The Future*, *A Summer Night*, *The Buried Life*, and *Philomela*. In these, irregularity of meter and rhyme or lack of rhyme brings, for Arnold, freedom from awkward compression or padding and seldom leads to sprawling looseness. The finest example is *Dover Beach*, a subtle mixture of short and five-stress lines with irregular rhymes; here the lines flow and ebb like the tide they describe. And we must not pass by the beautiful change of movement and tone from Empedocles' sermon to Callicles' song of Cadmus and Harmonia:

> Far, far from here,
> The Adriatic breaks in a warm bay
> Among the green Illyrian hills. . . .

The song continues in finely modulated lines, rhymed and un-rhymed, mainly of four or five stresses.

We may end with a late poem which seems to have no interest at all for most critics but has some in point of craftsmanship. While it is a commonplace that almost the whole body of Arnold's poetry is in some sense elegiac, there is the literal fact that

he wrote some eleven actual elegies on particular persons; a
sort of elegy on himself, *A Wish* (1865?); *Requiescat* (1849–
53?), on a nameless woman, real or imaginary, a graceful and
touching lyric véry typical in its theme of peace attained after
harassing life in the world; and three poems on family pets, two
dogs and a canary. The chief elegies we have noticed already.
The one on Dean Stanley, *Westminster Abbey* (1881), seems to
go unread and is described by Arnold's latest editor as "labo-
rious and unfeeling contrivance." The poem does not express
much personal grief, although Arnold had admired his father's
pupil, biographer, and powerful heir in the Broad Church movement, the historian as well as the Dean of the Abbey. The ceremonial tribute has positive attractions in its highly wrought design, its use of what Arnold called "a lovely legend of primitive
Westminster" and of classical myth, the play of light throughout, and the sustained elevation of tone: all this, as classical
scholars have recognized, constitutes a rare modern phenomenon, a really Pindaric ode. With all its artifice, the poem
touches ideas recurrent in Arnold's prose, for instance, the working of the *Zeitgeist* in terms of historical periodicity (here
imaged in the alternation of light and darkness):

> For this and that way swings
> The flux of mortal things,
> Though moving inly to one far-set goal.[21]

Leon Gottfried remarks that Stanley's "love of all things pure,/
And joy in light, and power to spread the joy" is a last echo
of Wordsworth ("Of joy in widest commonalty spread"); and
light recalls *Balder Dead* and Arnold's essay on Joubert as well
as Pindar.

[21] Bonnerot, 278–80. Arnold failed to catch and eliminate the echo of
Tennyson (the last lines of *In Memoriam*) in the last of the quoted lines.

# III: *Literary Criticism*

✧✧✧✧✧✧✧✧✧✧✧✧✧✧✧✧✧✧✧✧✧✧✧✧✧✧✧✧✧✧✧✧✧✧✧✧✧✧✧✧✧

ALTHOUGH, as a poet, Arnold ranked creativity above criticism and in letters of 1861–86 repeatedly expressed a hope of getting back to poetry, he had worked his way out of his spiritual malaise, and in finding relief from such anxieties he lost his chief inspiration; a number of his late poems tended to be impersonal essays. But he found also a new and progressively satisfying vocation in prose as "Physician of the iron age" (to use his poetic label for Goethe), as an apostle of enlightenment. Beginning, almost by accident, with literary criticism, and with a strongly ethical conception of that, he branched out into social, political, and religious writing, and he continued until his death to be active on these several fronts; they were all united in his conception of "culture."

Taking literature in general as a criticism of life, Arnold took literary criticism not only as an educator and guardian of public opinion and taste but as an intellectual and philosophical discoverer of ideas, a necessary precursor of valuable creative activity. Thus he imposed upon criticism a much weightier function than it had been accustomed to bear. And he gave it still further responsibility in exalting the role of poetry. In his view and experience, both Christian supernaturalism and the Romantic vision had lost their hold upon modern man, and in seeking a faith of enduring validity Arnold set up poetry, the greatest poetry, as one main agent of the spiritual and ethical life.

His importance has been not so much in his assessments of this or that writer (though his estimates gained wide authority) but in his general attitudes and seminal ideas, his position of classical centrality and sanity. His influence was commanding in his own century and in the earlier part of ours, as the names of his principal heirs indicate. In recent times, radical changes in the climate of civilization and of literature have led us further away from Arnold, and, so far as we have lost sight of his standards of ethical and artistic "adequacy," we have fared the worse. But he continues to appear frequently in print, either as an ally to be invoked or as an adversary to be reckoned with; and, if we sometimes grow tired of many literary intellectuals' compulsive need to be "with it," Arnold is restorative.

We observed, in his letters to Clough, Arnold's gradual shift from preoccupation with poetic style to preoccupation with content, with poetry as a *magister vitae*. In the Preface of 1853, starting from his reasons for withdrawing the "morbid" *Empedocles*, Arnold condemned both Romantic subjectivity and current demands that poets turn from "the exhausted past" to modern life; he pleaded for great actions, characters, and passions, for man's elementary, universal feelings, as the timeless material of poetry. And to Romantic diffuseness and excess of imagery he opposed severe, coherent economy of form and style.

In his inaugural lecture at Oxford, *On the Modern Element in Literature* (1857: Super, 1, 18 f.), Arnold outlined another dynamic principle of his classicism. The word "Modern" carries on the challenge of the Preface: it means, chiefly, any period in history in which critical and creative intelligence is capable of truly interpreting past and present. (In our time the word might mean chiefly preoccupation with the subjective self, conscious and unconscious, as the central or only reality.) Now, says Arnold, in an age of confusing change and complexity, the great need is for "intellectual deliverance," for philosophic comprehension of the general ideas behind multitudinous facts, "the collective life of humanity"—a view which helps to explain his turning to prose. A long and broad vision is essential: "no single event, no single literature, is adequately comprehended except in its relation to other events, other literatures." The Preface had ended by exalting study of the ancient classics as an experience of unique value, and the text of the lecture is that "the literature of ancient Greece is, even for modern times, a mighty agent of intellectual deliverance." The reason is that Greek literature, especially Greek poetry (poetry being the best interpreter of a civilization), was so greatly "adequate," that in the Periclean age we have "the coexistence, the simultaneous appearance, of a great epoch and a great literature." The poetry of Pindar, Aeschylus, Sophocles (Arnold recalls the famous line from his early sonnet), and Aristophanes "is most perfectly commensurate" with its epoch. Those who complain of Arnold's critical "solemnity" must be surprised to find Aristophanes in such company and "adequate"; Euripides, we note, is absent. The elaborate contrast drawn between Periclean Athens and Elizabethan England may be briefly postponed.

"The great period of Rome is, perhaps, on the whole, the greatest, the fullest, the most significant period on record; it is certainly a greater, a fuller period than the age of Pericles." Yet its literature is not commensurate. Lucretius, modern though he is in feeling (Arnold quotes the example of feverish ennui that he was to use in *Obermann Once More*), is not adequate because his morbid (and very modern) depression and his withdrawal from the activity of his age disable him as its interpreter. A similar though reluctant judgment is given of Virgil, whose epic remoteness and melancholy nature together made him an inadequate interpreter of his world. Horace lacks "interpretative and fortifying" seriousness. Arnold ends as he began: if we would understand the intellectual history of our own race and time, we must apply this method of inquiry "to other ages, nations, and literatures"; but he has said enough "to establish the absolute, the enduring interest of Greek literature, and, above all, of Greek poetry."

Although Arnold did not reprint the lecture and later apologized for the "sketchy and generalizing mode of treatment" and for a degree of dogmatism, his first regular "essay in criticism" is significant in its theme and its comparative—and selective—method. Persuasive lucidity is achieved at the cost of oversimplification, perhaps even unwitting sleight of hand, in the contrast between Athens and "the age of Elizabeth" (which becomes on occasion the age of James). Arnold's picture of Athens is as idealized as the famous Periclean speech in Thucydides (ii. 35–46), which he echoes. In Athens Arnold finds mature rationality, cultivation of the arts of peace, a tolerant spirit, refinement, simplicity; in Elizabethan England, immaturity, want of the common conveniences of life, fantastic extravagance in dress, religious intolerance (here Arnold's lifelong antipathy to Puritanism makes its first public appearance). Greek festivals and drama are set against the kind of pageantry shown at Kenilworth (as described by Scott); the proper comparison, one would have thought, would be with the theatre of Shakespeare and his fellows. Arnold sees catastrophic decay following the last years of the Peloponnesian War, but he does not mention the ruthless imperialism laid bare in Thucydides' Melian dialogue (v.84–113) or the intolerance that punished Protagoras and put Socrates to death. On the other hand, this decay in the fourth century is illustrated by the contrast between Aristophanes and Menander; it is not said that this was also the century of Plato and Aristotle—an error of focus Arnold later avoided (see Super, 4, 290). He puts the critical, "modern" Thucydides beside Sir Walter Ralegh's *History of the World* with its speculations about the firmament and the site of Paradise; but—not to mention Ralegh's critical realism in his large dealings with secular history—the argument would be modified or reversed if Herodotus were compared with William Camden. However, in spite of inadequate or illegitimate particulars, Arnold's main theme and ideas have some interest in themselves and much in relation to his subsequent writings.

A. E. Housman, who was not given to extravagance (except in anathemas), declared that Arnold's *On Translating Homer* (1861–62) outweighed in value "all the literary criticism that the whole nation of professed scholars ever wrote." In these lectures Arnold gave the earliest and fullest display of his very acute perceptions and sensitive taste, both in his choice of illustrative quotations and in his comments upon them; with these mainly brief specimens he exploited that most effective device, the "touchstone" method. A first reading of the small book gives one, as only rare books do, a real sense of enriched faculties and critical growth, and that sense is only confirmed by rereading. The experience is heightened by what we may begin to take for granted in Arnold, a pattern of exposition so orderly and clear that it immediately fixes itself in the reader's mind. Finally, in the style and tone of these discourses Arnold may be said to have got into his own stride; one feels the urbane ease of ripe (if amateur) authority and tact—although urbanity is strained in the relentless pulverizing of Professor Francis Newman (the brother of John Henry), whose translation of the *Iliad* (1856) avowedly made much of Homer "quaint, garrulous, prosaic, and low."[1]

Arnold said that his one object was "to give practical advice to a translator" (and he added, characteristically, that he would not in the least concern himself with theories of translation as such). The one proper aim of the translator should be to reproduce as nearly as possible the "general effect" of the original, and obviously the only qualified judges are critical readers of both Greek and English. Arnold sets up four axioms (Super, 1, 102):

... the translator of Homer should above all be penetrated by a sense of four qualities of his author: —that he is eminently rapid; that he is eminently plain and direct, both in the evolution of his thought and in the expression of it, that is, both in his syntax and in his words; that he is eminently plain and direct in the substance of his thought, that is, in his matter and ideas; and, finally, that he is eminently noble.

If emphasis on "nobility" seems now oddly superfluous, we may remember that for over a century Homer's sheer poetic greatness had been more or less refracted or slighted because of theories of ballad composition; Arnold put him in his place with,

---

[1] To Arnold's charge, says Basil Willey, "there can be only one reply, the reply Newman made: Homer is *not* noble, or not uniformly so; he is often 'quaint', 'garrulous', prosaic and low" (*More Nineteenth Century Studies*, London, 1956, p. 42). *Cf.* René Wellek below (and W. D. Anderson, *Matthew Arnold and the Classical Tradition*, Ann Arbor, 1965, pp. 85 f.). Such notable modern translations as those of Richmond Lattimore and Robert Fitzgerald do not seem to bear out this view.

indeed at the head of, the world's very greatest poets. The body of the lectures is the concrete application of his four criteria, a discriminating demonstration that none of the English translators live up to all four, though the better poets attain degrees of success in meeting one or two of them.

What we have, then, is a lesson in the poetic sensibility and style of Homer himself and in the taste of successive periods, the virtues and the kinds of un-Homeric texture, tone, and movement represented by the Jacobean Chapman, the Augustan Pope, the semi-Miltonic Cowper, and some translators of the nineteenth century, chiefly Newman. One of Newman's faults is associating Homer with the English ballad, and William Maginn is condemned for outright adoption of the ballad manner. Heroic couplets and blank verse both yield un-Homeric results. Dr. Hawtrey's hexameter version of *Iliad* 3.234–44 (the "most successful attempt hitherto made at rendering Homer into English") leads on—through Clough's *Bothie,* which has Homeric rapidity and plain directness of style—to Arnold's plea for the hexameter as the best English medium. He unluckily rendered some Homeric passages in hexameters of his own which do not strengthen the case for the meter (and on which Newman justly and joyfully pounced).

Newman's long and mainly obtuse *Reply* elicited a fourth lecture (enlarged and published by itself in 1862). With apologies for having wounded Newman, Arnold completed the annihilation of tasteless learning; the critic of poetry should be "the 'ondoyant et divers,' the *undulating and diverse* being of Montaigne." (He incidentally repeats his homage to "the master of us all in criticism, M. Sainte-Beuve.") Arnold here returned to "the grand style"; much less briefly, to the question of hexameters; and to the stylistically overrefined blank verse of Tennyson—whose first blank-verse rendering from Homer, by the way, was printed in 1863 (and whose *Ulysses* is here misquoted). Arnold also returned (with a partial misquotation) to the meretricious "falsetto" of Macaulay's *Lays of Ancient Rome*—which, it may be said, has in the past been a stirring introduction to verse for many children, including Yeats. Arnold followed up his earlier praises of Clough (who had died in November 1861) with a tribute not only to the *Bothie* but to "the Homeric simplicity of his literary life."

Several topics have an added interest because of their reappearance in Arnold; they belong to the main line of his criticism. He finds that "at the present hour" English literature "ranks only third in European effect and importance among the literatures of Europe" (that is, of course, after French and German)— a strange judgment, we may say, but we should observe the terms in which it is put. What has long distinguished the French and Germans has been "a *critical* effort; the endeavour, in all branches of knowledge,—theology, philosophy, history, art, science,—to see the object as in itself it really is." The lack of such an effort in England goes along with the eccentric individualism, the provincialism, of English writers (such as Francis Newman) and with the English failure to have an Academy like the French.

Arnold's much-discussed "touchstone" method is used not only with translations of Homer but in remarks on "the grand style" (a phrase borrowed from Sir Joshua Reynolds' *Discourses*?). Instead of attempting vain definitions, he quotes Scott and then Homer, Virgil, Dante, Milton, since "the presence or absence of the grand style can only be spiritually discerned." In his *Last Words*, while still insisting that it can only be felt, not analyzed, he defines, not the grand style in itself, but its prerequisites: it arises "when a noble nature, poetically gifted, treats with simplicity or with severity a serious subject." He distinguishes between "the grand style simple" in Homer (which is "the more *magical*") and "the grand style severe" in Milton; Dante exemplifies both; and he quotes lines from the three. René Wellek asserts that "The whole theory of the grand style is vitiated" by Arnold's "belief in form apart from meaning";[2] even though Arnold's primary concern here is with style, the charge does not seem to be warranted by his choice of quotations. Moreover, whether or not we think poorly of English hexameters in general, it is surely an absolute fact that rhymed couplets and ballad measures cannot possibly reproduce the effect of the Greek

[2] *History of Modern Criticism: 1750–1950*, 4 (New Haven and London: Yale University Press, 1965), 169.

hexameter. And when Wellek adds that "Arnold is convinced of the uniform nobility and elevation of Homer whatever the subject matter or theme," is he not ignoring Arnold's insistence that Homer treats "the plainest, most matter-of-fact subject" as he "always deals with every subject, in the plainest and most straightforward style" (Super, 1, 110)?

Finally, Arnold's later saying, of which many critics have made an enigma (or nonsense), that poetry is "a criticism of life," is anticipated here in his linking of Homer and Milton because "the noble and profound application of ideas to life" "is the most essential part of poetic greatness"—which carries us back to the later letters to Clough and forward to many things.

Critics have remarked that in these lectures "Homer" means the *Iliad*, that the *Odyssey* is barely mentioned. One practical reason appears on Arnold's first page, that two recent translations of the *Iliad*, one of them especially, furnished abundant ammunition. A more general reason was no doubt that Arnold felt a profoundly tragic strain in the *Iliad* and saw in the *Odyssey* only "the most romantic poem of the ancient world." It is idle to complain that he did not give a critique of even the *Iliad* as an epic whole, since he chose a quite different theme; at the same time the lectures reveal much more of Homer than his style—and more of Arnold than his view of Homer. A century later, classical scholars see some weaknesses, as in prosody (this Newman seized upon), and students of English poetry may see inadequacies in Arnold's discussion considered as historical criticism, which in part it is. He could not of course be expected to share modern knowledge of oral and formulaic poetry; nor could he be expected to recognize, for instance, the reverent zeal with which the "fantastical" Chapman emphasized and incorporated the ethical ideas of Renaissance humanism. But, whatever additions or qualifications modern scholarship might make, the lectures were an event in Victorian criticism, and they retain their illuminating vitality.

*Essays in Criticism* (1865) is another landmark in nineteenth-century literature. This first series contained three essays and six Oxford lectures of 1862–64, all more or less revised before and after 1865. Apart from *The Function of Criticism* and *The Lit-*

*erary Influence of Academies,* all the discourses, whatever they
included of English applications and comparisons, were on non-
English subjects: three French (the two Guérins and Joubert),
one Dutch (Spinoza), one German (Heine), one classical
(Marcus Aurelius)—all "mediocrities," according to one recent
critic of Arnold; one mainly classical (*Pagan and Mediaeval Religious Sentiment*), and *A Persian Passion Play* (added in 1875).
The mere table of contents enforced one of Arnold's central motives, his effort to deliver his countrymen from insularity and
provincialism and make them actively conscious of the mind of
Europe past and present. A likewise large and characteristic
purpose or result appears in Arnold's remark to his mother in
1865 that he has been "struck by the admirable riches of human
nature that are brought to light in the group of persons of whom
they treat, and the sort of unity that as a book to stimulate the
better humanity in us the volume has" (Russell, 1, 287)—a comment that recalls the work of his admired Sainte-Beuve. And,
as E. K. Brown observed, the portraits more or less resemble
"the human ideals presented in various guises in Arnold's poetry,"
the Scholar-Gipsy quality of Maurice de Guérin, the austere calm
of Marcus Aurelius, and so on—all of them "disinterested."[3]
Indeed the character of the majority of the essays would almost
warrant our taking the collection as the first of Arnold's religious
books, although he is not here engaged in a campaign.

The preface is one of Arnold's most felicitous mixtures of
earnestness and urbane irony. The first version (1865) included
the avowal that he had "never been able to hit it off happily
with the logicians": "They imagine truth something to be
proved, I something to be seen; they something to be manufac-
tured, I as something to be found" (Super, 3, 535). Arnold's
belief in the disinterested search for answers that cannot be final
is set forth in one sentence of his first paragraph. Having acknowledged the abundant criticism that had greeted several
essays on their first appearance, he says:

To try and approach truth on one side after another, not to strive or
cry, nor to persist in pressing forward, on any one side, with violence

---

[3] *Matthew Arnold: A Study in Conflict,* 85–90.

and self-will,—it is only thus, it seems to me, that mortals may hope to gain any vision of the mysterious Goddess, whom we shall never see except in outline, but only thus even in outline. (Super, 3, 286)

Here and at the end, Arnold's editor notes, the preface is somewhat akin to Renan's preface to his *Essais de morale et de critique* (1859), which contained the essay on Celtic poetry that Arnold was to praise and use; but it is also completely Arnoldian. Two particulars are quietly but strongly emotional: the "not to strive or cry" (Matthew 12.19) he had echoed in the concluding prayer of *Lines Written in Kensington Gardens*; and the latter half of his sentence may remind us not only of the "signal-tree" in *Thyrsis* but of the almost unattainable vision described in Plato's *Phaedrus* (250) and of the fable of Truth, Osiris, and Isis in *Areopagitica* (whose author could look for full illumination with Christ's second coming).

But most of the preface is an elegant demolition of Arnold's adversaries and antipathies. In his effort "to pull out a few more stops in that powerful but at present somewhat narrow-toned organ, the modern Englishman," he has always sought to stand by himself, and he does not want Oxford blamed for his professorial utterances. He had told his mother that the preface would make her laugh; however, she and many other people were not amused, and in later editions he cut out a good deal. Happily, enough remains. The "vivacity" for which Arnold apologizes "is but the last sparkle of flame before we are all in the dark":

Yes, the world will soon be the Philistines'! and then, with every voice, not of thunder, silenced, and the whole earth filled and ennobled every morning by the magnificent roaring of the young lions of the *Daily Telegraph*, we shall all yawn in one another's faces with the dismallest, the most unimpeachable gravity.

According to the *Saturday Review*, a persistent foe—and target—of Arnold's, "the British nation has searched all anchorages for the spirit, and has finally anchored itself, in the fulness of perfected knowledge, on Benthamism." But Benthamite salvation is not final: "No, we are all seekers still!" And this leads into the apostrophe to Oxford, "home of lost causes, and forsaken beliefs, and unpopular names, and impossible loyalties," the perpetual deliverer from Philistinism and "the bondage of *'was uns alle bändigt, Das Gemeine!'* ":

Beautiful city! so venerable, so lovely, so unravaged by the fierce intellectual life of our century, so serene!
"There are our young barbarians, all at play!"
And yet, steeped in sentiment as she lies, spreading her gardens to the moonlight, and whispering from her towers the last enchantments of the Middle Age, who will deny that Oxford, by her ineffable charm, keeps ever calling us nearer to the true goal of all of us, to the ideal, to perfection,—to beauty, in a word, which is only truth seen from another side?—nearer, perhaps, than all the science of Tübingen.

In 1885 Arnold could say that "Oxford is still, on the whole, the place in the world to which I am most attached" (Russell, 2, 332). Yet even the fervent apostrophe, one of the very few purple patches in Arnold's prose (and a parallel to his nostalgic poems), has its tinge of irony: the line adapted from Byron (in which the word "barbarians" suggests the Arnoldian sense) and "so unravaged by the fierce intellectual life of our century" are not quite ideal tributes to a university. In 1854, not long after *The Scholar-Gipsy* and a decade before *Thyrsis*, Arnold had hoped that "the infusion of Dissenters' sons" might "brace the flaccid sinews of Oxford a little" (Russell, 1, 45).

We may follow Arnold's evolving ideas by following the literary essays chronologically, a procedure that brings us in the end to the two general ones which have stood first in the many editions. Maurice de Guérin (1810–39) and his sister Eugénie (1805–48) were, in literary stature, very small figures in Arnold's gallery, but the nature of his interest soon becomes clear. The essay on Maurice (1862–63) makes the distinction between two kinds of interpretation that Arnold was to use again in *Celtic Literature.* Here, as later, he is concerned, not with the faculty of moral interpretation, but with the lesser yet rare gift for the "magical" rendering of nature. This does not mean a clear-cut "explanation of the mystery of the universe, but the power of so dealing with things as to awaken in us a wonderfully full, new, and intimate sense of them, and of our relations with them." Thus oppressive bewilderment is replaced by a calming sense of harmony between man and nature; whether or not this sense is illusive, poetry can awaken it, and "to awaken it is one of the highest powers of poetry." Such magical power is not in the scientists but in Shakespeare's March daffodils, Wordsworth's Hebridean cuckoo, Keats's "moving waters at their priestlike task" (here occurs another sad misquotation, "cold ablution"), in Chateaubriand, Senancour, and Guérin. Arnold proceeds, aided by an essay of Sainte-Beuve's, to describe Guérin's life and troubled soul and his turning away from a religious vocation to a mysticism of nature. Arnold links Guérin especially with Keats (his view of Keats, as we might expect, lacks modern dimensions): in both, "the faculty of naturalistic interpretation is overpoweringly predominant," and its results are "perfect" in creating "the thing's essential reality." Evidence is provided in extracts translated from Guérin's prose poem, *Le Centaure*. Eugénie de Guérin is the feminine embodiment of a likewise delicate and intense spirituality; and the ennui that could disturb her religious ardor did not touch her devotion to her brother. Arnold contrasts the Catholic Eugénie's refinement and the Protestantism of Emma Tatham, a poetess of Margate, who sings:

> My Jesus to know, and feel His blood flow,
> 'Tis life everlasting, 'tis heaven below.

It would not of course have suited the occasion or Arnold's mind to contrast a cultivated English Protestant—say Christina Rossetti—with a French Catholic vulgarian.

In the lecture (1863) on Heine, a vastly more important figure than the Guérins, Arnold stated and tried to fulfill what was to be his normal aim and method in dealing with individual authors:

To ascertain the master-current in the literature of an epoch, and to distinguish this from all minor currents, is one of the critic's highest functions; in discharging it he shows how far he possesses the most indispensable quality of his office,—justness of spirit. (Super, 3, 107)

I wish to mark Heine's place in modern European literature, the scope of his activity, and his value. (*Ibid.*, 117)

Carlyle, the great intermediary between Germany and England, had overemphasized German romanticism, whereas Heine, Goethe's chief successor, had been far more in the main current. Posterity will, in spite of Heine's disclaimer, continue to honor the poet, but, for nineteenth-century Europe, his significance is that he was, in his own words, "a brave soldier in the Liberation War of humanity." "Goethe's profound, imperturbable natural-ism," says Arnold, "is absolutely fatal to all routine thinking; he puts the standard, once for all, inside every man instead of out-side him." But Goethe's influence was not fully effectual; it was Heine who carried on "a life and death battle with Philistinism." Goethe, comments René Wellek, was not "a naturalist nor an en-emy of the old order" (4, 175).

It was Arnold, especially here and in *Culture and Anarchy*, who, following Carlyle, established Heine's word "Philistine" in the English language. "*Philistine* must have originally meant, in the mind of those who invented the nickname, a strong, dogged, unenlightened opponent of the chosen people, of the children of the light"; thus Philistinism is the intellectual equivalent—and frequent ally—of Arnold's "Hebraism." For the practical, unintellectual Englishman, Philistia appears as "the true Land of Promise . . .; the born lover of ideas, the born hater of common-places, must feel in this country, that the sky over his head is of brass and iron."

Heine failed to arouse Germany and migrated to France, where ideas were more highly valued. His career was in accord with Arnold's principles. Heine's "direct political action was null . . .; direct political action is not the true function of literature; and Heine was a born man of letters." He gave himself to "an intrepid application of the modern spirit to literature." Arnold illustrates the power of Heine's poetry and prose, in which "in-tense modernism" is so sharpened by unique wit. Yet his eulogy winds up: "He is not an adequate interpreter of the modern world. He is only a brilliant soldier in the Liberation War of hu-manity." The reason for his half-success is "want of moral bal-ance, and of nobleness of soul and character." The essay has been considered, by Sir Walter Raleigh, "perhaps the finest" in the volume,[4] and, by the learned René Wellek, "the least satis-factory." Wellek and other scholars have censured Arnold for inadequate knowledge and comprehension of German roman-ticism, Goethe, and Heine, and for establishing an inflated and largely erroneous estimate of Heine. At any rate the very attract-ive essay expressed, directly or obliquely, a good deal of Arnold himself.

Modern England, Arnold thinks, is in much the same stagna-tion as Heine's Germany was. After the age of Shakespeare "the great English middle class . . . entered the prison of Puritanism, and had the key turned on its spirit there for two hundred years." Arnold's abhorrence of Puritanism was intensified by his enforced familiarity with Victorian middle-class Dissenters. Here it leads him into a strange distortion of English history; he ignores not only the great effects of the Puritan revolution itself but all the awakeners of the ensuing two centuries. Then in a page and a half he runs through the English Romantic poets and finds the modern spirit wanting. Wordsworth—judged here much more sternly than in the elegiac poems—"plunged himself in the in-ward life, he voluntarily cut himself off from the modern spirit." "Coleridge took to opium"—a brusque verdict on the thinker whom Dr. Arnold had considered the greatest of his time and whose view of church and state Matthew inherited. "Scott be-came the historiographer-royal of feudalism"—although Scott (not to count his influence on the Oxford Movement) had cre-ated a *comédie humaine* which Balzac admired and emulated. Wordsworth, Scott, and the purely sensuous Keats, while they left "far more solid and complete works" than Byron and Shel-ley, "do not apply modern ideas to life; they constitute, there-fore, *minor currents*. . . ." Byron and Shelley, aristocratic rebels defeated by public inertia and resistance, did, despite "the in-adequacy of their actual work," make a "passionate" and "Titanic effort to flow in the main stream of modern literature." We may ejaculate that this sort of thing will not do, even in a lecture-essay (we may also remember that Arnold was to amend some of these estimates later); yet we must admit that he has a point,

[4] "Matthew Arnold," *Some Authors* (Oxford, 1923), 304.

a point which his contemporaries, more docile heirs of the Romantic tradition, could hardly have made.

In his Oxford lecture on the French moralist, Joseph Joubert (1754–1824)—a lecture Arnold barely managed to finish before breakfast on the day of its delivery, November 28, 1863—he again had England in mind. And in treating this minor though "life-giving" writer, he again—as with Maurice de Guérin—wishes to give an English view of a man already portrayed by Sainte-Beuve. Arnold defines and illustrates Joubert's quiet, "single-minded . . . pursuit of perfection," his awareness that "beauty and light are properties of truth" ("light" runs through the essay), "the soundness and completeness of his judgments" in religion, morals, literature, politics. The modern reader, whether or not he is drawn to reading more of Joubert than Arnold's extracts, is likely to remember two things. One is the parallel between Joubert and Coleridge (who is not here identified with opium): both celebrated talkers and sages, passionate thinkers and readers in areas off the beaten track, ardent seekers of truth, conservatives in religion and politics who had an antipathy "to the narrow and shallow foolishness of vulgar modern liberalism." "Coleridge had less delicacy and penetration than Joubert, but more richness and power." While very little of Coleridge's poetry or criticism can stand (a judgment which has not stood, however troublesome Coleridge has been to his modern interpreters), his "great usefulness" was and is "the stimulus of his continual effort,—not a moral effort, for he had no morals,—but of his continual instinctive effort, crowned often with rich success, to get at and to lay bare the real truth of his matter in hand, whether that matter were literary, or philosophical, or political, or religious; and this in a country where at that moment such an effort was almost unknown. . . ."

A second noteworthy item is the first appearance of one of Arnold's most debated phrases. Speaking of the immortal geniuses of literature and of the able writers famous only in their generation, he says that their work "is at the bottom the same,— *a criticism of life,*" which is the "end and aim of all literature" (not merely, we observe, of poetry). Writers of the first kind "are the great abounding fountains of truth, whose criticism of life is a source of illumination and joy to the whole human race for ever,—the Homers, the Shakspeares." Some minor writers, like Joubert, remain secure, for the few; but there is no future for such as "the great apostle of the Philistines, Lord Macaulay," a splendid, even an honest, rhetorician, but possessed of no organ for apprehending vital truth. For contrast, Arnold returns—possibly with a hope for himself—to the enviable lot of Joubert: "How far better, to pass with scant notice through one's own generation, but to be singled out and preserved by the very iconoclasts of the next, then in their turn by those of the next, and so, like the lamp of life itself, to be handed on from one generation to another in safety!"

*Pagan and Mediaeval Religious Sentiment* (1864) contains another central idea, distilled in another famous phrase, and the essay is a signal example of a neat pattern which immediately and indelibly fixes itself in the reader's mind. In brief, ancient paganism had a religion of the senses and understanding—illustrated by a lively translation from Theocritus' little drama of bustling, gossipy women at the festival of Adonis and the hymn they hear sung; medieval Catholicism was a religion of the heart and the imagination—illustrated by St. Francis' *Canticle* of love and praise for all God's creatures and things. But both are one-sided and, in their very different ways, inadequate; inadequate too is Heine, representing a sophisticated return to the senses and understanding. The only faith that can endure, "the main element of the modern spirit's life," is the fusion of intellect and feeling which Arnold calls "imaginative reason"—illustrated by the quartet of Greek poets he had cited in the *Modern Element* (with Simonides now in place of Aristophanes), and, specifically, by Sophocles' appeal to the laws that do not grow old (*Oedipus the King* 863–71; *cf. Antigone* 450 f.). When Arnold's persuasive clarity allows queries to obtrude, we may ask, for instance, if popular paganism is represented more adequately by the feast of Adonis than popular Christianity would be by an Anglican harvest-service or a church parade; if St. Francis represents the prime historical character of Catholicism; if "imaginative reason" did not have a principal exemplar in Plato. And yet—as in the case of Arnold's brief assessment of the English Romantics—our final reaction may be that, whatever our objections, the main argument is as suggestively valid as any such broad generalizing can be. And "imaginative reason" not only recalls "Who saw life steadily, and saw it whole" and Arnold's first two pieces of prose; it is another term for literature, for poetry, as a criticism of life, and it carries us on to "high seriousness" and to Arnold's insistent appeal to our "best self" and "right reason."

In this essay too, in spite of his subject, he has his eye on England, although in the printed version he left out "a good deal about Protestantism" that was included in the Oxford lecture, *Pagan and Christian Religious Sentiment*; but enough remains to indicate his smiling tolerance for Anglican bishops and his dislike of Philistine Dissenters, British and American. On the other hand, he shares the imaginative man's "weakness for the Catholic Church," which, with all its sins, suggests "the rich treasures of human life," "all the pell-mell of the men and women of Shakspeare's plays"—and Migne's vast collections of the church fathers and their successors, the work Arnold would choose if he had to pass his life with only one. (Having read in Migne perhaps more than Arnold had, I find his choice either playful or eccentric.) In regard to England we might observe his question whether, under the first emperors, the poor of Rome and the country were, "in comfort, morals, and happiness," worse off than those of London's East End and the country under Queen Victoria. (It was around this time that he wrote the humanitarian and religious sonnets noticed in the preceding chapter.) A very different item we might observe as a clue to Arnold's critical principles and methods: calling in Heine for an extended comment, he says: "I wish to decide nothing as of my own authority; the great art of criticism is to get oneself out of the way and to let humanity decide."

The essay ends with the quotation from Sophocles and "Let St. Francis,—nay, or Luther either,—beat that!" The journalistic exclamation might have been used in Arnold's next lecture as an example—rare in him—of the provincialism he criticized in English prose. That lecture, *The Literary Influence of Academies* (1864), owed something to reviews by Renan and Sainte-

Beuve of a history of the French Academy; Sainte-Beuve prompted such key words as "provincial." But, even more than in his usual dealings with foreign subjects, Arnold concerned himself with England and the English mind. He exalts the value of an Academy as "a recognised authority, imposing on us a high standard in matters of intellect and taste," because of the human and especially English reluctance to submit to external discipline. The classical humanist quotes Cicero (*De Officiis*, I. iv–v) on the ideal of perfection, on man's need for general standards of order, measure, and taste that will control the bent of his individual nature. He applauds Sainte-Beuve's remark that the French are not satisfied with responding to works of art or intellect but want to judge the rightness or wrongness of their responses. The chief spiritual characteristics of the English are energy and honesty; it is energy, "the life of genius," that has set English so far above French poetry. The power of France is in flexibility of intelligence and hence in prose. After the great "literature of genius . . . stretching from Marlow [*sic*] to Milton" came "our provincial and second-rate literature of the eighteenth century," whereas the French literature of that period was "one of the most powerful and pervasive intellectual agencies that have ever existed." (The words "provincial" and "second-rate" cover Swift, Pope, Berkeley, Fielding, Sterne, Johnson, Gibbon, Hume, Burke, Blake, *et al.*; elsewhere of course Arnold attests his admiration for some of these.) What is lacking in England is a standard of rational intelligence that curbs irrationality of idea and style, that establishes a classical temper and "Attic prose." Arnold cites "Asiatic" passages from Jeremy Taylor (contrasted with the classical Bossuet) and even from Burke, "our greatest English prose-writer." On the other hand, Addison's prose is Attic but his ideas are commonplace, in contrast with those of a first-rate moralist like Joubert. At present, Newman is almost alone in his intellectual delicacy and urbanity; Ruskin ranges from prose poetry to freakish etymologizing; and there are other exemplars of provincial vagaries without genius.

At the end, rather unexpectedly, Arnold says—probably with reference to a recent proposal by Lord Stanhope—that England is not likely to have an Academy of intellectual and literary opinion and taste, and perhaps ought not to wish for one, although English writers need to remember its functions. (Such a conclusion is just as well, since the record of the French Academy hardly warrants extreme deference.) In general, Arnold reveals something of his almost lifelong tendency to overestimate French and underestimate English intellectual virtues; complaint has been made about his inadequate recognition (perhaps influenced by Sainte-Beuve) of French poets, including Baudelaire, but at least he can be credited with a low opinion of Victor Hugo. For English readers the essay was an astringent caution against insularity, complacency, and provincialism. As Lionel Trilling shrewdly says, "whenever Arnold talks about style he is talking about society,"[5] and in this Arnold is carrying on the old humanistic tradition of order and standards that are not only intellectual and aesthetic but ethical and social.

Of all Arnold's critical essays, *The Function of Criticism at the Present Time* (1864) and *The Study of Poetry* (1880) have been much the most often cited by modern critics, whether for endorsement or for questioning. Nowadays, when criticism— not as a rule of Arnoldian scope—is a huge and mainly academic industry, we may take some points of the *Function of Criticism* as a matter of course, but in England it was Arnold who, while setting criticism below creation, raised it from a camp follower of literature to be the vanguard of thought. In his obituary tribute (1869) to Sainte-Beuve he declared—here differing from the critic he had long ranked as the finest of the age—that "first-rate criticism has a permanent value greater than that of any but first-rate work of poetry and art." He starts from what he had said at the end of his second lecture on Homer: that the main effort of the modern European mind has been a critical effort, "the endeavour, in all branches of knowledge, theology, philosophy, history, art, science, to see the object as in itself it really is." This was the "Modern Element" in Arnold's inaugural lecture at Oxford. He recognized, more clearly than most of his contemporaries, that the edifice of beliefs and ideas in

[5] *Matthew Arnold* (New York: Norton, 1939), 168; (Cleveland: World Publishing Co., 1968), 154.

which mankind had lived for many centuries was now crumbling, or crumbled, and that modern man must build a new one (though keeping the best of the old materials); on this great problem we noted, in the essay on Heine, a self-revealing dictum about Goethe. Arnold the critic, as we have observed all along, does not now, like Arnold the poet, wander unhappily between two worlds, one dead, the other powerless to be born; he can be one of the midwives.

The *Function of Criticism* was written as an introduction to the collected essays, and ideas we have met before become parts of a fresh whole. As often, Arnold has some debts to Renan and Sainte-Beuve and Newman. In some points he anticipates T. S. Eliot, who, for all his antagonism, was his chief heir: both see criticism as discovering new ideas, creating the atmosphere the imaginative writer needs to carry on his "work of synthesis and exposition." Here the *Zeitgeist* comes into play, the necessary concurrence of "the power of the man and the power of the moment." But Arnold soon, and characteristically, takes leave of large abstractions for another brief survey of the English Romantics: "the English poetry of the first quarter of this century, with plenty of energy, plenty of creative force, did not know enough." Arnold distinguishes mere "reading" (of which Shelley had much and Coleridge an infinity) from both "the nationally diffused life and thought of the epochs of Sophocles or Shakspeare" and the culture and critical thought of Goethe's Germany. (The characterization of Elizabethan England here— as in the essay on Heine—is very different from that given in the *Modern Element.*) As before, we may, with qualifications, agree on the insufficiency, in the English Romantics, of what Arnold means by the modern critical spirit: theirs was too much "a great movement of feeling, not . . . of mind." And we recognize the generalizing insight and remarkable independence of a critic who had to detach himself from his own strong Romantic roots and affinities.

The French Revolution was "the greatest, the most animating event in history," and one inspired by intelligence; why did it not bring such a crop of works of genius as came from great earlier movements, that of Greece or the Renaissance and the

Reformation? Arnold's answer is that those movements "were, in the main, disinterestedly intellectual and spiritual," whereas "The French Revolution took a political, practical character." Whether or not the contrast is valid (we might compare Arnold's account of the Revolution in his poem of this time, *Obermann Once More*), it brings us to the main theme of the essay. Burke, in an epoch of concentration, was a great and very "un-English" exemplar of "living by ideas"; now that an epoch of expansion seems to be opening, advances in material welfare may lead the Englishman to remember that he has a mind. And criticism must lead the way by inaugurating a rule of disinterestedness, "By keeping aloof from what is called 'the practical view of things;' by resolutely following the law of its own nature, which is to be a free play of the mind on all subjects which it touches." (The idea of disinterestedness had appeared, for example, in the early *Resignation* and the first *Obermann* poem.) There is no such disinterested play of mind in the polemical partisanship of the Whig *Edinburgh Review*, the Tory *Quarterly*, and other journals. Here and in what follows we are on the way to *Culture and Anarchy*, "Hellenism," and the prejudice and complacency that obstruct the path toward "perfection." Mr. Roebuck, the M.P., has complacently asked: "Is not property safe? Is not every man able to say what he likes? . . . I ask you whether, the world over or in past history, there is anything like it? I pray that our unrivalled happiness may last." On top of Mr. Roebuck's song of triumph Arnold cites a newspaper report of the strangling of an illegitimate child and the arrest of its workhouse mother: "Wragg is in custody." (Arnold's feelings are stirred, but he might have left his added complaint about hideous English names—"by the Ilissus there was no Wragg, poor thing!"—to be made by Oscar Wilde, who quoted it, incorrectly.)

In its war with the Philistines disinterested criticism is bound to have slow effects, but its method is sure—unlike that of the angry prophets, Cobbett, Carlyle, and Ruskin, or that of bustling liberalism with its shallow substitutes for thought. At present there are difficulties and dangers in resisting the popular "liberal" voice. Arnold recalls the hard knocks he had recently received after demolishing Bishop Colenso's wrongheaded work on the Pentateuch, a work which is "the critical hit in the religious literature of England," while the corresponding works in Germany and France are those of Strauss and Renan. The present essay evidently grew out of the claims he had made at that time for the function of literary criticism in the religious domain (a principle he was to apply at large in his religious books).[6]

Arnold ends by enunciating, and repeating, his definition of criticism: "a disinterested endeavour to learn and propagate the best that is known and thought in the world, and thus to establish a current of fresh and true ideas." This implies—as Arnold's whole book does—that the English critic "must dwell much on foreign thought," and that not much contemporary English writing comes under his definition. The critic must see authors in "relation to a central standard" (as the word "best" requires); he must have "ever fresh knowledge" and judgment; and he must not become abstract. He must (like Goethe) look at

Europe as being, for intellectual and spiritual purposes, one great confederation, bound to a joint action and working to a common result; and whose members have, for their proper outfit, a knowledge of Greek, Roman, and Eastern antiquity, and of one another.

Criticism can only help in "growth towards perfection," towards such epochs as those of Aeschylus and Shakespeare.

That promised land it will not be ours to enter, and we shall die in the wilderness: but to have desired to enter it, to have saluted it from afar, is already, perhaps, the best distinction among contemporaries; it will certainly be the best title to esteem with posterity.

This essay (along with remarks cited elsewhere) prompts a reminder of Arnold's more or less poor opinion of many of his chief English contemporaries: Macaulay, Carlyle, Ruskin, Mill; Charlotte Brontë, whose mind "contains nothing but hunger,

6 Below, Chap. V, *passim*. Arnold's essays, *The Bishop and the Philosopher* and its defensive sequel, *Dr. Stanley's Lectures on the Jewish Church* (Super, 3, 40–55, 65–82), had appeared in 1862–63. The whole matter is set forth by S. M. B. Coulling, "The Background of 'The Function of Criticism at the Present Time,'" *Philological Quarterly* 42 (1963), 36–54.

rebellion, and rage" (Russell, 1, 34), and Thackeray; Mrs. Browning, Tennyson, Swinburne; the historians Freeman, Stubbs, Kinglake; F. D. Maurice, the egregious Bishop Colenso; and others. Carlyle had done much to fire the thought and feeling of Arnold and his generation (as Arnold acknowledged in his American discourse on Emerson), and his deep influence continued to work in Arnold's writing after he had rejected some of the prophet's doctrines. Tennyson, "with all his temperament and artistic skill, is deficient in intellectual power," is not "a great and powerful spirit in any line" (Russell, 1, 147, 278). We saw how Arnold's poetic theory and practice conflicted with his friend Clough's. In an early letter to Clough he had spoken of Browning's "moderate gift" and "confused multitudinousness"; in 1867 he could say, whether or not he had greatly changed his opinion, that he was reprinting *Empedocles* "at the request of a man of genius, Mr. Robert Browning."

Most of Arnold's adverse comments are made in letters, where —like other people—he is briefer, sharper, and more unqualified than he would be in print. His relatively few comments in print are in general qualified and moderate in tone, as they are on Tennyson and Ruskin; with Macaulay (who had died in 1859) he is quite severe. Mill he criticized with an intellectual respect he did not extend to "Millism." We may more or less agree with his private or public judgments, though we may see virtues that Arnold either does not see at all or sees dimly. One thinks of only four contemporary writers in English who are highly praised: although Newman's dogmatic creed was "impossible," Arnold was to name him as one of four men who had profoundly influenced him, the others being Goethe, Wordsworth, and Sainte-Beuve;[7] the lecture on Emerson, though it

---

[7] Whitridge, 65–66. This acknowledgment, obviously sincere, must have startled many readers. Arnold specifies the learning of "habits, methods, ruling ideas, which are constantly with me." A little earlier (November 29, 1871: Whitridge, 56), he had written to Newman that "nothing can ever do away the effect you have produced upon me, for it consists in a general disposition of mind rather than in a particular set of ideas. In all the conflicts I have with modern Liberalism and Dissent, and with their pretensions and shortcomings, I recognize your work." See below, Chap. IV, n. 2.

denied him first rank, was a strong testimony of personal and enduring gratitude; Dean Stanley he praised in prose and verse;
and to Dickens, at least to *David Copperfield*, he paid warm
tribute.

There are some obvious reasons for Arnold's estimates of most
eminent Victorians. As a devout classicist who derived his
standards chiefly from the greatest ancients, he was predis-
posed to find his contemporaries much inferior (not that he had
an exaggerated notion of his own importance). Then classical
standards were reinforced by Arnold's European outlook, his
demand that to be really great a writer must be in the main
stream of European ideas, and his feeling that Victorian Englishmen
(like even the Romantic poets) were almost bound to be
outside that stream; and his war on English provincialism was
salutary, however much he may have overrated Continental
and underrated English authors. Throughout his life he read a
good deal of modern writing, in both literature and thought
and newspapers and periodicals, as his abundant readiness of
topical reference indicates. But professional busyness, literary
and social engagements, severely limited time for reading, and
selective concentration on authors and books he thought most
valuable for himself and on general grounds, all this helps to
account for his relatively scanty dealings with contemporary
English (and American) writing. There was besides a very
practical reason: Arnold said in 1888 that in general he did not
write about his contemporaries, and much earlier he had re-
sisted the temptation to discuss Tennyson because of the "odious
motives" that would be imputed to a fellow poet (Russell, 1,
277–80; 2, 438).

Arnold's later Oxford lectures, *On the Study of Celtic Literature*, were delivered in 1865–66 and published in the *Cornhill
Magazine* in 1866 and as a book in 1867. Not unnaturally, this

---

In regard to Dickens, who is mentioned just below, it is painful to find,
in the original full text (1865) of the preface to *Essays in Criticism* (Neiman, 96; Super, 3, 538), that *Little Dorrit* is named in an ironical list of
"modern, intelligible, improving" books. If he had read the novel, Arnold
would surely at least have recognized the morbid Hebraism of Mrs. Clennam
and delighted in the Circumlocution Office.

was and probably remains the least popular of his literary books, yet various recent experts agree that it was, and remains, "a spectacular achievement in the combination of scholarship and taste" (Super, 3, 496).[8] Moreover, it had positive results. As a writer who had the ear of the cultivated public, Arnold hoped and helped to widen general interest in a part of the British heritage which had been pretty much unknown outside a band of scholars, and his plea for an Oxford chair of Celtic was fulfilled in 1877. (One member of his final audience, the undergraduate John Rhys, was to be the first incumbent of the chair.) A more remarkable result Arnold could not have foretold: that his book would affect at least the lesser writers of the Irish renaissance (and Yeats, with reservations, was happy to echo it).

As for Arnold's own evolution, his novel theme was more striking proof than *Essays in Criticism* of the breadth of his horizons. Along with his general curiosity, three impulses in the Celtic direction were his mother's Cornish descent, an exploration of Wales in 1864, and his poetic sympathy with the temperament he sought to define. As an amateur who did not know the languages and much of the literature (and there were more translations than he read), Arnold got up the complex subject as best he could, and he freely admitted the tentative character of what he had to say. While he used the best available authorities, some parts of his book have long been out of date or retain only a modicum of interest as a partial picture of the transition from uncritical speculation to critical scholarship. His dexterous and dubious juggling with racial and national characteristics reflected a long and large English and European debate. (His father, by the way, was labeled "that Teuton of Teutons, the Celt-hating Dr. Arnold," by the *London Quarterly Review* 31, 1868-69, 48).

The great attraction of the lectures is in the intuitive insights,

[8] See J. V. Kelleher, "Matthew Arnold and the Celtic Revival," *Perspectives of Criticism*, ed. Harry Levin (Harvard University Press, 1950); F. E. Faverty, *Matthew Arnold the Ethnologist* (Northwestern University Press, 1951); Rachel Bromwich, *Matthew Arnold and Celtic Literature: A Retrospect 1865–1965* (Clarendon Press, 1965).

however hazardous at times, of Arnold the literary critic. On
the interpretative side, he acknowledged debts to Renan's "beautiful essay," *La Poésie des races celtiques*: like Renan, he linked
together Irish, Welsh, and Breton literatures, and, on his own
lines, he elaborated Renan's suggestions concerning Celtic spirituality and melancholy and the Celtic treatment of nature. He
finds in the Celts a dominant strain of sentiment, of emotional
and spiritual intensity, a "style" they possess "in a wonderful
measure," and "penetrating passion and melancholy"; Arnold
felt it legitimate to draw evidence of melancholy (and the
epigraph of his book) from Macpherson's *Ossian*, since it was
in keeping with the Celtic genius. The "Titanism of the Celt,
his passionate, turbulent, indomitable reaction against the despotism of fact" reminds Arnold of Byron and even of Milton's
Satan. The mysterious "magic" of the Celtic rendering of nature
prompts quotations from Keats's odes and Shakespeare; these are
sometimes Greek, sometimes Celtic (three lines from the *Grecian
Urn* have two misquoted words). Yet, with all his unique combination of gifts, the Celt lacks "steadiness, patience, sanity,"
the *architectonicé* which shapes great works, the wide, deep
grasp of fact and idea which—as in Shakespeare—can achieve
the moral interpretation of life. Whatever may be thought of
Arnold's ethnological divinations, we can say that he defined a
recognizable type of sensibility and provided us with a useful if
vague adjective.

Other things in the lectures enlarge the perspective by relat-
ing themselves to Arnold's central doctrines. In later essays he
was to develop what is here touched briefly, the disastrous
view of the Irish commonly held in England. Some ideas and
phrases anticipate *Culture and Anarchy* or recall *Essays in
Criticism*. Arnold condemns "Saxon" Philistinism, though a dash
of this, he suggests, might have steadied the Celtic genius in
politics as well as in literature. The way to "perfection" is
through "culture," that is, through disinterested inquiry into
the nature of things as they really are; one result of the process,
beneficial for Ireland, might be "a new type" of Englishman,
"more intelligent, more gracious, and more humane." The
*Zeitgeist* is at work: the several peoples of Great Britain and the

nations of Europe are moving irresistibly toward merging into a great whole. In contrast with the purely religious Semitic genius, "the Indo-European genius places its highest spiritual life in the imaginative reason." Although Arnold seeks to reduce the Teutonic and exalt the Celtic inheritance, he declares that "Our great, our only first-rate body of contemporary poetry is the German" (that is, Goethe); this alone, since the Greeks, has got on with "the grand business of modern poetry,— a moral interpretation, from an independent point of view, of man and the world."

The second series of *Essays in Criticism*, published in 1888 after Arnold's death, comprised nine pieces selected by himself, all of much later date than the first series; five were written in 1879–81, four in 1887–88. Only two were on foreign writers (Amiel, Tolstoy), and, apart from *The Study of Poetry*, all the rest were on individual English poets. Also, whereas the first set of subjects had been entirely of Arnold's own choice, the second set of essays were composed for purposes that affected his mode of treatment: three (*The Study of Poetry, Thomas Gray*, and *John Keats*) were contributions to the large anthology, *The English Poets* (1880), edited by T. Humphry Ward, the husband of Arnold's niece, the novelist; *Wordsworth* and *Byron* were the introductions to his own anthologies of those poets (1879, 1881); *Shelley* (1888) was a review of Dowden's biography; and *Milton* (1888) was a ceremonial speech. In these essays, except *The Study of Poetry*, there is not much specific criticism; Arnold is trying, as before, to revise conventional estimates and define each author's character and central significance.

Early personal acquaintance with Wordsworth went along with a degree of temperamental affinity or nostalgia to give a special niche in Arnold's poetical pantheon to that Romantic survivor (whom, says Leon Gottfried, he quoted more than any other poet)—even though he had admitted that Wordsworth turned away from "half of human fate," from "the modern spirit." The poet Arnold mourned in his elegies—the irreplaceable poet of simple feeling who re-created "The freshness of the early world" —was not quite the Wordsworth we have in mind but the kind of physician the troubled Arnold had needed. In the essay of

1879 his piety reappears, though he is naturally more objective. Wordsworth's hold upon lovers of poetry has steadily lessened, the later generations have been won over by Tennyson, and Wordsworth has not, "up to this time, at all obtained his deserts." Arnold declares his firm belief that Wordsworth's achievement "is, after that of Shakespeare and Milton, . . . undoubtedly the most considerable in our language from the Elizabethan age to the present time." He catalogues the chief poets of England (with the two exceptions), of Germany (except Goethe), and of France (since the death of Molière), and sets Wordsworth above them all.

But if Wordsworth is to have general recognition, the first necessity is to separate his best from the mass of his inferior work. (At the end Arnold avows himself such a Wordsworthian that he can read, "with pleasure and edification," everything from *Peter Bell* to the address to Mr. Wilkinson's spade, "everything, I think, except *Vaudracour and Julia*": did this single exception remind Arnold of Marguerite?) As anthologist he admits only three short extracts from *The Prelude*, which all critics nowadays take as Wordsworth's central edifice. "His best work is in his shorter pieces," but these need drastic winnowing. What remains—largely of 1798–1808—is a "body of powerful work" in which Wordsworth accomplishes "the most essential part of poetic greatness," "the noble and profound application of ideas to life." These are moral ideas because moral ideas are really so main a part of life; and, as we noticed earlier, "moral" is not to be construed narrowly or didactically. Wordsworth's superiority to almost all other modern poets is that "he deals with more of *life* than they do; he deals with *life*, as a whole, more powerfully"; and "poetry is at bottom a criticism of life" (the phrase used in *Joubert* of literature in general). In these last famous words, as I. A. Richards remarked,[9] Arnold was saying something so obvious that it is constantly overlooked. And his insistence on humane values was a virtual rejection of the current gospel of art for art's sake.

Arnold takes issue with those who make Wordsworth into a

[9] *Principles of Literary Criticism*, 2nd ed. (London: Routledge & Kegan Paul; New York: Harcourt, Brace, 1926), 61.

systematic philosopher; "we cannot do him justice until we dismiss his formal philosophy" as it is set forth in *The Excursion*, which offers preaching, not poetry. But in his many short poems Wordsworth feels and shares joy in nature and the affections, and in these idea and expression are one; the perfection of Wordsworth's styleless style—which owed something to Burns— is illustrated by the line in *Michael*: "And never lifted up a single stone." Arnold warmly admires *Laodamia* and *Intimations of Immortality*, yet he finds something artificial in the former and some fanciful and declamatory elements in the latter; the best of Wordsworth is in such poems as *Michael, The Fountain, The Solitary Reaper*. Arnold hoped that his selection (which was in fact to have a large, rapid, and continuing sale) contained "everything, or nearly everything," that the majority of readers would and should welcome, the many pieces that— in Wordsworth's own words—"will, in their degree, be efficacious in making men wiser, better, and happier." Many modern critics and readers recoil, here as elsewhere, from Arnold's habitual concern with such benefits; but, in this particular case, one might call a perhaps unexpected witness, Paul Goodman, who in his own way reaffirms Arnold's belief in Wordsworth's healing power, his ability to "cope with everyday vicissitudes," to feel and communicate "the beauty of the world and simple human affections that develop great-souled and disinterested adults" (*New York Times Book Review*, January 12, 1969).

One bit of this essay is so interesting, in regard to general changes in perspective, that it cannot be passed by. As the orthodoxy of his time Arnold names the chief English poets from the Elizabethan age onward (Shakespeare, Milton, Wordsworth, and living poets being omitted): Spenser, Dryden, Pope, Gray, Goldsmith, Cowper, Burns, Coleridge, Scott, Campbell, Moore, Byron, Shelley, Keats. We, no doubt, would drop Gray, Goldsmith, Cowper, Scott, Campbell, and Moore, and would add—at least—Marlowe, Donne, Jonson, Herbert, Vaughan, Marvell, and Blake. Although Arnold did not openly dissent from the conventional canon, it is clear that, as Leon Gottfried says, "The line of Shakespeare, Milton, and the Romantics was for him, as for most of his contemporaries, *the* tradition in English poetry. . . ." And, as earlier pages (and Mr. Gottfried) remind us, that often inadequate English tradition needed the discipline of Continental literature, ancient and modern.

Arnold's anthology from Byron (1881) was prompted by the same motive as his *Wordsworth*, the feeling that a now under-valued poet needed to be reestablished through selection. As a matter of fact, Byron's stock had been rising in recent decades, and it cannot be said to have been advanced by either Arnold's choice of poems or his excerpts, large and small, from the long ones. Thirty years before, in *Memorial Verses* and the *Grande Chartreuse*, Arnold had pregnantly summed up the nature and the impact of Byron's melancholy and Titanism, and for the elderly anthologist *Childe Harold* and *Manfred* still rank far above the works now chiefly prized, *Don Juan* and *The Vision of Judgment*. The selections do not adequately express the poetic personality exalted in Arnold's introduction. He freely admits that the poet, like the man, was often a child, a barbarian, and a poseur; but he appeals to Goethe, who, while making such admissions, nevertheless considered Byron "the greatest talent of the century." Arnold contrasts Byron with Leopardi and Wordsworth in "the criticism of life," and develops Swinburne's assertion of Byron's essential excellence as "sincerity and strength." It was these qualities which, with all his faults and his lack of ideas, made Byron the supreme assailant of the old order in Europe and even, at moments, an artist. Arnold concludes that Wordsworth and—somewhat below him—Byron rank first among the century's English poets. F. R. Leavis declares that he was right in his placing of Byron and right in his reasons—as Sir Leslie Stephen had pretty much said in his essay on Arnold (*Studies of a Biographer*, 1898, 2, 92).

*The Study of Poetry* (1880) has probably provoked more controversial comment than any other of Arnold's literary essays. The most central question was launched in his opening words, which he adapted from his introduction to the first volume of *The Hundred Greatest Men* (1880: Neiman, 239):

The future of poetry is immense, because in poetry, where it is worthy of its high destinies, our race, as time goes on, will find an ever surer and surer stay. There is not a creed which is not shaken, not an accredited dogma which is not shown to be questionable, not a received tradition which does not threaten to dissolve. Our religion has materialised itself in the fact, in the supposed fact; it has attached its emotion to the fact, and now the fact is failing it. But for poetry the idea is everything; the rest is a world of illusion, of divine illusion. Poetry attaches its emotion to the idea; the idea *is* the fact. The strongest part of our religion to-day is its unconscious poetry.

This is a reaffirmation of Arnold's early remark to Clough that modern poetry must become a *magister vitae*, like the ancient, by including religion. It is also his version, sharpened by reaction to the Victorian religious problem, of Romantic claims for poetry and the imagination[10]; and Arnold's word "idea" would be translated by modern readers as "myth" or "symbol." He has been accused, notably by T. S. Eliot, of substituting poetry for religion; A. H. Warren, with scholarly objectivity, finds him here perhaps most modern and most misleading because, seeking a panacea and having an inadequate idea of religion, he confused it with art. But Arnold seems to have had more modern allies—among them Santayana and Wallace Stevens—than opponents; and I. A. Richards used the quoted declaration as an epigraph for his *Science and Poetry* (1926). That declaration may be thought something of an overstatement of Arnold's actual position; if he had thought that genuine religion was, or ought to be, superseded by poetry, he would hardly have written four earnest books on religion, books in which no such thought or wish appeared. In them his plea was that the Bible, in its essential parts a supreme guide to life, must be read and assimilated with the interpretative understanding that all great writing demands. In a letter to his mother of June 25, 1870 (Russell, 2, 41), he spoke of literature as the great intermediary between religion and physical science. The grand questions cannot be readily resolved, at any rate not here, but, granted that poetry is not a substitute for religion, it can be said that poetry has in modern

[10] It is taken as a radical extension of Newman by D. Butts, *Notes and Queries* 5 (1958), 255–56, and DeLaura, *Hebrew and Hellene*, 139–40. They cite Newman's "Prospects of the Anglican Church" (1839), reprinted in *Essays Critical and Historical* (1871), 1, 290–91.

times brought many people closer to a religious state of mind than they would otherwise have come. It is surely true—whatever the often crude aberrations of the latest poetic radicalism—that "More and more mankind will discover that we have to turn to poetry to interpret life for us, to console us, to sustain us." And Arnold ends with the claim that currency and supremacy are ensured to poetry, "not indeed by the world's deliberate and conscious choice, but by something far deeper,—by the instinct of self-preservation in humanity."

More immediately, Arnold's doctrine warrants his dismissing as fallacious both "the historic estimate" (the weakness of scholars) and "the personal estimate" (the bias due to "personal affinities, likings, and circumstances"), which affects especially the reading of modern poets. He was one of those who, as he said elsewhere, do not live to read but read to live. His view explains "criticism of life" and the semi-Aristotelian equivalent, "high seriousness," which becomes, along with artistic excellence, the prime criterion in Arnold's judgment of poets. The "laws of poetic truth and poetic beauty" are not explicitly defined and, as his examples indicate, are variable in their application; but they clearly comprehend "absolute sincerity," the coherent ordering of significant experience, and the power to evoke valid imaginative, emotional, and aesthetic responses.

A notoriously disputed point of method has been Arnold's use of brief quotations, even single lines, as "an infallible touchstone for detecting the presence or absence of high poetic quality, and also the degree of this quality, in all other poetry which we may place beside them." The method is in keeping with Arnold's dislike of abstractions, and, when used with tact, it is surely far more potent and economical than many of the relentless pages of modern analysis. Even Eliot—who used touchstones with similar effect—admitted that "to be able to quote as Arnold could is the best evidence of taste."[11] Eliot's complaint that Arnold is more concerned with the greatness of poetry than with its genuineness would seem to be met by his insistence on sincerity and by the declared use of touchstones for distinguish-

[11] *The Use of Poetry and the Use of Criticism* (Cambridge, Mass.: Harvard University Press, 1933), 111.

ing kinds and degrees of "poetic quality." Eliot wrongly said that Arnold never emphasizes the fundamental element of rhythm; in this essay Arnold makes it even more important than diction, and his touchstones notably exemplify that as well as idea, language, and tone. Other critics, such as Raleigh and lately Wellek, have objected that the use of atomistic touchstones contradicts the idea of a work's thematic and structural totality and unity. While the method can be abused, and sometimes is by Arnold, it may be said, for one thing, that an essayist cannot quote or summarize the whole of the *Iliad*, the *Divine Comedy*, *Paradise Lost*, or a Shakespearian play. For another, such a complaint ignores what we just noted as Arnold's purpose, the distinguishing of kinds and degrees of poetic quality, since even a line or two may recall the texture and total character of a long poem—which he assumes that his readers know. In the words of F. R. Leavis (which Wellek quotes but disagrees with), a touchstone "is a tip for mobilizing our sensibility; for focussing our relevant experience in a sensitive point; for reminding us vividly of what the best is like."[12]

Another objection has been that Arnold's touchstones, reflecting his "personal estimate," tend to be uniformly "solemn" in their preoccupation with human suffering—as his own poetry had been. But surely the greatest poetry *is* solemn, in the best sense of the word, the sense of a tragic vision of life; and, from the Preface of 1853 onward, Arnold had maintained that poetry should give "joy," as great tragedy can. He enthusiastically praised Burns's *Jolly Beggars* and *Tam o'Shanter*, but should he have classed these with the works of Homer, Dante, and Milton? He does say that the "breadth, truth and power" of *The Jolly Beggars* make the scene in Auerbach's Cellar, in *Faust*, "seem artificial and tame" (Arnold seldom finds fault with Goethe), and can be matched only by Shakespeare and Aristophanes. Lionel Trilling, who presses the charge of solemnity, remarks: "One must indeed have a strange notion of laughter to make it a bar to seriousness—as Arnold does when he excludes Rabelais, Molière and Voltaire from the company of Sophocles,

[12] "Arnold as Critic," *Scrutiny* 7 (1938), 328.

Homer, Vergil, Horace and Dante."[13] The facts are that Arnold expressly bars Horace from that company, for his want of true seriousness (*The Modern Element*), and expressly joins Molière, "by far the chief name in French poetry," with Shakespeare and Sophocles "in depth, penetrativeness, and powerful criticism of life," in his "profound seriousness" (*The French Play in London*); and he ranked even his beloved Wordsworth below "Shakespeare, Molière, Milton, Goethe" (*Wordsworth*). And why, in discussing great poets, should he have named Rabelais and Voltaire? Moreover, we recall that Arnold linked Pindar, Aeschylus, Sophocles, and Aristophanes as the Greek poets "most perfectly commensurate" with their great age.

Burns, we are surprised to find, gets more space than any other poet; next to him comes Chaucer. It is painful to have high seriousness denied to Chaucer; we may suspect that the hard-pressed critic had not read *Troilus and Criseyde* (it is not named in his reading lists), although he says that the last stanza of Villon's most famous *Ballade* has more of that supreme virtue than "all the productions of Chaucer." And we regret his choosing a line from the Prioress's Tale—"O martyr souded in virginitee!"—for contrast with *In la sua voluntade è nostra pace* and in association with "Absent thee from felicity awhile" and "And what is else not to be overcome"; the Wife of Bath would have supplied some far more poignant lines than the Prioress. Finally, there has been much head-shaking over Arnold's view of "our excellent and indispensable eighteenth century" and his labeling of Dryden and Pope as "classics of our prose," poets of intelligence, not of soul. This view is commonly taken to represent Arnold's Romantic weakness or bias, but it had been expressed, for instance, by the generally anti-Romantic Francis Jeffrey (in his essay on Swift). However greatly and justly Dryden and Pope have risen in modern critical esteem, do even their strongest admirers read either as a *magister vitae*? At any rate, to quote Eliot again, "The essay is a classic in English criticism: so much is said in so little space, with such economy and with such authority."[14]

---

[13] *Matthew Arnold* (1939), 375; (1968), 341.
[14] *The Use of Poetry and the Use of Criticism*, 111.

The essays on Gray and Keats (1880) were quite general and seldom touched the poems to which they were prefixed. In each case Arnold tries to discern the core of his subject's personal and poetic character. The essay on Gray is, in a limited sense, an historical inquiry, an attempt to explain the nature and the scantiness of his poetry by placing him in his age. Arnold finds a clue in the casual remark of Gray's friend that "He never spoke out" (concerning his expectation of untimely death) and gives it a much larger meaning. Gray was immensely and variously learned, his qualities of mind and soul were high, but, as a man and as a poet, "he never spoke out" because, though "a born poet," he "fell upon an age of prose"; not "Chill penury," we might say, but a climate of prosaic rationalism "froze the genial current" of his soul. Arnold's fallacious half-Romantic theorizing, however, does not explain either Gray or the sparks of "soul" and "natural magic" in the contemporary William Collins and Christopher Smart.

The essay on Keats is wholly personal, not historical. In 1848–49 Arnold had been upset by Milnes' *Life and Letters of John Keats* (Lowry, 96), and we have observed both his early censures of the "style and form seeker" and his later tributes to Keats's powers. In this essay he is at pains to show—as indeed Milnes had been—that Keats was not a febrile aesthete but a man who had "flint and iron in him" as well as an acute and sensitive intelligence and extraordinary poetic gifts. Arnold does, like most other people at the time (including Swinburne), recoil from the lately published letters to Fanny Brawne, the "under-bred," unrestrained love letters of "a surgeon's apprentice." But Keats was "by his promise, at any rate, if not fully by his performance, one of the very greatest of English poets. . . ." Arnold proceeds with his main purpose, to illustrate, from Keats's letters to his brothers and friends, the strength of his character and the clearness of his judgment. In view of what Keats had become for the Pre-Raphaelites, all this is not otiose. Keats's passion for beauty "is not a passion of the sensuous or sentimental poet. It is an intellectual and spiritual passion." Arnold speaks for himself when he affirms—as he had affirmed in his apostrophe to Oxford and in *Joubert*—that "to see things in their beauty is to see things in their truth, and Keats knew it." Using the distinction made in *Celtic Literature*, Arnold says that, although he was not ripe for the kind of moral interpretation given by Shakespeare, Keats, in spite of his short and harassed life, "accomplished so much in poetry, that in one of the two great modes by which poetry interprets, in the faculty of naturalistic imagination, in what we call natural magic, he ranks with Shakespeare." Arnold ends by explaining that he has dealt chiefly with the man because Keats's "perfect" shorter poems prove his genius far better than any comments could.

The essay on Shelley (1888), being a review of Dowden's biography, sticks closely to the poet and his circle. Arnold's ejaculation, "What a set! what a world!," has sometimes been said to have revealed a priggish moralist, although it might seem not unwarranted (we may wonder how he would have reacted to Michael Holroyd's *Lytton Strachey*). But the purpose of the review is "to mark firmly what is ridiculous and odious in the Shelley brought to our knowledge by the new materials, and then to show that our former beautiful and lovable Shelley nevertheless survives"; the second part of that purpose is not entirely forgotten. In general, and with reason, Arnold is annoyed by Dowden's adoration and special pleading (and Dowden's being Irish reminds him of Gladstone and Home Rule). Of poetical criticism there is nothing except the concluding phrase (taken over from the conclusion of the essay on Byron), which for later critics has been a target more commonly than a text: "a beautiful *and ineffectual* angel, beating in the void his luminous wings in vain." A page of more critical comment had appeared in the *Byron*, where Shelley, with far more loveliness and charm than Byron, is said to suffer from "the incurable want, in general, of a sound subject-matter, and the incurable fault, in consequence, of unsubstantiality." This view modern Shelleyans of course reject. Arnold apparently intended to write a critical piece on Shelley, but he did not get around to it; he might perhaps not have repeated the odd prophecy made in the essay on Byron, that Shelley's "delightful Essays and Letters" might come to outrank his poetry.

*Milton* was an address delivered at the unveiling of a memorial window in St. Margaret's Church, Westminster, on February 13, 1888, two months before Arnold's death. In this brief discourse Milton is seen as unique among English poets because, unlike even Shakespeare, he was a perfectly disciplined artist. Arnold dwells on the "soul" of Milton's power, which "resides chiefly in the refining and elevation wrought in us by the high and rare excellence of the great style." Since increasing multitudes do not know Greek and Latin, Milton is the only English poet who can give such readers a sense of the power and charm of the great ancients. This is what Arnold had said or assumed forty years earlier in his letters to Clough and in later public utterances. The tacit assumption that the theme and substance of *Paradise Lost* have no meaning for the modern reader had been made explicit in Arnold's fuller critique of 1877, *A French Critic on Milton* (*Mixed Essays*, 1879). There he damned at length the young Macaulay's famous essay as rhetorical panegyric on Milton and the Puritans; Addison's account of *Paradise Lost*, "all based upon convention," is thrown away "on the positivism of the modern reader"; Dr. Johnson's good sense was often limited and warped. But Edmond Scherer, notwithstanding his "historical" approach, is a critic akin to Sainte-Beuve. We need not follow Arnold as he more or less follows the mixture of insight, inadequacy, and ineptitude in Scherer's exposition of the lifelong conflict in Milton between the Renaissance and Puritanism. The contents of the epic "are given by Puritanism" (that is still a popular error) and if the story is to be effective it must be taken literally. Thus the poem is false, grotesque, and tiresome; so far as it lives, it lives only in the unfailing power of style and rhythm, which links Milton with the great Greeks, Virgil, and Dante, and which, in spite of Milton's Puritan temper, is strengthened by the "absolute sincerity," elevation, and moral purity of his mind and life. It was no doubt inevitable, though it is disappointing, that the chief Victorian critic, the chief classicist critic of the century, did not have it in him to break down that century's conventional dichotomy between the sublime organ voice and what that voice so earnestly strove to say, his grand "criticism of life." One partly explanatory fact, touched on earlier, is that, through many years of acquaintance with Philistine Dissenters of his own age, Arnold had conceived such a prejudice against the early Puritans that, in their vicinity, he lost nearly all his critical disinterestedness, and not even the presence of Milton could restore it. At any rate, he was less obtuse than some of his well-known successors in our century.

Five other late essays show Arnold's habitual effort to discern and appraise an author's central value. We have often observed his profound respect for Goethe, whom he, like Carlyle before him, somewhat made over in his own image; his only rounded estimate is *A French Critic on Goethe* (*Mixed Essays*, 1879). The French critic is again Scherer, whose cool but generally judicious discrimination is contrasted with other critics' adulation. His own final and characteristic verdict is this:

Goethe is the greatest poet of modern times, not because he is one of the half-dozen human beings who in the history of our race have shown the most signal gift for poetry, but because, having a very considerable gift for poetry, he was at the same time, in the width, depth, and richness of his criticism of life, by far our greatest modern man.

In a letter of 1876, written just after George Sand's death, Arnold said that "she was the greatest spirit in our European world from the time that Goethe departed" (Russell, 2, 151–52). His account of her (*Mixed Essays*) explains his early devotion. George Sand's "ruling thought" was "the sentiment of the ideal life, which is none other than man's normal life as we shall some day know it," and the "grand elements" of her writing are "the cry of agony and revolt, the trust in nature and beauty, the aspiration towards a purged and renewed human society." To a very different writer, an academic solitary, the Swiss Henri Amiel (1821–81), Arnold came late. He was drawn to the *Journal* by Scherer's introduction and the translation by his niece, Mrs. Humphry Ward. Arnold gives Amiel a lower rating than other critics have agreed upon. As a philosopher, he is bedazzled by a vague sense of the infinite, which is not the kind of idea one can live with; on that plane, Amiel is a case of "mental pathology," decidedly less valuable than Arnold's early master, Senancour. What is penetrating is Amiel's criticism, literary, social, political, and religious.

*Emerson* is Arnold's one discussion of an American author (his views of American civilization are noticed in the next chapter). This lecture, written hurriedly for delivery in the United States, fulfilled a literary guest's obligation to his hosts. It was also—like *George Sand*—a reassessment of an old favorite, and in the preface to *Discourses in America* (1885) Arnold was uneasy about his candor, although he believed that what he said would not "finally be accounted scant praise." Recalling Oxford and the dominant teachers of his youth, he links Emerson with Newman, Carlyle, and Goethe. He proceeds, however, to deny Emerson a place among great poets, great men of letters, and great philosophical writers, and gives his reasons. None the less, Emerson is said to be, like Marcus Aurelius, "the friend and aider of those who would live in the spirit"; and, considered from that standpoint, his shortcomings are not absolute. There is incalculable value in Emerson's "holding fast to happiness and hope." In an early—and enigmatic—sonnet Arnold had saluted the "voice oracular" of Emerson's *Essays*, and he is able to say now that he thinks that book "the most important work done in prose" during the century.

Arnold's essay of 1887 was the virtual introduction of Tolstoy to English readers (*Essays in Criticism, Second Series*, 1888). Tolstoy had called on him in 1861 (he was clearly the "Russian count" of Russell, 1, 155), and became a faithful admirer of Arnold's prose writings.[15] The essay, more than half of which is given to *Anna Karenina*, was prompted by Arnold's interest in Tolstoy's religious ideas. As he sees things, French fiction, since *Madame Bovary*, has grown scientific, hard, and unattractive; the famous English novelists have left no comparable successors; and the Russian novel has come to the fore. Its distinctive qualities are fully exemplified in *Anna Karenina*; characters and incidents, even if overcrowded, have the rare naturalness, the intimate reality, of "a piece of life." An outline, done with sympathy and respect for Anna (even if her complete surrender to passion is said to startle an ordinary English reader), leads into Tolstoy's

[15] Marion Mainwaring, "Arnold and Tolstoi," *Nineteenth-Century Fiction* 6 (1952), 269–74; Ernest Simmons, *Leo Tolstoy* (Boston, 1946); V. O. Buyniak, "Leo Tolstoy and Matthew Arnold," *Wascana Review* 3, ii (1968), 63–71.

presentation of himself in the person of Levine and the process of his conversion. Arnold would naturally be struck by the peasant's phrase that sounded in Levine's ears, "living by the rule of God, of the truth," since that had been the essential theme of his own religious verse and prose. And he repeats here his emphasis on "access to the spirit of life through Jesus" and Jesus' "temper of sweetness and reasonableness."

This survey began with Arnold's account of "the Modern Element in Literature" as the timeless critical spirit, which had distinguished the Greeks, and it may end with his view of a related yet different kind of modernism. In *The Literary Influence of Academies* he had affirmed that "the highest reach of science is . . . an inventive power, a faculty of divination, akin to the highest power exercised in poetry"—a generality certainly true so far as it goes but one often invoked in our time to reconcile (in fact, to blur) the profound difference between human and nonhuman materials and inquiries. That difference is the theme of Arnold's well-known lecture, *Literature and Science* (1882: *Discourses in America*, 1885). It had been the main theme of a little-known but more concretely grounded discussion, the twenty-second chapter of *Schools and Universities on the Continent* (1868). Here, reflecting on the mass of data he has gathered, Arnold weighs the conflict between the old classical curriculum and the modern scientific one. Both are essential, because the prime object of education "is to enable a man *to know himself and the world.* Such knowledge is the only sure basis for action. . . ." (Super, 4, 290). The humanities, above all the ancient classics, present "the most powerful manifestations of the human spirit's activity" and thus feed and quicken our own. "But it is also a vital and formative knowledge to know the world, the laws which govern nature, and man as a part of nature." Partisan and exclusive claims on both sides damage sound and balanced education; after the same basic training for all, the choice of direction must depend upon individual aptitudes and aims. Arnold admits that, like others brought up in the old way who know nothing except the humanities, he may be biased, but he believes that the study of human rather than nonhuman activities and forces still fits men to play a prominent part in human affairs, even though scientific knowledge is so important that humanists suffer from the lack of it. He goes on to urge more humane teaching of the classics, more concentration on the literature and less on verbal scholarship and composition.

By the time of *Literature and Science* Arnold is more concerned to defend his traditional faith, which seems in danger, conspicuously in the modern industrial United States, of being swept away by the rising tide of science. As these last paragraphs, and indeed the book as a whole, should make manifest, for Arnold the classics were never a "genteel tradition," which he abhorred. His faith is a sophisticated version of the Renaissance and especially the English humanists' ideal of "virtue and good letters" as the nursery of wisdom and right action; and to that is added the moral emphasis of his later years and writings. He defends Plato's belief in those studies which result in man's soul "getting soberness, righteousness, and wisdom," though he acknowledges that traditional education is in bad odor in the world of modern industry. But Huxley, the eminent spokesman for the new, has reduced to *belles lettres* Arnold's ideal of classical literature, thought, and civilization studied in all their breadth and depth. Instead, Huxley would prescribe science and only modern literature; and, as Arnold says (and said in a letter to Huxley), modern literature and general and scientific thought and the arts had been embraced in his definitions of criticism and culture, "the best which has been thought and said in the world." Granting the interest and the intellectual and practical benefits of science, he rebels against a predominantly scientific education because it is at odds with the ethical and aesthetic constitution and the felt necessities of man. The study of Greek and Latin, like the "Sea of Faith," was, as Arnold knew and said, rapidly ebbing, yet the classics, and letters generally, cannot die:

We shall be brought back to them by our wants and aspirations. And a poor humanist may possess his soul in patience, neither strive nor cry, admit the energy and brilliancy of the partisans of physical science, and their present favour with the public, to be far greater than his own, and still have a happy faith that the nature of things works silently on behalf of the studies which he loves, and that, while we shall all have to acquaint ourselves with the great results reached by modern science, and to give ourselves as much training in its disciplines as we can conveniently carry, yet the majority of men will always require humane letters; and so much the more, as they have the more and the greater results of science to relate to the need in man for conduct, and to the need in him for beauty.

However old-fashioned Arnold's language may sound in some ears, his basic principle is surely right—as Lionel Trilling said, in broad terms, in the words quoted at the end of the introduction above.[16] Arnold could not foresee that the twentieth-century world would be made over by science and technology, that the infinite practical benefits would be accompanied not only by infinitely destructive powers created for the use of uncivilized man but by the dehumanizing pressures of ordinary life in a civilization dominated by machinery and computers. The current revolt of youth has, by some inquirers, been seen as in part a revolt against the scientific view of life. And many of their elders, including some scientists, had already been asking how far either pure science or technology has promoted "soberness, righteousness, and wisdom."

The great critics have seldom been scholars, in the common meaning of the term, and Arnold never wished or pretended to be one. Apart perhaps from Dante, he had no more than spotty knowledge of European and English culture and literature between Marcus Aurelius and Shakespeare. But, in spite of his wearing extraliterary life, he managed to read and think and

---

[16] In his full and judicious analysis of "The Leavis-Snow Controversy" (*Beyond Culture*, 1965, p. 146) Mr. Trilling remarks that "In its essential terms, the issue in debate has not changed since Arnold spoke," and he shows that both of the modern spokesmen, in their very different ways, considerably obscured that issue. However, granted Mr. Leavis' faults of focus and ferocity, he was on the side of the angels. Lord Annan (*Matthew Arnold: Selected Essays*, London: Oxford University Press, 1964) observes that *Literature and Science*—and Huxley—"should have been read by C. P. Snow before he reopened the issue in his shallow lecture on the Two Cultures"; yet, he says on the next page, Arnold's essay "reinforced for two generations the prevailing complacency and disdain for science and technology"—which may be so, but, as everyone knows, recent years have brought increasing antagonism to the tyranny of science and, on more obvious practical levels, increasing fear of the results of uncontrolled technology.

write a great deal, and to put what he knew and thought to potent use. Along with a considerable amount of later English literature, he knew the major and some minor figures in Greek, Latin, French, German, and Italian, in the original languages. His equipment compares very well with that of his predecessors and successors, and not many of the latter have been brash enough to disparage the quality of his intelligence. Modern critics who have found grave defects in Arnold's critical theory and practice are wont to begin—as John Holloway shows (*The Charted Mirror*, 1960)—by missing or misrepresenting what he said and thought. Like other critics, Arnold could, as it appears to posterity, go wrong at times in point of knowledge or judgment, though his sins of this kind are perhaps not more numerous and serious than those of, say, T. S. Eliot or F. R. Leavis. Moreover, whether we agree or disagree with him, Arnold's writing is almost always highly attractive and enjoyable, and the reading of some more abstruse modern criticism, murky with jargon and faint in luminosity, is, to mix metaphors, like wading through glue.

One complaint is that Arnold wrote very little criticism of specific works, which in general is true enough (though not of his Homeric lectures). But it is important to remember that he was not addressing the modern army of literary specialists (which had hardly begun to exist); that he was intent upon creating the right intellectual and spiritual climate for the whole body of educated readers as well as for the fruitful working of the creative imagination; and that he did more than anyone else to quicken and refine critical sensibility throughout the English-speaking world. Not many modern literary critics have essayed that large role—apart from some recent engagement with political and social issues. Nonacademic criticism has been largely restricted to contemporary writing; and in much modern academic criticism the narrowing of focus, the doctrine of the enclosed autonomy of literature, has tended to divorce literature from life. That all-important relation Arnold never forgot; for him literature is not an end in itself, it is a main agent in man's effort toward perfection, toward the achievement of a discriminating, integrated totality of experience and insight, emotional, intellectual, ethical, and social.[17]

Some modern critics of Arnold have seen a serious inconsistency between "learn" and "propagate" in his definition and practice of criticism, on the ground that the missionary endeavor involves a betrayal of "disinterestedness." It is hard to understand how the propagation of ideas can be so regarded; on such a view, Socrates and Jesus and all other teachers of mankind, all great writers, indeed all who express opinions to other people (including the aforesaid critics of Arnold), would have to be classified as "interested" propagandists. Arnold did not require that his critic should take vows of silence and commune only with himself; he was following the way of Erasmus rather than Luther, the way of enlightenment rather than partisan argument or ill-considered action. His watchword means, as René Wellek says, "a denial of immediate political and sectarian ends, a wide horizon, an absence of prejudice, serenity beyond the passions of the moment." The individual critic of literature and society should, so far as he can, perform the function of an academy or university. His intellectual curiosity, his free play of mind, must be a discriminating quest of truth and wisdom in which he is guided by the past and present toward the future. If Arnold propounds an unattainable ideal, he lives up to it better than most men; it can be said both that he speaks with more than personal authority and that his lapses are usually no more than inevitable signs of human warmth and frailty—and vivacity.

It has sometimes been said that "to see the object as in itself it really is" means seeing a work as it appears to Matthew Arnold, a cultivated but fallible person immersed in the second half of the nineteenth century. But the complaint would apply

[17] This idea of literature as a large part of the all-embracing conception of culture has been expounded with sympathetic understanding by David Perkins, "Arnold and the Function of Literature" (*ELH: A Journal of English Literary History* 18, 1951, 287–309) and W. J. Bate, "Arnold" (*Prefaces to Criticism*, New York: Doubleday, 1959, pp. 177–87). Philip Rahv's essay, "Criticism and the Imagination of Alternatives," ends with praise of Arnold's *Function of Criticism* as a timely model for modern critics in the broad but essential "educative and preparative" work which "is as much a criticism of the larger context of literature as of its specific texts" (*Literature and the Sixth Sense*, Boston: Houghton Mifflin, 1969, pp. 255–57).

to all critics of all ages and does not detract from Arnold's express aim. For one thing, his attitude is in accord with his professions. He does not talk about seeing the object as in itself it really *was*, since he objects to "the historical estimate" as narrow and prejudiced and asks of an idea or a work of art (as he says Goethe asked), "But *is* it so? is it so to *me*?" This must surely be the position of any critic (a disciplined mind and taste being assumed), unless he is merely a mechanical echo of tradition. At the same time, as Wellek says, and as essay after essay has shown, "Contrary to the usual opinion, Matthew Arnold is . . . primarily a historical critic who works with a historical scheme in his mind." But now and then he failed to realize that the critic must read works of the past with bifocal lenses, or he lacked the knowledge and sympathy to do so adequately. For example, much recent criticism of *Paradise Lost* starts from scholarly and sympathetic understanding of Milton's theme, beliefs, and background and works into a modern and total appreciation, ideological and aesthetic, which is thoroughly valid and shows the wrongness of the dichotomy made by Arnold and other critics between Milton's grand style and deplorable theme —a dichotomy which, as we saw, he had not made in his *Homer*.

There have been various other complaints. Sir Walter Raleigh, for instance, said that Arnold never understood the English character and had too little affection for the English people: "He stands among them, a well-bred, highly-cultivated stranger, and tries to win them to the light." His approach to literature, Raleigh says further, is too purely intellectual and dogmatic; and his evangelistic efficiency suffers from his "invincible air of superiority" (*Some Authors*, Oxford, 1923). Such strictures should be considerably qualified by more accurate recollection of Arnold's writings and in particular by recognition of his critical strategy, his effort to awaken and stimulate, not so much by head-on assault (which would be self-defeating) but by indirect and often irritating suggestion, as in his frequent appeals to French and German writers and culture. If Arnold had not greatly loved his country and the mass of his countrymen, he would not have labored so zealously to chasten and improve them.

Some main characteristics of Arnold's literary criticism have been consistently if inadequately illustrated: the strength that comes from a few coherent and deeply felt principles; high standards of judgment based on the greatest ancient and modern writers and their combination of artistic power and moral value, their "criticism of life"; a view of England and Europe, past and present, as one great cultural confederation, a view which requires active correction of English insularity and provincialism and habitual use of comparison and contrast; a deliberate effort to maintain a disinterested outlook, to shun partisan prejudice; sensitive taste and perceptiveness and a special exaltation and understanding—a poet's understanding—of poetry; a capacity for suggestive generalizing, which yet refuses to become involved with vague abstractions; temperate rationality and clarity of thought; a thoroughly civilized style and tone, the expression of a mind of breadth and balance, of delicacy and sanity.

Such virtues explain why Arnold can be called the last great critic in English who addressed and engaged the educated public. While our main concern in this book is Arnold's present interest and value, we should not forget his large historical importance. René Wellek—who never overrates an English critic— ends his account of Arnold by saying that he, "almost single-handedly, pulled English criticism out of the doldrums into which it had fallen after the great Romantic Age." But the first conspicuous manifestation of his influence was a plain perversion. For Walter Pater (despite his moral and religious seriousness) and Oscar Wilde and their followers, Arnold's plea for disinterestedness, his warnings against direct action, and his antipathy for Philistinism became a sanction for withdrawal from the bourgeois world into the ivory tower of aestheticism; this attitude was reinforced by Arnold's Hellenism, as sentimentally reinterpreted and divorced from its essential helpmate, Hebraism. Eliot's essay, "Arnold and Pater," is a prejudiced picture, in these terms, of master and disciple. A recent critic, W. A. Madden (*Matthew Arnold: A Study in the Aesthetic Temperament in Victorian England*, 1967), sees Arnold as a poet by temperament and vocation and as an agent in the evolution of "the belief that the aesthetic consciousness was capable of organizing and transfiguring the whole of human experience," although he was regrettably drawn into the ethical and intellectual currents of his age. For all its scholarly and acute presentation, this view may seem to be a perversion of the same kind as Eliot's, and to approach what has been, in some modern interpretations of various writers from Tennyson to Mark Twain, a too facile formula, that of the free spirit corrupted by pressures from outside. D. J. DeLaura, in his impressive study of Newman, Arnold, and Pater, while he stops well short of Madden, avowedly looks in the Eliot direction (p. x), and, in his conclusion, lumps Arnold and Pater together as exponents of "a self-regarding 'culture'"—a notion which, with reference to Arnold, was put forth by the first critics of *Culture and Anarchy* and should have died with them; one may also think, in spite of what Mr. DeLaura seems to say, that Arnold was much more in touch with the main currents of life and thought than Newman, and that he remains so.

At the opposite pole from Victorian aestheticism was the later American and mainly academic manifestation of Arnold's influence, the "New Humanism" of Irving Babbitt, Paul Elmer More, and others. This group, while closer to the authentic Arnold than the aesthetes, tended to upset his balanced totality by emphasizing Hebraism, moral ideas and conduct, and slighting or blunting his positive literary and aesthetic responsiveness and sensitivity. These two examples of one-sided influence will serve to show that Arnold's real place was in the middle: his approach to literature combined the aesthetic and the ethical and both elements were parts of his essential self.

Such opposed movements, the later one much less public than the earlier, suggest also the progressive shrinkage of Arnold's general audience. Especially in the last half-century, with the growth of the natural and social sciences (which promised all the answers to modern problems), the once relatively homogeneous educated public has become more and more an aggregation of distinct tribes which have little common interest or possibility of communication with one another. Even the literary tribe, to speak only of its higher levels, has been divided into academic scholars (with their many separate domains) and highbrow *literati*. Arnold's most recognizable successors have been

T. S. Eliot, I. A. Richards, F. R. Leavis, and Lionel Trilling, who have all differed more or less from Arnold and from each other. Eliot, who combined qualified respect for Arnold with a particularly religious hostility, had a partly similar classicist and European outlook, a similar comparative method and similar felicity in the persuasive use of quotations, a similar urbanity of style and tone; his more specific criticism has more subtlety than Arnold's, and also more disabling dogmas. During the same period I. A. Richards had a potent influence on critical theory and practice; he touched Arnold's principles chiefly in his doctrine, more psychological than directly ethical, that poetry exerts a saving power through its aesthetic organization of our responsive attitudes and impulses. Leavis' great bond with Arnold has been his earnest emphasis on the moral force of literature; he has been decidedly remote from Arnold in other ways too well known to rehearse. Trilling has carried on Arnold's cultural, social, and moral concern, with urbane, flexible openness of mind in regard to modern developments.

The breadth and depth of Arnold's influence cannot be measured or even guessed at because, from his own time onward, so much of his mind and outlook became part of the general educated consciousness; and if, to a modern reader making his first acquaintance with Arnold, some ideas seem commonplaces, it is because he made them so. He was one of those critics who, as Eliot said, arrive from time to time to set the literary house in order; Eliot named Dryden, Dr. Johnson, and Arnold. And if some of Arnold's attitudes and judgments now seem dubious or wrong, we may remember that the world has never had a critic—or any other kind of thinker—of impeccable and enduring infallibility, and that Arnold's "errors," inadequacies, and inconsistencies are such as have attended all critical efforts. More than any critic after Johnson, Arnold united active, independent insight with the tried authority of an immemorial humanistic tradition. He carried on, in his more sophisticated way, the serious Renaissance humanist's faith in good letters as the teacher of wisdom and virtue, in great literature, above all great poetry, as a supremely illuminating, animating, fortifying aid in the difficult endeavor to become or remain fully human. Nowadays, if we have been benumbed and befogged as well as stimulated by minute analyses of imagery and myth and symbol, and overworn by abstract jargon, and if we are sick of sick art and of the tawdriness of the literary marketplace, it is refreshing to come back to Arnold, as to other great critics, and encounter central questions about literature and life as these are seen and felt by a mature and civilized mind.

# IV: *Education, Society, and Politics*

I N HIS LETTERS to Clough and increasingly in his poetry Arnold had shown his concern about society at large; it was strong in *Essays in Criticism* and appeared even in the lectures on Celtic literature. One explicit statement of his belief in the social function of criticism is made in a context of special interest, his obituary article, written in 1869, the year of *Culture and Anarchy*, on Sainte-Beuve, whom he had long admired as the chief of modern critics and had taken, in his earlier essays, as a model and aid for his own. Arnold's admiration is still high, but he is impelled to acknowledge that Sainte-Beuve, because of his character and especially "his date, his period, his circumstances," "stopped short at curiosity, at the desire to know things as they really are, and did not press on with faith and ardour to the various and immense applications of this knowledge which suggest themselves, and of which the accomplishment is reserved for the future" (Super, 5, 309). Arnold's own "Hellenic" ideal, "to know things as they really are," is a prerequisite, not a final goal; the difference is elaborated in the opening paragraphs of the first chapter of *Culture and Anarchy*. Arnold himself did not stop short at "curiosity"; because of his period and circumstances and especially his character and heritage, he was moved to press on with faith and ardor (and abundant wit) to apply his knowledge and wisdom to the enlightening and refining of his countrymen. Obviously the second stage was, in principle if not always in practice, no less "disinterested" than the first.

In 1851 (the significant year of the Great Exhibition), a few days after he took up his duties as an inspector, Arnold, as we observed in the first chapter, had written to his wife about the immense importance of the schools "in civilising the next generation of the lower classes, who, as things are going, will have most of the political power of the country in their hands" (Russell, 1, 20). That prophetic conviction goes far to explain not only Arnold's many years of wearing educational labor but his continuing efforts to give a changing society the counsel it needed for new problems and responsibilities. In his prose writings on all fronts he was always an educator; and, with all his serious purposes, he enjoyed his role and his sense of growing power. In the field of education, as in literary criticism, one aim was to correct insular complacency and inertia by comparing England with other countries. But his long and solid reports on Continental education can barely be touched in relation to his larger concerns. *Democracy*, the introduction to his first official report, *The Popular Education of France* (1861), is in many ways, as R. H. Super says (2, 330), "the keystone of his thinking about politics and education"; Arnold indicated his own view of its significance by reprinting it as the initial piece in *Mixed Essays* (1879).

To postpone *Democracy* for the moment, the practical thesis of the report is that the education of the English middle class must be greatly improved and can be only through schools created by the State. As Arnold said twenty years later, elementary education—of which, as an inspector, he had expert knowledge—was in relatively good shape, and his continual preoccupation was with secondary schools: the upper class had its more or less old and illustrious "public" schools (in the English sense), while the middle class was largely left to what he called "private adventure schools." In France the establishment of State secondary schools by Napoleon has contributed greatly to make the French people, "in spite of their almost incredible ignorance" (Super, 2, 153), the most intelligent in Europe, and to lessen or bridge the gulf which in England separates upper and middle classes. "Our middle classes are nearly the worst educated in the world" (*ibid.*, 88). And whereas in France comparatively few children slip through the educational net, England has "a schoolless multitude" of 2,250,000 (*ibid.*, 109–10). The French lyceums "may not be so good as Eton or Harrow; but they are a great deal better than a *Classical and Commercial Academy*" (*ibid.*, 22). In 1881, coming belatedly to praise of Dickens and *David Copperfield*, Arnold vouched for the complete authenticity of Mr. Creakle's school—and for the Murdstones as representatives of middle-class "Hebraism" (*The Incompatibles*, in *Irish Essays and Others*).

The introduction, *Democracy*, is designed to remove or allay traditional English fear of State action, which had been strongly aroused during the previous fifteen years or so. Arnold took great pains with it, and it is a model of persuasive rationality. There is of course none of the satirical liveliness with which he was to treat aristocratic "Barbarians" and middle-class "Philistines" in *Culture and Anarchy* and *Friendship's Garland*; here the virtues and defects of the two classes are presented with temperate sobriety. The spirit of democracy, Arnold says, is inevitably asserting itself in the modern world, and in England the long sway of aristocratical government is ending. The English aristocracy, the best that all history can show, has displayed a "grand style" but an incapacity for ideas. "Protestant Dissent, that genuine product of the English middle class," has done invaluable service in establishing liberty of conscience and opinion, but it has not been civilizing in its social action and has been insignificant in positive intellectual action. It needs culture, and culture is not a mere varnish. "Culture without character is, no doubt, something frivolous, vain, and weak; but character without culture is, on the other hand, something raw, blind, and dangerous." Ancient Athens retains profound interest for a rational man because it offers "the spectacle of the culture of a *people*."

The cherished virtues of the English middle class, industry and love of liberty, cannot of themselves rise to "a high reason and a fine culture," because "The difficulty for democracy is, how to find and keep high ideals." These ideals can be realized only through the enlightened guidance and power of the State, which "is properly just what Burke called it—*the nation in its collective and corporate character*," "its best self." The English being what they have been and are, there is no ground for either the old fear of governmental despotism or a new fear of vulgar Americanization. The great changes in progress must be faced, by every country according to its special needs: "one irresistible force . . . is gradually making its way everywhere, removing old conditions and imposing new, altering long-fixed habits, undermining venerable institutions, even modifying national character: *the modern spirit*." "Openness and flexibility of mind are at such a time the first of virtues"; at present, to use Arnold's later terms, England has far more need of Hellenism than of Hebraism. "Perfection will never be reached," but honest and rational adaptation to change "is perhaps the nearest approach to perfection of which men and nations are capable."

The urgent necessity of State secondary schools was the theme also of Arnold's small book, *A French Eton; or, Middle Class Education and the State* (1864), addressed to the public, not officialdom; here sober earnestness allows some sparks of vivacity. He begins with accounts of two representative French schools, the Toulouse Lyceum and a private school administered by the eminent ecclesiastic Lacordaire. Both, as he had said before, are less good than Eton but much better than the middle-class academies of England. He tries again to break down the English belief that State power must not go beyond police functions, an inveterate prejudice held most stubbornly by the middle class (and not unwarranted by history). But enlargement of the State's powers is coming, and responsibility for wise use rests with the middle class. State schools are a prime need. They will bring, not humiliation to pupils and families, but enhanced dignity through participation in democracy. The middle class will become the center of culture, of intellectual life (which has been decaying in the aristocracy and the aristocratic schools and universities), if it has the will to "*transform itself*" and not merely to "*affirm itself*," as it has done hitherto (Super, 2, 317). The middle class now has no better ideal than pushing its way up to a share of aristocratic privilege. Its alleged devotion to "Business

and Bethels," or to "Business without the Bethels," is a charge
that slights the real strength of its religion, which, though coars-
ened and stiffened, can renew its spiritual vitality, but it is as
yet a large obstacle on the way to self-transformation (and
Anglicanism is no Jerusalem). The United States, where the
same kind of devotion reigns, is perhaps now being transformed
"in the furnace of civil war." In England the great question is
whether the middle class can see and fulfill its destiny. And if
"a middle class, narrow, ungenial, and unattractive," can become "a cultured, liberalised, ennobled, transformed middle
class," it will carry the lower class upward with it. Arnold is not
indulging in utopian dreams; he is making a concrete plea for
State schools as essential agents of deliverance and enlightenment. It is not his fault if such schools, either in England or in
the United States, have fallen short of his hopes.

Arnold's official statement and *A French Eton* clearly anticipate some doctrines of *Culture and Anarchy* (1869), but we
may postpone that central book to pursue his direct campaign
for middle-class schools. In 1878 a French report on French
schools apparently prompted the essay *Porro Unum Est Necessarium* ("But one thing is needful": from the story of Mary and
Martha, Luke 10.42). Arnold quotes his own reports of 1861 and
1868 and says that "middle-class education remains just as it
was": "our body of secondary schools is suffered to remain the
most imperfect and unserviceable in civilised Europe, because
our upper class does not care to be disturbed in its preponderance, or our middle class in its vulgarity" (*Mixed Essays: Irish
Essays and Others*, New York: Macmillan, 1894, pp. 112–13).
In the twenty-two planks of Gladstone's Liberal platform "there
is not a word of middle-class education." A statistical and quali-
tative comparison with French schools shows up the great in-
feriority of the English. In France, "Aristocracy and middle class
are brought up in schools of one equal standing"; the French
middle class is "larger, more homogeneous, and better educated,"
and it is *"happier,"* than the English. "If there is one need more
crying than another, it is the need of the English middle class
to be rescued from a defective type of religion, a narrow range
of intellect and knowledge, a stunted sense of beauty, a low
standard of manners" (133).

In 1879 Arnold repeated his plea, with others, in *Ecce, Convertimur ad Gentes* ("Lo, we turn to the Gentiles": Acts 13. 46), an address delivered to the Ipswich Working Men's College—and, in substance and style, well above what would be given now to such an audience. English civilization, he declares,

the humanising, the bringing into one harmonious and truly humane life, of the whole body of English society,—that is what interests me. I try to be a disinterested observer of all which really helps and hinders that. (*Mixed Essays: Irish Essays and Others*, 1894, p. 361)

During the twenty years since he first studied Continental education, he has felt the necessity of three things:

a reduction of those immense inequalities of condition and property amongst us, of which our land-system is the base; a genuine municipal system; and public schools for the middle classes.

Arnold repeats what he had boldly and firmly argued in the notable address, *Equality* (*Mixed Essays*), that the English system of landed inheritance "tends to materialise our upper class, vulgarise our middle class, brutalise our lower class."[1] On the third point, he repeats that the future lies with the middle class, but that at present it is quite incapable of assuming power; it must be educated, and can be only in State schools. The conclusion explains his title: the "Judaic" middle class "is of no present service" to that end, and "We turn to the Gentiles," the working class, to lead reform. The last words of the address, which might serve as an epigraph for most of Arnold's prose, come from Ulysses' exhortation to his fellow voyagers in Dante (*Inferno* 26): "Consider whereunto ye are born! ye were not made to live like brutes, but to follow virtue and knowledge." In the use of this quotation a good critic finds—oddly, one may think—the tone of Coriolanus.

In most of the areas of education that he treated Arnold had expert knowledge, the result of both professional experience and wide research, but he did not write in the manner of most modern educationists and bureaucrats (or their recent "romantic"

---

[1] Trollope's ducal prime minister, weighing conservative and liberal views, affirms that "Equality would be a heaven, if we could attain it," but "its perfection is unattainable" (*The Prime Minister*, 1876, v. 3, ch. 15).

opponents). He was of course one of the great masters of Attic prose, of lucid exposition and persuasion, and he wrote with the large philosophic perspectives and aims of a liberal, highly cultivated humanist who was moved by profound concern for the quality of individual and national life. The most pragmatic proof of his insight and foresight is that, although in his own time he met chiefly frustration, the main course of educational policy in England down to the present (including the establishment of provincial universities) has been along the lines he urged. We might add related items also in keeping with subsequent developments and with Arnold's whole egalitarian outlook: his plea for the production of books, new as well as old, in a form both cheap and attractive (*Copyright*, 1880: *Irish Essays*), and his plea for a national theatre in the East as well as the West End of London (*Irish Essays*, 455–56).

Arnold's continuing anxiety for the future of England, his reasons, and his degree of prophetic intuition, can be most directly illustrated from his letters. In May 1848 he wrote to his sister Jane: "I am not sure but I agree in Lamartine's prophecy that 100 years hence the Continent will be a great united Federal Republic, and England, all her colonies gone, in a dull steady decay" (Russell, 1, 10). In 1865, when he was well launched in critical prose, he wrote to her:

Indeed, I am convinced that as *Science*, in the widest sense of the word, meaning a true knowledge of things as the basis of our operations, becomes, as it does become, more of a power in the world, the weight of the nations and men who have carried the intellectual life farthest will be more and more felt; indeed, I see signs of this already. That England may run well in this race is my deepest desire; and to stimulate her and to make her feel how many clogs she wears, and how much she has to do in order to run in it as her genius gives her the power to run, is the object of all I do. (Russell, 1, 285–86)

Writing to Jane from Prussia in the same year, Arnold said that all he saw abroad made him "fonder of England" (Russell, 1, 340); yet a few months later he wrote to another sister of his conviction

that there is a real, an almost imminent danger of England losing immeasurably in all ways, declining into a sort of greater Holland, for want of what I must still call ideas, for want of perceiving how the world is going and must go, and preparing herself accordingly. This conviction haunts me, and at times even overwhelms me with depression; I would rather not live to see the change come to pass, for we shall all deteriorate under it. While there is time I will do all I can, and in every way, to prevent its coming to pass. (*Ibid.*, 1, 360)

Here, as always, Arnold is concerned, not about England's being a great political and economic power, but about the quality of English civilization, the only measure of true greatness, as he was to urge in the first chapter of *Culture and Anarchy*.

*Culture and Anarchy* (1869) became a book as a series of articles, bearing the general title *Anarchy and Authority*, grew under Arnold's hand. The book opened with *Sweetness and Light*, which, under the title *Culture and its Enemies*, had served as his last Oxford lecture (June 7, 1867). Its publication in the *Cornhill Magazine* (July 1867) evoked especially notable replies from two men, Henry Sidgwick, a young Cambridge philosopher, and Frederic Harrison, the English apostle of Comtist Positivism. Harrison's satirical *Culture: A Dialogue*, done in the vein of Arnold's "Arminius" letters, made its victim laugh till he cried; but, as Sidney Coulling has pointed out (*Studies in Philology* 60, 1963), Arnold was really disturbed by an earlier piece of Harrison's in which contempt for ineffectual "culture" went along with a "Jacobinical" argument for the transfer of political power to the working class, the "best part" of which was of all classes the most capable of exercising it. These and other responses, violent or scornful, helped to stimulate Arnold's desire—which had long been fed by the fatuous complacency of newspapers, politicians, and Nonconformist spokesmen—to give a true account of English and in particular middle-class culture, its grave deficiencies and excesses and its urgent needs, to find a true center and agent of authority, to expound standards by which the inward life and the whole quality of English civilization might be raised and refined. Dover Wilson affirmed that "but for Newman's *Idea of a University* it is likely that *Culture and Anarchy* would never have seen the light; different as the two works are in tone and in the circumstances which produced them, their hearts beat as one."[2] Arnold's first—and only—extended work of political and social criticism may also, without much stretching, be called the first of his religious books (unless *Essays in Criticism* preempts that label). Indeed his editor remarks that the long preface (written after the completion of the book) may seem strange to a reader who begins with it, that it "is in fact a transition from the book it introduces to Arnold's next work, *St. Paul and Protestantism*," which began to appear a few months later (Super, 5, vi).

One large historical fact must be remembered. As early as 1848, the year of revolutions in Europe, Arnold had written to his mother that "the hour of the hereditary peerage and eldest sonship and immense properties has, I am convinced, . . . struck" (Russell, 1, 5).[3] In *England and the Italian Question* (1859), in his report on French education (1861), and at large in *Culture and Anarchy* Arnold amplified his conviction that the sun of aristocratic government had set and that the dubious dawn of middle-class power had risen. The second Reform Act of 1867, which, by adding a million new voters, doubled the electorate (and created a Nonconformist majority), gave concrete force to Arnold's warnings about the incapacity of the middle-class mind to meet its new responsibilities unless or until it

---

[2] *Culture and Anarchy*, ed. J. Dover Wilson (Cambridge University Press, 1932; repr. 1963, p. xiii). D. J. DeLaura, in his close and elaborate study, already cited, of Newman, Arnold, and Pater, sees Newman's total and largely unexplored influence as "more central and more essential to Arnold's development than is generally believed. The precise weight and tone of Arnold's attitudes toward a number of crucial matters—criticism and the qualities of the critic; culture, Liberalism, Philistinism; religious 'development,' the Oxford Movement, the Roman Catholic Church; the relation of religion to poetry—cannot be caught without reference to Arnold's relation to Newman" (6–7).

[3] In the same year Arnold's brother Tom, now in New Zealand, wrote to their mother with vehement sympathy for the revolution in England that many people feared: "the whole rotten system" must come down, and there will be a fearful day of reckoning when power falls into the hands of the lower classes, "maddened and brutalized as they are by suffering." And he adds what sounds like some utterances of 1968–70: "Yet anarchy itself, which implies the agitations and movements of life, would be better than this Order, which is Death; and the faithful heart would see, even in it, the promise of a brighter day." (*New Zealand Letters of Thomas Arnold*, ed. James Bertram, London and Wellington, 1966, p. 96)

strove to transform itself and ceased to be content with affirming itself.

Another large fact behind Arnold's book, though much less conspicuous in it, was the urban and rural poverty and misery which, in spite of humanitarian agitation and legislation, were still, for those who could see and feel, a dark blot on the triumphant record of industrial progress. The elegant exponent of culture—aloof, as his enemies said, from all vulgar actuality— had shown his unhappy awareness of poverty and misery in his earlier poetry and prose, and the occasion of a late sonnet, *East London* (1863?), is perhaps recalled in a paragraph of *Culture and Anarchy* (Super, 5, 217). In one of London's poorest districts Arnold saw "a multitude of children . . . eaten up with disease, half-sized, half-fed, half-clothed, neglected by their parents, without health, without home, without hope." His companion said that the one thing needful was to teach these children to help one another, whereas throughout the country the cry was for "knowledge, knowledge, knowledge!" Yet, says Arnold, they multiply in their misery, and, whether or not they help one another, "the knowledge how to prevent their accumulating is necessary, even to give their moral life and growth a fair chance!" One of Arnold's critics, the young Robert Buchanan, rhapsodized about "divine philoprogenitiveness," a quality, Arnold observed, shared with God by the British Philistine, the poorer class of Irish, and the inhabitants of East London (Super, 5, 214). (Was this passage, by the way, a source of "Polyphiloprogenitive" in T. S. Eliot's poem?)

A partly affluent society, founded on a broad base of callous exploitation, political and economic sophistry, and belief in the divine arrangement of classes and incomes, had been attacked by various modern gadflies from William Cobbett up to Ruskin (not to mention Marx and Engels). In *The Future of Liberalism* (1880: *Irish Essays*, 1882) Arnold, speaking once more of ineffectual Liberal nostrums, praised the now neglected Cobbett and remarked that "what Cobbett called a Hell-hole" "Lord Derby and Mr. Bright would call a centre of manufacturing industry." "You seem to think," he had said in *My Countrymen*, "that you have only got to get on the back of your horse Freedom, or your horse Industry, and to ride away as hard as you can, to be sure of coming to the right destination" (Super, 5, 22). But, though he spoke urgently of economic injustice, Arnold was less qualified to deal with immediate than with long-range remedies. He concerned himself with fundamental qualities, chiefly shortcomings and excesses, of the English mind and character and civilization, on all levels from top to bottom. The three classes of society, the aristocracy, the middle class, and the lower class, whom he christens Barbarians, Philistines, and Populace, all have their distinctive virtues and defects, but they have one quality in common, imperviousness to ideas—a quality especially reprehensible and disastrous in the two classes that have power, and manifested in the lower class, which is now challenging its oppressors, by occasional recourse to violence.[4] With mixed irony and candor Arnold presents himself as "properly a Philistine" ("David, the son of Goliath," as Swinburne had called him), who finds in his own "ordinary self" the baneful impulses of all three classes. "All of us, so far as we are Barbarians, Philistines, or Populace, imagine happiness to consist in doing what one's ordinary self likes" (Super, 5, 145). In each class, to be sure, there are some fine spirits who recognize a "best self," who have a vision of perfection and the will to follow it; yet English civilization gives all but complete encouragement to the ordinary, uncritical, and often foolish or dangerous self.

*Culture and Anarchy* was the first full-scale work in which Arnold employed his journalistic skill in exposition and argument, on a level well above conventional journalism. In continuing his effort to "pull out a few more stops in that powerful but at present somewhat narrow-toned organ, the modern Englishman," he—"a plain, unsystematic writer, without a philos-

---

[4] Arnold's quoting of his father's harsh prescription for the treatment of rioters, which he later deleted (Super, 5, 131–33, 430, 526), has often been brought up against him. Trilling's suggestion that Arnold's quotation was used "possibly with irony" is not repeated in another reference (1939: pp. 55, 278; 1968: pp. 53, 253). R. H. Super also thinks that Arnold's quotation from his father's letter was intended as a joke (and perhaps by Dr. Arnold himself), and that it was deleted because the joke fizzled (cited by F. G. Walcott, *The Origins of Culture & Anarchy*, Toronto, 1970, p. 130, n. 70). While insisting on the preservation of order, Arnold had no great esteem for the ways of authority.

ophy"—enlivened and reinforced his serious message with the kind of satirical wit he had praised in Heine, that soldier in the liberation war of humanity. In an age of vociferous clap-trap, he said in a letter of December 5, 1867, he had an effective weapon in quiet irony, in the Greek sense, "the saying rather less than one means" (Super, 5, 414). Two months later he wrote to his mother that "the one arm they [the Barbarian aristocrats] feel and respect is irony . . .; whereas the Puritan Middle Class, at whom I have launched so much, are partly too good, partly too gross, to feel it. I shall tell upon them, however, somehow before I have done" (Russell, 1, 450).

So, along with earnest preaching, Arnold's ironic wit punctures complacent torpor, inflated cant, fanatical fervor of devotion to mistaken ideals. As G. K. Chesterton happily observed, he kept an insulting "smile of heart-broken forbearance, as of the teacher in an idiot school." Arnold might have anticipated the declaration attributed to that once well-known exponent of American Hebraism, the evangelist Billy Sunday: "They say I rub people's fur the wrong way; I say, 'Let the cats turn around.'" Arnold knew the value of catchwords for fixing ideas in his readers' minds and as a counterweight to the Liberal slogans he held up to ridicule. Many of his phrases—notably the chapter headings added in 1875 to *Culture and Anarchy*—became parts of the language (often, it is true, in sadly debased meanings). "Sweetness and Light" was quoted to Arnold across a dinner table by Disraeli; at another dinner Arnold heard the word "Philistines" at least a hundred times, and "Barbarians" very often. One of his devices, repetition, was used seriously (and sometimes excessively) to drive points home; but it was also a weapon of lethal mockery, aimed at such individual victims as Mr. Roebuck the politician, Mr. Spurgeon the evangelist, and Mr. Murphy the anti-Catholic rabble-rouser, and at such general targets as "children of the established fact" (the aristocracy), "The Dissidence of Dissent," and marriage with one's deceased wife's sister—"that annual blister," in the words of *Iolanthe* (1882).

*Culture and Anarchy* remains a living book because, while it includes topical and faded (though often piquant) items, it puts enduring issues in a large perspective and treats them with wisdom that is still very relevant in our own chaotic and anarchic world. We are not less depressed than Arnold by social unrest and its uncured causes, by the sway of empty or vicious slogans, by the unenlightened power of Philistine "Hebraism," by the "Thyesteän banquet of clap-trap" so abundantly provided by many prominent politicians, and we readily see modern parallels for the objects of Arnold's general and particular judgments. More important than such cold comfort is Arnold's positive ideal of a society in which all individuals may attain full and harmonious development of all their powers. Although that ideal is nowadays widely upheld in theory and action, its fulfillment may seem hardly less remote than it was a century ago —unless it is translated into what Herbert Muller has called "the highest standard of low living in all history."[5] But, even for our vastly altered world, Arnold raises, in regard to the individual person, fundamental questions which tend to get lost in our computers or to be answered in terms of "Doing as One Likes." Some of his premises and principles have already been touched in his earlier writings, especially those on education, and the most important chapters of *Culture and Anarchy* are such canonical reading that their contents may be taken largely for granted; one must, regretfully, resist the continual temptation to quote.

In modern times the word "culture" is used mainly in the anthropological sense; if used in Arnold's sense, it is likely to be derisive. This supercilious hostility is an inheritance from Arnold's early opponents, lowbrow, middlebrow, and highbrow, represented by newspapers, John Bright, and Henry Sidgwick, Frederic Harrison, and Huxley. In various terms they pictured him as "an elegant Jeremiah," an embodiment of sheltered literary gentility who was quite ignorant of actual conditions and who (said Sidgwick, the young Cambridge don) offered his pouncet-box of culture to the Hotspurs on the battlefield, thinking to cure the nation's ills by a general sprinkling of classical

[5] *The Children of Frankenstein: A Primer on Modern Technology and Human Values* (Bloomington and London: Indiana University Press, 1970), 5.

*belles lettres.* This was of course a travesty. And it may seem odd that such charges could be brought against a man who knew far more about the condition of England than most of his critics, a man who for nearly twenty years had been going up and down the country inspecting Nonconformist schools and absorbing firsthand knowledge of the middle and lower classes. But attacks on intellectualism and snobbery, however unfounded, are always a popular line, and Arnold can still be a victim. As John Gross says, "nothing is more misleading than the fairly widespread legend of an impersonal Arnold, eternally detached, eternally aloof."[6] A second point is that, whatever the importance of knowledge, the essence of culture is not bookish: "If a man without books or reading, or reading nothing but his letters and the newspapers, gets nevertheless a fresh and free play of the best thoughts upon his stock notions and habits, he has got culture" (Super, 5, 529; Dover Wilson, 6–7).

English society and the middle class, the new repository of power, being what they are, Arnold's title *Culture and Anarchy* presents alternative choices: are the half-blind going to learn to see and know and think, or is the nation to blunder on in its accustomed darkness and dividedness? Where is to be found a basis, not for raw, unthinking power, but for genuine authority and genuine progress? Certainly not in any one of the three classes in their present state. It is significant, as regards the coherence of Arnold's principles, that his definition of culture is virtually identical with his earlier definition of criticism, though it must work on a broader scale and seek to touch all people, in all areas of their lives:

The whole scope of the essay is to recommend culture as the great help out of our present difficulties; culture being a pursuit of our total perfection by means of getting to know, on all the matters which most concern us, the best which has been thought and said in the world; and through this knowledge, turning a stream of fresh and free thought upon our stock notions and habits, which we now follow staunchly but mechanically, vainly imagining that there is a virtue in following them staunchly which makes up for the mischief of fol-

[6] *The Rise and Fall of the Man of Letters* (London: Weidenfeld and Nicolson; New York: Macmillan, 1969), 46.

lowing them mechanically. This, and this alone, is the scope of the following essay. And the culture we recommend is, above all, an inward operation. (Preface, Super, 5, 233–34)

This inward operation is "a study of perfection," the quest of "Sweetness and Light," which Swift had called "the two noblest of things." It is of necessity an endless quest, but men must never cease striving toward a goal they can never reach. Culture "consists in becoming something rather than in having something." Hence it cannot be satisfied with the drab, uncivilized self-righteousness of Nonconformist chapels or with the popular nostrums of "Our Liberal Practitioners"—"reliance on freedom, on muscular Christianity, on population, on coal, on wealth,— mere belief in machinery, and unfruitful." As for technological progress, "machinery" in the literal rather than the Carlylean sense, Arnold is not impressed by the glory of frequent and rapid trains which carry people "from an illiberal, dismal life at Islington to an illiberal, dismal life at Camberwell" (*My Countrymen*, Super, 5, 22)—a remark which applies still more to the age of automobiles and airplanes. Far from accepting external and material proofs of well-being, as Barbarians, Philistines, and Populace do in their several ways, culture aims at harmonious development and direction of all human powers and opposes overdevelopment of any one. The one-sided overdevelopment which now most needs correction is middle-class Philistine "Hebraism," the sacrifice of all sides of human nature—or all except acquisitive industriousness—to the religious side, to *strictness of conscience.* " Hebraism means, in Victorian England, a narrow, crude, rigid, antiintellectual, antiaesthetic inheritance from Puritanism which both energizes and darkens Nonconformity, "The Dissidence of Dissent and the Protestantism of the Protestant Religion" (the motto of the chief Nonconformist newspaper). If Shakespeare or Virgil had been on board the *Mayflower*, how intolerable they would have found the company of the Pilgrim Fathers! And while in England there is still some leaven, there is next to none in the United States, which is almost wholly populated by middle-class Philistine disciples of Hebraism.

The opposite ideal, the much-needed corrective of Hebraism,

is Hellenism, *"spontaneity of consciousness,"* the free, critical, disinterested play of the informed mind on all issues and traditions. And yet, as the late phases of ancient Greek history showed, Hellenism by itself, intellectual curiosity, the free play of ideas, could not survive without moral stability,[7] which is the best fruit of Hebraism. If Arnold could fall short of both sweetness and light when he touched the Puritan tradition, he never condemned the religious ideal of perfection in its higher and purer forms. In his lectures on Celtic literature he had even exclaimed "But what a soul of goodness there is in Philistinism itself!" (Super, 3, 348). And at the end of the preface to *Culture and Anarchy* he says:

To walk staunchly by the best light one has, to be strict and sincere with oneself, not to be of the number of those who say and do not, to be in earnest,—this is the discipline by which alone man is enabled to rescue his life from thraldom to the passing moment and to his bodily senses, to ennoble it, and to make it eternal. And this discipline has been nowhere so effectively taught as in the school of Hebraism.

These sober words, which look forward to Arnold's religious books, recall some of his poems, and also, among other things, the dirge for Mignon in *Wilhelm Meister's Apprenticeship* (book 8, chapter 8), which he was to quote much later in his lecture on Emerson: "Travel, travel back into life! Take along with you this holy Earnestness:—for Earnestness alone makes life eternity." We need not fuss about the full historical validity of Arnold's two labels—the fact that his account of "Hebraism" is tailored to fit Victorian middle-class Protestant Dissenters, or that modern scholars might modify the rationality of his "Hellenism" by stressing the active presence, in ancient Greece, of irrational elements and of a strong sense of sin and evil. Arnold's labels, however qualified, are sufficiently valid signs for the dominant strains, religious zeal and detached intellectual curiosity, in ancient Hebraism and Hellenism and the Western tradi-

[7] *Cf.* Arnold's fuller analysis of Athenian greatness and decline in his reviews (1868–76) of Ernst Curtius' *History of Greece*, especially pp. 133–52 in Neiman, pp. 268–94 in Super, 5.

tions derived therefrom. For Arnold, both, ideally, seek perfection, the "partaking of the divine life."

To walk staunchly by the best light one has is a real but incomplete virtue, and it can be a menace. Arnold likes to quote a double maxim from that eighteenth-century Bishop Wilson whose counsel he so much admired (and whom some of his readers took to be his Mrs. Harris): "First, never go against the best light you have; secondly, take care that your light be not darkness." Modern Hebraism follows the first injunction but slights the second; Hellenism followed the second but slighted the first. The English middle class, having a large surplus of Hebraism, needs a large infusion of Hellenism. But for Arnold, who hated "all over-preponderance of single elements" (Russell, 1, 287), ideal balance and totality require an equipoise. In our so-called post-Christian era Victorian Hebraism has largely disappeared, but the Hebraist set of mind has not; an absolute assurance of rightness can animate those who are determined on radical change as well as those who resist it. Arnold himself, of course, was avowedly intent upon changing other people, but he had earned the right to try: when his favorite sister told him he was becoming as dogmatic as Ruskin, he half-playfully replied that the difference was that Ruskin was "dogmatic and *wrong*" (Russell, 1, 233).

Thus Arnold, "a Liberal, yet . . . a Liberal tempered by experience, reflection, and renouncement" (Super, 5, 88), could not join the contemporary Liberal chorus in celebration of the liberties enjoyed by Englishmen, a chorus which included the newspapers and the great parliamentary orator, John Bright. That smaller parliamentarian, John Roebuck, was not a fool, but his inspiring question, "May not every man in England say what he likes?", Arnold put to mocking use: the important thing is the value of what is said, not the right to utter nonsense. As we might expect, though he and Mill had some kindred attitudes, Arnold's praise of *On Liberty* (1859) was genuine but lukewarm (Russell, 1, 111). Mill inculcates liberal tolerance for diversity of opinion but sees liberty as only absence of constraint; it has no positive content or direction. For Arnold it has. "I . . . venture . . . to inquire what we do with ourselves when we are free to do just what we like. . . ." (*A Courteous Explanation*, Super, 5, 35). Mere personal liberty is quite inadequate: the glorification of it as an end in itself partakes of the English worship of "machinery." Coming after his discourse on *Sweetness and Light*, the very heading *Doing as One Likes* takes the wind out of a number of sails. It echoes, and deflates, not only such Liberal and Radical politicians as Bright and Roebuck but the high-minded philosopher (whose use of the phrase Arnold politely does not refer to). "Doing as One Likes," which is the motto of all three classes, Barbarians, Philistines, and Populace, is only the law of the nursery or the jungle and entails a variety of consequences, from selfish indifference to anarchy and violence. Arnold is much less concerned with natural rights than with duties, duties as understood by enlightened minds.

Intellectual curiosity, the appetite for fruitful knowledge, disinterested examination of old and new ideas, these are high and essential virtues, but they are not enough; and they may be merely self-regarding. Arnold urged not only the righting of monstrous economic injustices but more and better education for the sake of intellectual and cultural illumination, harmony and fullness of life, happiness—a matter of less concern in his time and perhaps not of prime concern even now, when the State's interest in public welfare is taken as a matter of course. Culture necessarily begins with the individual, with his search for knowledge and wisdom, and that requires unceasing self-scrutiny; but the main part of the study of perfection is "the noble aspiration to leave the world better and happier than we found it," "the moral and social passion for doing good," as guided by informed intelligence. Culture must be (to change the focus of Wordsworth's phrase) "in widest commonalty spread," "because," says Arnold, "men are all members of one great whole." Although—unlike Carlyle—he saw the existing aristocracy as a great obstacle in the way of civilization, he was, as Stuart Sherman said, so passionately aristocratic that he, "a Liberal of the future," wanted all men to be aristocrats in the true sense. "The men of culture are the true apostles of equality" (Super, 5, 113).

All this and more is contained in the words of Bishop Wilson that Arnold reiterates, "To make reason and the will of God prevail." His meaning has been much misunderstood, and he has been charged with a blandly arrogant disposition to identify the will of God with the will of Matthew Arnold. The charge is quite unwarranted and it is important to recognize the meaning and the history of a principle so central in Arnold's later writings. The first and simplest meaning of "reason" is reasonableness, that flexible, tolerant open-mindedness which is essential to civilized man and which Arnold saw—for instance in *A Speech at Eton* (1879: *Irish Essays*)—as a precious (though inadequate) quality that distinguished ancient Athens at its best. I do not recall that he ever quoted Cromwell's famous appeal to intransigent Presbyterians, but he would have happily applied it to middle-class Hebraists: "I beseech you, in the bowels of Christ, think it possible you may be mistaken." That state of mind or mindlessness Arnold had attacked before, and, with an excursus on early Puritanism, he attacks it again in the preface to *Culture and Anarchy*.

But the full historical and Arnoldian meaning of "reason and the will of God" is much larger and deeper than "reasonableness." One main clue appears early in the chapter *Sweetness and Light*:

> The moment this view of culture is seized, the moment it is regarded not solely as the endeavour to see things as they are, to draw towards a knowledge of the universal order which seems to be intended and aimed at in the world, and which it is a man's happiness to go along with or his misery to go counter to,—to learn, in short, the will of God,—the moment, I say, culture is considered not merely as the endeavour to *see* and *learn* this, but as the endeavour, also, to make it *prevail*, the moral, social, and beneficent character of culture becomes manifest. (Super, 5, 93)

The reference to ancient Stoic doctrine, to the wise man's effort to go along with the providential order of the world, recalls Arnold's early and continued attachment to Epictetus. (Marcus Aurelius, a lesser influence, he celebrated in a sonnet and, in an essay, as "perhaps the most beautiful figure in history," an *anima naturaliter Christiana*.) Arnold's God may indeed seem much more in the Stoic than in the Judeo-Christian tradition, but

Arnold, who was also an *anima naturaliter Christiana*, was able, like many men before him, to fuse the two: "At the bottom of both the Greek and the Hebrew notion is the desire, native in man, for reason and the will of God, the feeling after the universal order,—in a word, the love of God" (Super, 5, 165). This sentence is in the line of Christian Stoicism and perhaps especially Spinoza. It recalls too, in *The Function of Criticism*, the praise of Burke's ability to acquiesce in "this mighty current in human affairs" (what Burke elsewhere terms "the known march of the ordinary providence of God"). And this suggests that half-abstract entity we have met before: "Goethe remarks somewhere how the *Zeit-Geist*, as he calls it, the Time-Spirit, irresistibly changes the ideas current in the world" (Super, 3, 77).

Behind these utterances is the age-old concept not merely of reason but of "right reason," a phrase Arnold uses continually throughout *Culture and Anarchy*. "Right reason" is, in fact, the one valid source of authority, the one valid defense against anarchy. Since Arnold is such a model of lucid exposition, it is odd that he takes its meaning and long history for granted; and even his best modern interpreters seem to follow him in that. The concept of right reason, at least implicit in Plato and Aristotle, was formulated by the ancient Stoics (and codified, more literally, in Roman law), and was readily assimilated into Christian thought. The church father Lactantius pronounced well-nigh inspired Cicero's assertion that morality is founded on the universal law of right reason written in every human heart (*De Re Publica* III.xxii.33; *De Legibus* I.vi–viii). The basic premise is that there are ethical absolutes which man can comprehend. Right reason (*recta ratio*) is a kind of philosophic conscience implanted by God in all men, pagan and Christian alike, which can distinguish right from wrong. The right reason of mankind, its collective wisdom through the ages, has agreed upon fundamental principles, and these constitute natural law, which is universally binding. In the words of Richard Hooker (whom Arnold cites, in other connections, in his preface), words which may seem startling from an Elizabethan divine, "The general and perpetual voice of men is as the sentence of God himself." As Arnold says, summarizing Spinoza in his earlier essay,

"Scripture itself teaches that there is a universal divine law, . . . common to all nations alike," and for him "who truly conceives the universal divine law . . . moral action has liberty and self-knowledge. . . ." "Reason gives us this law, reason tells us that it leads to eternal blessedness, and that those who follow it have no need of any other" (Super, 3, 164–66). And "right reason" is everywhere in the Cambridge Platonists, of whom Arnold was later to write.[8]

Thus Arnold was not assuming divine authority, he was speaking in accord with concepts which had been a dynamic force for some two thousand years, even if in our day they have been replaced by opinion polls—"instant right reason," as it were. In *Culture and Anarchy* and later Arnold uses "right reason" interchangeably with his own phrase, "our best self" (as opposed to "our ordinary self"); possibly he would appear more modern and scientific if his terms had been *Id, Ego,* and *Super-ego.* At any rate right reason provides, not rules of thumb, but an ideal standard of thought, feeling, and action. Historically, the idea of right reason and natural law had been a conservative, even at times a reactionary, force, but Arnold was a liberal conservative; his constant endeavor was to fuse the best of the old with the best of the new. His definition of culture insists upon fresh knowledge and critical scrutiny, so that traditional wisdom is always subject to revision.[9] We may remember that assertion which, if invalid with respect to Goethe, is in its second half quite valid with respect to Arnold: "Goethe's profound, imperturbable naturalism is absolutely fatal to all routine thinking; he puts the standard, once for all, inside every man instead of

[8] Right reason and two of the Cambridge Platonists, Whichcote and Smith, are touched in the next chapter. On the history of the concept see Robert Hoopes, *Right Reason in the English Renaissance* (Cambridge, Mass., 1962), C. A. Patrides' introduction to his anthology, *The Cambridge Platonists* (London, 1969), and J. Hicks, *The Stoicism of Matthew Arnold,* University of Iowa Humanistic Studies 6 (1942), 38 f.

[9] Raymond Williams, while recognizing Arnold's acute discernment and high importance, sees a final breakdown or confusion in his thinking between relativist and absolutist attitudes (*Culture and Society 1780–1950,* London: Chatto & Windus, 1959, 128–29). If I understand his argument, I cannot agree with it, in view of what is said here about right reason.

outside him." Needless to say, Arnold does not make every man either a god or an anarchist.

At a moment . . . when it is agreed that we want a source of authority, and when it seems probable that the right source is our best self, it becomes of vast importance to see whether or not the things around us are, in general, such as to help and elicit our best self, and if they are not, to see why they are not, and the most promising way of mending them. (Super, 5, 146)

Arnold was wholeheartedly opposed to the Utilitarian and laissez-faire doctrines of his age, and, as we have seen, a central part of his social and political gospel was the Burkeian principle that the State should be the corporate expression of—and hence the grand support for—the best selves of its citizens. He sees the Welfare State as not merely redressing economic and social injustice but as promoting the good life—aims which are as yet more or less unfulfilled. Arnold defined civilization as "the humanisation of man in society," and to read him, even in our greatly altered age, is to ask ourselves how far the humanizing process has advanced, or, if it has gone some way into dehumanizing, how that momentum might be reversed.

*Friendship's Garland* (1871), though it has a good deal of the topical and ephemeral, contains also the liveliest and most tartly satirical writing Arnold ever did. The title of the pungent *jeu d'esprit* glanced at the usually insipid literary annuals that were a feature of the age. The contents were largely the series of letters (three being omitted) that Arnold wrote for the *Pall Mall Gazette* during 1866-67 and 1869-70. With these were joined *My Countrymen* (1866)—a generalized reply to Sir James Stephen's *Mr. Matthew Arnold and His Countrymen* (*Saturday Review*, December 3, 1864), a protest against the view of England set forth in Arnold's *Function of Criticism*—and *A Courteous Explanation*. (Arnold had already replied briefly to Stephen and others in the preface to *Essays in Criticism*.) Thus the composition of *Friendship's Garland* went along with and somewhat beyond that of *Culture and Anarchy*. In both, Arnold, who abhorred philosophic abstractions, delighted to echo Frederic Harrison's satirical arraignment of his lack of a system with "principles . . . coherent; . . . interdependent, subordinate, and derivative."

In *My Countrymen* Arnold used the ironical method he was to carry further in the body of *Friendship's Garland*. He presents himself as a humble, docile inquirer anxious to revise, if need be, the severe judgments of British Philistinism for which he has been taken to task. He cites from newspapers and politicians fulsome eulogies of Britain and the great middle class that governs it, and—fresh from a prolonged educational mission abroad—reports that very different, quite unfavorable, even contemptuous views are held by Continental observers. These become Arnold's real spokesmen. In the era of Waterloo Britain was great because of the energy the British aristocracy had; but (as Arnold had been saying for years) aristocratic government, with its resistance to ideas, belongs to the past; the present era needs intelligence, of which, foreigners say, the British middle class has "absolutely none." Arnold, posing as the conventional complacent Liberal, is "aghast" at such notions; he quotes one of his favorite whipping boys, Robert Lowe (a lineal descendant of Voltaire's Pangloss, according to Arnold's Arminius), on the prosperity and the perfect civilization England now enjoys. But, ask the foreigners, where does England stand in relation to "the modern spirit, the modern time?" For Arnold "modern," in a political and social context, means "in the current of ideas engendered by the French Revolution." The "modern problem" "is to make human life, the life of society, all through, more natural and rational; to have the greatest possible number of one's nation happy." What Arnold saw as England's failure to respond to that challenge, and the reasons for it, we have met in his most philosophic analysis, *Culture and Anarchy*, and the letters of *Friendship's Garland* are a sportive version. But his underlying seriousness, the depth of his critical patriotism, is made clear by his concluding *My Countrymen* with his own lines, from *Heine's Grave* (1858–63?), on England, "The weary Titan," "Staggering on to her goal;/Bearing . . . the load . . ./Of the too vast orb of her fate."

In *Friendship's Garland* the method of ironic dialogue is given dramatic focus and immediacy: Continental opinion is embodied in the forceful and picturesque Prussian visitor Arminius, an imagined member of "the noble family of Von Thunder-ten-Tronckh" described in *Candide*. He—against the background of the Austro-Prussian and Franco-Prussian wars—attacks English ways and institutions and some individuals, and Arnold, in his assumed role of conventional Liberal, defends them; the defense can be as blighting as the attack. When Arminius applies to the *Daily Telegraph* Dryden's dictum on Elkanah Settle, "that its style is boisterous and its prose incorrigibly lewd," Arnold remonstrates: though he does "think its prose a little full-bodied," he cannot bear Arminius' strong language: " 'No, Arminius,' I always say, 'I hope not *incorrigibly;* I should be sorry to think that of a publication which is forming the imagination and taste of millions of Englishmen' " (Super, 5, 67). However, early readers in general were not amused; perhaps there were few whose withers were unwrung.

The method and ideas owe a good deal to Heine, whose deadly irony Arnold had praised, and something to Carlyle's *Sartor Resartus*. While Arminius can make straightforward onslaughts, he as well as his host has a full share of Arnoldian irony. And he is the mouthpiece for Arnoldian ideas (even the "better self") expounded more soberly in *Culture and Anarchy* and elsewhere. Some main objects of castigation are the English lack of the *Geist* ("intelligence") which animates French democracy and Prussian education; the raw power of English Philistinism, its "fetish-worship" of personal liberty, industry, and publicity—"*the beatification of a whole people through clap-trap,*" which pours from newspapers and politicians; the belligerent bigotry of Nonconformists; the state of education; and so on, down to marriage with a deceased wife's sister. When Arnold glorifies the transatlantic telegraph as far beyond Prussian and professorial *Geist*, Arminius exclaims: "Pshaw! . . . that great rope, with a Philistine at each end of it talking inutilities!"

What may be called the most famous purple patch is the cross section of English society personified in the Whig Lord Lumpington, the Tory (and sporting) clergyman, Reverend Esau Hittall, and the Radical Mr. Bottles, the manufacturer (who had been a Particular Baptist but in becoming a millionaire became an Anglican). Arnold's irony can take in what, in its authentic forms, he often celebrates, "the grand, old, fortifying, classical curriculum." Lumpington had been at Eton and Oxford, and Hittall once made "some longs and shorts . . . about the Calydonian Boar." The pyrotechnical display is reserved for Bottles, who lauds his old school and its principal:

Original man, Silverpump! fine mind! fine system! None of your anti-quated rubbish—all practical work—latest discoveries in science—mind constantly kept excited—lots of interesting experiments—lights of all colours—fizz! fizz! bang! bang! That's what I call forming a man.

Pressed by Arminius for a description of the kind of man thus formed, Arnold is somewhat at a loss:

Bottles has certainly made an immense fortune; but as to Silverpump's effect on his mind, whether it was from any fault in the Lycurgus House system, whether it was that with a sturdy self-reliance thor-oughly English, Bottles, ever since he quitted Silverpump, left his mind wholly to itself, his daily newspaper, and the Particular Baptist minister under whom he sate, or from whatever cause it was, cer-tainly his mind, quâ mind—" "You need not go on," interrupted Arminius, with a magnificent wave of his hand, "I know what that man's mind, quâ mind, is, well enough."

Since these three men sit together on the county bench, passing judgment on poachers, Arminius affirms that "to administer at all, even at the lowest stage of public administration, a man needs instruction." " 'We have never found it so,' said I."

Fifteen years later, in 1882, addressing a Liverpool audience, the man who had mocked others could—not for the first time—mock himself. Instead of the eminent man of science who had been promised for the occasion, he said,

You have, . . . many people would tell you, a nearly worn-out man of letters, with one nostrum for practical application, his nostrum of public schools for the middle classes; and with a frippery of phrases about sweetness and light, seeing things as they really are, knowing the best that has been thought and said in the world, which never had very much solid meaning, and have now quite lost the gloss and charm of novelty. (A Liverpool Address, in Five Uncollected Essays of Matthew Arnold, ed. K. Allott, Liverpool, 1953)

Arnold gave a considerable part of his later writing to that thorny complex of religion, economics, and politics, the Irish question. In *Culture and Anarchy* he had used the disestablishment of the Church of England in Ireland as his first example of the way in which "Our Liberal Practitioners" do right or partly right things for wrong reasons—in this case, the strong pressure of English Nonconformists' antipathy to all church establishments and endowments. Arnold treated the matter again in a letter he did not include in *Friendship's Garland* (Super, 5, 319–24, 471).

In *Irish Catholicism and British Liberalism* (*Mixed Essays*, 1879) the remedies Arnold had urged for English education and society are extended to Ireland. The right of Ireland to have a Catholic university has been refused because Britain's Irish policy is determined by a "Puritan middle class" whose narrow rigidities we know: the standard formula is that the Liberal party condemns religiou; endowments and that British Protestants will not endow Cath licism in any form. Arnold labors to uproot such stubborn prejudice by arguing, in the spirit of *Literature and Dogma*—a spirit more likely to alarm than to persuade—that

the prevailing form for the Christianity of the future will be the form of Catholicism; but a Catholicism purged, opening itself to the light and air, having the consciousness of its own poetry, freed from its sacerdotal despotism and freed from its pseudo-scientific apparatus of superannuated dogma.

Irish Catholicism is far below that level, thanks to the miserable lack of education and to British ill-government. The Irish need Catholic secondary schools and a Catholic university "with a public character," under national, not clerical, control. Arnold parts company with secular Liberals in his insistence on the powerful "germ" of good in the "immense poetry, the gradual work of time and nature, and of that great impersonal artist, Catholic Christendom." A similar reply might be made to those "Puritan reproachers and attackers" who would disestablish the Church of England in England. Puritanism cannot satisfy man's need for beauty, "Catholicism and the English Church can"— though neither can satisfy his need for intellect and knowledge.

Arnold ends by affirming that "The Puritan middle class, with all its faults, . . . is the best stuff in this nation, and in its success is our best hope for the future. But to succeed it must be transformed." He repeated and enlarged some of his more practical arguments in a letter to the *Times*, July 31, 1879 (reprinted in Neiman, 212–15).

In his preface to *Irish Essays and Others* (1882) Arnold apologized, as a man of letters, for his incursion into politics; the Irish pieces had received "no great favour" when they first appeared, and he expects no more now. His "great contention" in both "Irish Essays" and "Others" is that, if the English are to win Ireland away from its inveterate hatred, they must not only act differently but be different; they must make England and its civilization more attractive. The double essay, *The Incompatibles*, combines history with analysis of current problems. The best of all witnesses, Burke, saw that "Irish misery and discontent have been due more to English misgovernment and injustice than to Irish faults." "Burke thought, as every sane man must think, 'connection between Great Britain and Ireland essential to the welfare of both'" (284, 287). Some now say that Ireland must be either governed despotically or given its independence. Arnold rejects both extremes: if the English set about the task seriously, Ireland can be blended with England as Scotland, Wales, and Cornwall have been. Both material and moral wrongs must be righted, with enlightened sympathy. The Land Acts of 1870 and 1881 have improved the wretched lot of Irish tenants, but not enough: tenants must be converted into owners through expropriation of bad landowners' land. Disestablishment of the English Church in Ireland (1869) was also an advance, but not of a kind to conciliate Irish Catholicism; and, as Arnold had urged before, the Irish must have Catholic schools and a Catholic university. In the last third of the essay he argues that the Irish become acquainted with the quality of English life and manners through the English middle class and are naturally repelled. Here, as we noted earlier, Arnold invokes *David Copperfield*, because Mr. Creakle and his school and the Murdstones are perfect representatives of middle-class education and hard, sour Hebraism, while Mr. Quinion is "the jovial, genial man of our middle-class civilisation"—all antipathetic to "Irish quick-wittedness, sentiment, keen feeling for social life and manners." So, if Ireland is to be won, the English middle class, as Arnold had so often insisted, must transform itself. And he winds up with another plea for what is not a panacea but an "indispensable preliminary" to such transformation, public schools for the middle classes. This last theme is taken up again in *An Unregarded Irish Grievance*, in which he makes full use of a report on Irish schools by the eminent classicist, Professor Mahaffy.

Arnold's chief late utterance, *The Nadir of Liberalism* (May 1886: reprinted, with its sequel, *The Zenith of Conservatism*, in Neiman), was a vehement attack—"magnificent," according to Sir James Knowles, who printed it in the *Nineteenth Century* —on the Irish policy of the Liberals and their leader, who had just brought in his Home Rule Bill. Though long acclaimed as a great statesman, Gladstone, in Arnold's judgment, is only a consummate party and parliamentary manager, and a dangerous one; for all his "victories," he and the Liberals have signally failed, both abroad and at home, and in their handling of the Irish problem have now reached their nadir. "The project of giving a separate Parliament to Ireland has every fault which a project of State can have. It takes one's breath away to find an English statesman propounding it." Arnold reiterates some of the arguments already encountered, all based on the Burkeian doctrine that Britain and Ireland are essential to the welfare of each other. What Ireland needs is not a separate parliament but a good system of local government—which, he says, England needs also.

With our knowledge of subsequent history, we may say that Arnold, in opposing Home Rule, forgot that larger Burkeian doctrine of acquiescence in the "mighty current in human affairs" which was carrying Ireland toward independence. On the other hand, we may think that his program for just and generous conciliation, seriously pursued, might have prevented the bloody hostilities of later years, even if it could not have checked the rising spirit of nationalism; and the Ulster troubles of 1969–71 surely confirm what Arnold had often said about "the Dissidence of

Dissent" and cries of "No Popery." His friend John Morley, whose support of Gladstone Arnold repeatedly criticized (and who much earlier had repeatedly attacked Arnold), gave the retrospective verdict that "In truth, his insight into the roots of the Irish case, and the strong persistence with which he pressed that case upon unwilling ears, were in some ways the most remarkable instance of his many-sided and penetrating vision" (*Recollections*, New York: Macmillan, 1917, 1, 129).

The first of Arnold's American lectures, *Numbers; or, The Majority and the Remnant* (1883: *Discourses in America*, 1885), was his last general pronouncement on the state of the modern world, and, for our view of his evolution, it is significant in at least two respects. It is a sober admission that time—and, in England, his own efforts—have not brought nearer that transformation, that humanization of man in society, which in earlier years Arnold had set up as a remote but essential goal. Even ancient Athens, so often presented in the past as the highest model of a civilized people, is now seen chiefly in Plato's picture of decay; Isaiah and the other Hebrew prophets, like Plato, were right in their parallel pictures. In those small ancient states the remnant of the wise and righteous was too small to make head against the ways of the majority, but in the modern world there is one ground of hope: if the unsound majorities are very large, the saving remnants are also large, large enough to work with some effect toward salvation. Thus, like many sages and prophets before him, Arnold has lost much of his faith in the will of men in the mass to transform themselves, yet he still has faith in individuals. His position is akin to that of the modern liberal, who, if not a Plato or Isaiah or Arnold, has no great confidence in majorities. And the "remnant" (Isaiah 1.9, etc.) may carry us back to "that small, transfigured band," "The Children of the Second Birth," in the first *Obermann* poem or to the "Servants of God" on their Alpine march in *Rugby Chapel*.

The second point, like the first, is not a recantation but does involve a shift of emphasis. In *Culture and Anarchy* Arnold had seen in the English a dangerous excess of Hebraism, a dangerous want of Hellenism; now, as before, both elements are necessary, but the prior need is for Hebraism. Nations are saved by loving

study of "Whatsoever things are true, whatsoever things are ele-
vated, whatsoever things are just, whatsoever things are pure,
whatsoever things are amiable, whatsoever things are of good
report. . . ." (Arnold's version of Philippians 4.8). Arnold's
shift of emphasis is summed up in the preface to the *Discourses*.
England is in the same old mess, but the individual Englishman
does his duty "with the old energy, courage, virtue." As a people,
the English have believed,

more steadfastly and fervently than most, this great law that moral
causes govern the standing and the falling of men and nations. The
law gradually widens, indeed, so as to include light as well as honesty
and energy; to make light, also, a moral cause. Unless we are transformed we cannot finally stand, and without more light we cannot
be transformed.

Arnold's emphasis on Hebraism (not really new, to be sure, if
we recall his growing concern with "conduct" in his religious
books and elsewhere) led on to one topic in *Numbers* which has
brought some odium upon him. In the past he had been rebuked—as indeed he says here—for exalting French intelligence,
French civilization, as a model for provincial England; but now,
when French fiction, drama, and newspapers are what they are
and when Arnold's admired (and personally irreproachable)
Renan can declare that "Nature cares nothing for chastity," it
would seem that France is largely given over to worship of the
great goddess Lubricity.[10] The sophisticated modern reader, who
is accustomed to writing in English that leaves Zola far behind
and who has changed the name of Arnold's divinity to Dionysus,
is shocked by such Victorian prudery in a supposedly great
critic. In 1858, conversing with Clough and his brother Tom,
Arnold had brushed off as unimportant the charge of sensuality

[10] *Cf.* Arnold's remarks in letters of 1871, 1873, 1883, 1884, and 1885
(Russell, 2, 55–56, 121, 250, 309, 339); his review of Renan's *La Réforme
intellectuelle et morale de la France* (1872: Neiman, 188); *Literature and
Dogma*, xi.5 (Super, 6, 390–92); and his essay on Tolstoy (1887) in
*Essays in Criticism, Second Series* (ed. 1896, 253–54, 275–76).
    The anecdote about Arnold and Voltaire, mentioned below, was recorded
by Tom Arnold in his sketch of Clough (*Nineteenth Century* 43, 1898, 115).
Clough had "bluntly replied, 'Well, you don't think any better of yourself
for that, I suppose.' "

in Voltaire; in *Friendship's Garland* he referred ironically to English notions of "France and its immoral people" (Super, 5, 50: Arnold's note); and, though he exclaimed over Shelley's circle, in his essay on George Sand (1877) he uttered no word of censure on her amatory career, and he avowedly refrained from touching Byron's.

No doubt, like most people, Arnold grew somewhat more conservative, more "Hebraic," as he grew older and as his age grew more emancipated (or "decadent," to use the official term of literary history). But his attitude in *Numbers* must be judged in comparison with the attitudes of his contemporaries. If we are not much surprised by the unwonted vehemence with which John Morley denounced Swinburne as "the libidinous laureate of a pack of satyrs" (*Saturday Review*, August 4, 1866), we may be by Swinburne's including grossness in his attack on "Whitmania" (*Fortnightly Review* 248, 1887; reprinted in *Studies in Poetry and Prose*, 1894). Tennyson, who praised Whitman, with reservations, denounced "the troughs of Zolaism"—a phrase Swinburne thought unfair to pigs. To crown, and cut short, the catalogue, the modern, ultrasophisticated Francophile, Henry James, recoiled as strongly as Arnold from the French goddess Lubricity. And at a significant time, July 1940, André Gide (not perhaps the most impressive of witnesses) in some measure confirmed Arnold's prophecies by condemning his country's tradition of moral slackness in contrast with Puritan rigor, though his focus was broader than Arnold's.[11] If Victorian reticence had its foolish or hypocritical side, it none the less carried more genuine respect for life and love and privacy than our current belief in the transcendent virtue of publicity for all things: and it is possible to prefer Arnold's moral concern and honesty to the hypocrisy which, in the name of art, so often masks commercial exploitation of sex and violence.

Finally, something must be said about Arnold's view of the United States. His earliest references, in letters of 1848, set the tone for later ones, private and public: he quotes to Clough

---

[11] *Journals*, tr. J. O'Brien, 4 (New York, 1951), 39: quoted by William Robbins, *The Ethical Idealism of Matthew Arnold* (Toronto and London, 1959), 133

Michelet's "superb" characterization, *La dure unintelligence des Anglo-Americains* (Lowry, 66); and, he tells his mother, he sees "a wave of more than American *vulgarity*, moral, intellectual, and social, preparing to break over us" (Russell, 1, 5; *cf.* 1, 180)—a remark followed by a contrast between the uniquely civilized French and the "fictitious" manners and civility of the English. *Culture and Anarchy*, as we have seen, includes similar comments. Philistine Hebraism, so strong in England, is still stronger throughout the United States, because of the powerful, unimpeded working of Puritan religiosity and industry and because of complacent acquiescence in educational mediocrity which, as Renan noted, has no corrective in "serious higher instruction"; and the American past has lacked the civilizing influence of an established priesthood and an aristocracy (Russell, 1, 133). England has more leavening elements than Arnold discerned in the United States. In the American lecture, *Numbers*, conscious of the large growth of the country, he could hope for the leaven, there as elsewhere, of "the remnant"—to which P. T. Barnum "was determined to belong" ("that term," said Arnold, "is going the round of the United States": Russell, 2, 269). His American tour, which brought personal acquaintance with many cultivated Americans (and other kinds), modified his earlier wholesale charges.

His final estimate was given in the last three of the four essays, *General Grant* (1887), *A Word about America* (1882), *A Word More about America* (1885), and *Civilisation in the United States* (1888), which were collected in Boston under the title of the latest piece (1888). *General Grant* was a biographical essay based on the General's *Personal Memoirs*, which Arnold wanted to make better known in England; it was a tribute to a man of ability, integrity, and modesty, a man he—very strangely, in our view—preferred to Lincoln, whose high virtues did not include "distinction." The other three essays are a tentative but considered appraisal of the United States, far briefer and slighter of course than Tocqueville's famous work (which Arnold had found too abstract). *A Word about America*, written before the American tour, begins—while taking account of such patriotic spokesmen as J. R. Lowell, T. W. Higginson, and a Boston newspaper—with a statement of the view Arnold had learned from Burke and long held, that "the Americans of the United States are English people on the other side of the Atlantic." However, if we are inclined to read no further, we are reminded that Burke had shown the "immense consequences" of that transplantation, and Arnold proceeds to indicate some. Even without his premise, it would be natural to make comparisons with England, so that we get here a late estimate of his countrymen also (and repetition of many of his earlier judgments and allusions, from John Bright and Renan to Murdstone and Quinion). If the American people are the English "with the Barbarians quite left out, and the Populace nearly," the great mass of Philistines manifest, as in England, a defective type of religion, a narrow range of intellect and knowledge, a stunted sense of beauty, a low standard of manners. On the other hand,

Perhaps America, with her needs, has no very great loss in not having our special class of gentlemen. Without this class, and without the pressure and false ideal of our Barbarians, the Americans have, like ourselves, the sense for conduct and religion; they have industry, and they have liberty; they have, too, over and above what we have, they have an excellent thing—equality.

(Equality, we might recall, was the theme launched in the first sentence of Tocqueville's introduction to his work; modern native observers may be less assured.) The question is whether, or when, the saving remnant can leaven and refine the mass. Arnold ends with the plea he had so often made in England: what English and American civilization most urgently requires is good secondary schools, with a serious program "really suited to the wants and capacities" of pupils. He was much pleased to hear that Henry James, when asked by the editor of the *Nineteenth Century* to write a reply, had said that he could not, that Arnold's discourse "was so true, and carried him so along with it" (Russell, 2, 232–33), James was not perhaps the most unbiased of judges.

In *A Word More*, written after the tour, Arnold acknowledged the justice of an American friend's dictum, that his first essay, though true, had missed something important. In the second he argues that American political institutions, notwithstanding defects and corruption, do suit the country and work well. The great fact is equality and homogeneity: "politically and socially the United States are a community living in a natural condition, and conscious of living in a natural condition." The House of Commons is not working easily and successfully; the House of Lords is a feudal anomaly far inferior to an elected Senate; the English vision and English thinking, unlike the American, are fuzzy and foggy because the people "are living in an unnatural and strained state," because they are not, like the Americans, a homogeneous society. Arnold returns to his "old thesis: inequality is our bane." Thus he sees far more to praise than he had seen before, though the United States has not yet solved "the human problem," is not yet an ideal home for the sensitive and cultivated.

The "human problem" is the theme of the last essay. Certainly the United States has brought about a far wider and more even distribution of "the comforts and conveniences of life," but these are not the measure of happiness and of civilization. The prime want in American civilization is that it is savorless and not *interesting*, that it lacks "the great sources of the *interesting* . . . distinction and beauty." Americans cannot have before their eyes such venerable monuments of beauty as English cathedrals and parish churches, castles and houses. (Henry James had given a longer list of such wants in his *Hawthorne*, 1879, pp. 43–44.) One might quote or imagine Americans' indignant responses to such complaints, responses already made, after a fashion, by Whitman. Americans' want of "the discipline of awe and respect," says Arnold, appears glaringly in the vulgarity of their newspapers, and such newspapers are a matter of great pride. In general, there is uncritical glorification of all things American, and the critical, of whom there are plenty, "let the storm of self-laudation rage, and say nothing." American civilization is most in need of "a steady exhibition of cool and sane criticism by their men of light and leading" (Arnold could not foresee that self-criticism would reach an explosive point in our time). England has much to learn from the United States, and increasingly feels its influence; but "the ideal society of the future," the life of the spirit, must "be born *from above*." This relatively unfamiliar discourse is an excellent example of Arnold's critical insight and urbane, tactful persuasiveness, and it contains enough of his characteristic ideas to be a substantial valedictory.

# V: *Religion*

❖❖❖❖❖❖❖❖❖❖❖❖❖❖❖❖❖❖❖❖❖❖❖❖❖❖❖❖❖❖❖❖❖❖❖❖

By the time of our first real contact with Arnold, in his letters to Clough (1845 f.), he had evidently given up orthodox Christian faith; but religion, his own evolving version of Christianity, remained a matter of ultimate concern throughout his life. Every chapter of this book has touched more or less on the subject, and a fair outline of Arnold's attitudes and ideas could be drawn from his poems and from the first series of *Essays in Criticism*—essays on the Guérins, Marcus Aurelius, Spinoza, Joubert, *Pagan and Mediaeval Religious Sentiment, A Persian Passion Play* (this last of 1871)—and from *Culture and Anarchy*. The main theme of his religious books appeared, for instance, in the deeply felt essay on Marcus Aurelius, where Arnold emphasized "the necessity of an inspiration, a joyful emotion, to make moral action perfect"; "The paramount virtue of religion is, that it has *lighted up* morality" (Super, 3, 134). In other pieces of 1862–63 (Super, 3, 40–55, 65–82) he contrasted Bishop Colenso's biblical operations with Dean Stanley's liberal focus on essentials and with Spinoza, who treated the Bible and religious problems with the fruitful insight of a great philosopher. Spinoza —to whom, Arnold wrote to Huxley in 1878, he owed more than he could say—he discussed more fully in the later essay: the Jews of the Amsterdam synagogue who anathematized him "remained children of Israel, and he became a child of modern Europe" (Super, 3, 158). It was almost inevitable that Arnold, being himself and the son of a prominent religious liberal, should feel impelled to deal more directly and adequately with the issues of belief which were disturbing more and more people as the advance of both biblical criticism and science made those issues inescapable. (Of course Arnold moved well beyond his father's position.) And, since belief or unbelief of any kind has a large bearing on conduct, at least on motives (Victorian skeptics were in general exemplary), Arnold was no less involved with that.

The quickest reminder of the growth of Victorian skepticism —which brought so much distress as well as emancipation— might be a partial list of more or less well-known names and books. There was, to go no further back, the rationalistic legacy of the eighteenth century (Hume, Paine, Godwin, *et al.*); and Gibbon stood on every respectable bookshelf. That bulwark of orthodoxy, Paley's *View of the Evidences of Christianity* (1794), came perhaps to alienate more readers—including Coleridge, who appealed to inward experience—than its cool rationality fortified; his *Natural Theology* (1802) was a strong formative influence on Darwin. Sir Charles Lyell's *Principles of Geology* (1830–33), though he was discreet, undermined the biblical story of Creation and set the earth and its creatures in a time-less continuum of natural process; the work left its impress on *In Memoriam*. The gritty Utilitarianism of Jeremy Bentham helped to awaken the volcanic thunders of Carlyle (who was a fiery force on both sides of the religious question) and later the hostility of such diverse spirits as Dickens and Arnold. Charles Hennell's earnestly skeptical *Inquiry concerning the Origin of Christianity* (1838)—which was praised by the German David Strauss—accomplished the "conversion" of the young Mary Ann Evans (George Eliot). She herself translated Strauss's *Life of Jesus* (1846)—with an image of Christ set up before her—and Feuerbach's *Essence of Christianity* (1854). Robert Chambers' *Vestiges of the Natural History of Creation* (1844), a popular —and prudentially anonymous—account of evolution was widely read and attacked; it even inspired an amusing dialogue in Disraeli's *Tancred* (1847: chap. 9). Continuing and widening disquiet brought *The Nemesis of Faith* (1849), a grim novel by

J. A. Froude, the future historian and biographer of Carlyle, who was a friend of Arnold and whose brother was an early leader of the Oxford Movement; *The Soul* (1849) and *Phases of Faith* (1850) by the classical scholar, Francis Newman, brother of the chief Tractarian and future Cardinal and author of the Homeric translation that Arnold was to demolish;[1] and, from the three great poets of the age, *In Memoriam, Christmas-Eve and Easter-Day*, and *Empedocles on Etna*; and we cannot forget the arch-skeptic, Clough.

*The Origin of Species* (1859) stimulated and confused religious and scientific debate, a result notoriously dramatized in the encounter between Bishop Wilberforce ("Soapy Sam") and Huxley; Huxley, by the way, feeling, in the Metaphysical Society, like the tailless fox, coined the word "agnostic."[2] Along with Darwin and Huxley there was the general influence of Mill (in his earlier phases), Herbert Spencer, and H. T. Buckle, and of Comtist Positivism, "the religion of humanity." The strength of orthodoxy among the educated can be measured by the outcries over *Essays and Reviews* (1860). The seven authors, all but one clerical—"the Seven against Christ," as they were labeled—included Arnold's friends Jowett and Temple; he found nothing fresh in their essays (Super, 3, 53–54), though he praised the "unction" of Jowett's "On the Interpretation of Scripture." A major premise of the group was the idea of historical development; like a number of men before and after them, they were intent upon saving the inwardness rather than the outworks of Christianity.

Some further landmarks were Colenso's *The Pentateuch* (1862), Renan's *Vie de Jésus* (1863), W. E. H. Lecky's history of European rationalism (1865); the anonymous *Ecce Homo* (1866) by Sir John Seeley (later a historian), a reverent presentation of a human Jesus which raised another storm; the Belfast

[1] It was apparently Newman's second and better-known book that Arnold read or looked through in 1850 and reported on to Clough with undue harshness (Lowry, 115). *The Soul* anticipated, at times with eloquence, the argument of *Literature and Dogma* and *God and the Bible* (Basil Willey, *More Nineteenth Century Studies*, 40).

[2] Huxley, *Science and Christian Tradition* (London, 1894), 239.

address, *The Advancement of Science* (1874), by the eminent John Tyndall; William Hale White's *Autobiography of Mark Rutherford* (1881), the drab and painful story of a young Dissenting minister cut loose from his moorings; *Robert Elsmere*, published in the year of Arnold's death by his niece, Mrs. Humphry Ward, a novel set in a much higher milieu than White's, about a clergyman who, after losing his conventional faith, is reborn in the spirit of Christ; and Sir Edmund Gosse's *Father and Son* (1907), which takes us back to a scientist of note who was also a fundamentalist—and, in his way, impressive. On the other side, we must remember that during the earlier nineteenth century traditional Christianity, Nonconformist and Anglican, had been strongly reanimated by Methodism, Evangelicalism, and the Oxford Movement, and by the seminal influence of Coleridge.[3]

Arnold's most elaborate writings in this area were *St. Paul and Protestantism* (1870), *Literature and Dogma* (1873), *God and the Bible* (1875), and *Last Essays on Church and Religion* (1877). Some of his later critics, untouched by the Victorian crisis, deplored his spending so much time and energy on books they automatically consigned to oblivion. But such dismissal would leave us with a very imperfect understanding of Arnold because it fails to recognize the depth of his religious concern, his conception of the significance of his task; and this has been recognized by his best recent interpreters. In 1869, congratulating his old friend Temple on being appointed bishop of Exeter, Arnold made what may seem—though perhaps not on second thoughts—a surprising statement: "In the seventeenth century

---

[3] Readers will forgive an appendage to this paragraph from H. G. Wells, a caricature presumably of Edward Clodd (1840–1930): "Dodd is a leading member of the Rationalist Press Association, a militant agnostic, and a dear, compact man, one of those Middle Victorians who go about with a preoccupied, caulking air, as though, after having been at great cost and pains to banish God from the Universe, they were resolved not to permit Him back on any terms whatever. He has constituted himself a sort of alert customs officer of a materialistic age. . . examining every proposition to see that the Creator wasn't being smuggled back under some specious new generalization. Boon used to declare that every night Dodd looked under his bed for the Deity, and slept with a large revolver under his pillow for fear of a revelation." (*Boon*, New York: Doran, 1915, pp. 46–47).

I should certainly have been in orders, and I think, if I were a young man now, I would take them."[4]

In the preface to the popular edition (1883) of *Literature and Dogma* Arnold spoke of this as, among all his books in prose, "the one most important (if I may say so) and most capable of being useful" (Super, 6, 141). (It might not be stretching too far to recall Milton's speaking of his *Christian Doctrine* as "my best and richest possession.") We may note the concrete fact that the first two of these religious books were the first of Arnold's that sold well: whereas *Essays in Criticism*, *Culture and Anarchy*, and *Friendship's Garland* took four, six, and twelve years respectively to reach a second edition, *St. Paul and Protestantism* had its second within a year and in several decades the total sale of *Literature and Dogma* exceeded a hundred thousand copies, far beyond that of any other book of Arnold's. (It was, by the way, a favorite of Tolstoy's.) Even before 1870 Arnold's influence—partly through periodical publication—had become great, and it can be confidently surmised that he did much more than any other writer of the age to provide a saving creed that could withstand corrosive skepticism. He was naturally indebted to various predecessors, English and Continental, and he claimed only to be giving a popular synthesis, but his own head and heart were deeply engaged. Arnold may be charged with radical failure of insight and foresight by those who would point to the continuing (if diminished) strength of traditional Christianity and the vitality of modern theology, but, at least in the Anglo-Saxon world, a large proportion of people seem to hold a religious position more or less in line with Arnold's.

*St. Paul and Protestantism* carries on the religious and moral strain of *Culture and Anarchy*, especially as that had been distilled in the preface. In the preface to the later book Arnold said (Super, 6, 124):

What we, whose greatest care is neither for the Church nor for Puritanism, but for human perfection, what we labour to show is, that the triumph of Puritanism will be the triumph of our ordinary self, not the triumph of Christianity; and that the type of Hebraism it will

[4] *Memoirs of Archbishop Temple*, ed. E. G. Sandford (London and New York, 1906), 1, 278.

establish is one in which neither general human perfection, nor yet Hebraism itself, can truly find their account.

One major premise is that critical minds have increasingly rejected the fundamentalist conception of God. (Tennyson remarked that "The general English view of God is as of an immeasurable clergyman; and some mistake the devil for God": *Memoir*, 2, 90). Arnold's definition of God as "That *stream of tendency by which all things seek to fulfil the law of their being*" (Super, 6, 10), an Aristotelian and Thomistic principle, has from the first been often misread: Arnold offered it, not as his own chosen definition, but as one that would be acceptable to scientists. (The phrase "stream of tendency" presumably came from Wordsworth's *Excursion* 9.87.) The definition would hardly nourish the religious "warmth" that Arnold so greatly valued, and his own conception, while it included this principle, was not cold. He was showing the way to "joy," "joy whose grounds are true."

A first necessity, he urges, is to shake off the age-old incubus of Protestant and Puritan misinterpretation of St. Paul. English Nonconformity, aided by the language of the English Bible, has turned St. Paul's utterances, with their Oriental and Jewish coloring, into a set of "formal scientific propositions" and has thus twisted and smothered "the master-impulse of Hebraism,—*the desire for righteousness*."

The end and aim of all religion, *access to God*,—the sense of harmony with the universal order, the partaking of the divine nature, that our faith and hope might be in God, that we might have life and have it more abundantly,—meant, for the Hebrew, access to the source of the *moral* order in especial, and harmony with it. (Super, 6, 24)

This is the main road toward man's proper totality and perfection. "In this conformity to *the will of God*, as we religiously name the moral order, is our peace and happiness" (*ibid.*, 6, 32). The echo of Dante's famous line (*Paradiso* 3.85)—one of Arnold's critical "touchstones"—is very audible. In the next few sentences we hear echoes of Arnold the troubled poet of earlier years:

But how to find the energy and power to bring all those self-seeking tendencies of the flesh, those multitudinous, swarming, eager, and incessant impulses, into obedience to the central tendency? Mere commanding and forbidding is of no avail, and only irritates opposition in the desires it tries to control. It even enlarges their power, because it makes us feel our impotence; and the confusion caused by their ungoverned working is increased by our being filled with a deepened sense of disharmony, remorse, and dismay.

"Religion is that which binds and holds us to the practice of righteousness" (33); faith is "a power, pre-eminently, of *holding fast to an unseen power of goodness*" (44). Puritanism has never properly got beyond the sense of sin and the fear of a punitive Jehovah; "Sin is not a monster to be mused on, but an impotence to be got rid of." Some of these positive counsels, so far as they go, might have been acceptable to "the heavy-handed Protestant Philistine," but not of course Arnold's fusillade against materialized and legalistic theology. One of his reinterpretations, already urged in *Culture and Anarchy* (and not altogether novel), was that, while St. Paul undoubtedly had complete belief in Christ's resurrection, his final message "for himself and others was a resurrection *now*, and a resurrection to *righteousness*" (52). Arnold's friend Huxley—like some Christians—doubted whether Paul would own his expositor.[5]

About a third of the book, entitled *Puritanism and the Church of England,* was historical in method and ecumenical in aim. Arnold recalled Archbishop Tillotson's proposals, in 1689, for a comprehensive union of Protestants, but he would take in Roman Catholics as well. Anticipating, with perhaps undue optimism, the modern ecumenical movement, he could foresee in time "a general union of Christendom." "But this union will never be on the basis of the actual *Scriptural Protestantism* of our Puritans" (Super, 6, 107). Here Arnold is most obviously carrying on the spirit of his father, whose liberal and historical attitude he so often praised in his letters. The Church of England,

---

[5] Without venturing into modern Pauline exegesis, one may cite E. V. Arnold, *Roman Stoicism* (Cambridge University Press, 1911, pp. 420–21) on the doctrine of "spiritual resurrection" in Origen and Bishop Westcott, and his approving quotation (435) of the last three sentences of *St. Paul and Protestantism* (Super, 6, 71).

"in many aspects so beautiful, calming, and attaching," not least in its liturgical symbolism, must be renewed as a broad *via media* between the stunted, rigid Hebraism of Dissent and the perverted Hellenism, the anti-Christian shrillness, of Mill and his truculent followers. Arnold saw the Church—borrowing a phrase from a correspondent—as "a great national society for the promotion of goodness" (*Last Essays*, ed. New York, 1883, 209, 315); and he urged that, along with a revamping of its creeds, it should cease to be mainly a branch of the establishment and should develop a social conscience in regard to the alienated working classes.

In all his religious writings Arnold was animated by a fervent zeal for righteousness, but—like Renan, for instance—he approached his subject as a literary critic conscious of the need of literary sensibility and tact for the essential work of reinterpreting the Bible. It was avowedly as a man of letters, concerned with the effect of books upon general culture, that he had in 1863 pulverized Bishop Colenso, whose criticism of arithmetical data in the Pentateuch (*e.g.*, three priests having to eat 264 pigeons a day) had drawn "a titter from educated Europe" (Super, 3, 40)—though we may respect the bishop's integrity in what was for him "a matter of life and death." "The object of this treatise," Arnold said in *St. Paul and Protestantism*, "is not religious edification, but the true criticism of a great and misunderstood author" (Super, 6, 46). *Literature and Dogma* was certainly a work of edification (as indeed *St. Paul* had been) because it was a broad attempt at a true criticism of a much misunderstood book. Two things, Arnold said in the preface to *God and the Bible*, were unmistakably clear: that men cannot do without the Christian religion, and that they cannot do with it as it is. We must remember the dogged strength of fundamentalism in both Nonconformity and the Church. In 1863 Arnold had said:

He [Bishop Colenso] quotes Mr. Burgon [later a professor of divinity who became Dean of Chichester] as expressing the common belief of English Christians when he says: "Every verse of the Bible, every word of it, every syllable of it, every letter of it, is the direct utterance of the Most High." And so, too, since the publication of the

Bishop of Natal's book, a preacher in the Oxford University pulpit has declared, that if the historical credit of a single verse of the Bible be shaken, all belief in the Bible is gone. (Super, 3, 45)

*Literature and Dogma* was written during a time when a good part of the nation was involved in acrimonious religious controversies.

The object of the book, Arnold said in his preface to the popular edition of 1883, "is to re-assure those who feel attachment to Christianity, to the Bible, but who recognise the growing discredit befalling miracles and the supernatural" (Super, 6, 142–43). This statement may be briefly expanded. The spirit of Christianity, the *sine qua non* for man's full and true development and happiness, is in the example and the ethical teaching of Christ; this is the uniquely powerful agent of deliverance from the self and the world and of participation in the divine life. But if Christ is to be understood and followed, the prime necessity is to get free from the anthropomorphic supernaturalism and the codified and repellent theology which through the centuries have obscured and perverted the central and saving truth, since modern man, no longer receptive to fabulous and legalistic dogma, may turn away from Christianity altogether and embrace no better guide than his ordinary, animal, mundane self. The text of the book, we might say again, is what Arnold had urged in the poem *Progress*: "Leave then the Cross as ye have left carved gods,/But guard the fire within!" The "object of religion is *conduct*," and conduct "is three-fourths of human life"; it is also "the hardest thing in the world" (Super, 6, 172–75). But religion is not mere morality, it is *"morality touched by emotion"* (176), that is, a love of righteousness (the religious word) that kindles the heart.

To make clear the difference Arnold uses "touchstone" quotations (177–78), and this Arnoldian method is a specific reminder that understanding of the Bible demands the historical and critical exegesis of the sophisticated student of literature. He is in line with such predecessors as Hennell, Strauss (he thought Strauss too negative), Francis Newman, and the liberal theologians of Oxford in seeking to disengage spiritual essence from mythic accretions. The books of the Bible were written by men; they record and create, in a nation of unique religious genius, a movement from external observances to inwardness, a process culminating in Jesus and his interpreter, St. Paul. The authors' modes of reflection and presentation are inevitably literary, metaphorical, poetic: the Bible must not be taken as a set of scientific propositions, or "as a sort of talisman given down to us out of Heaven, with all its parts equipollent"—which became the Jewish view and is now the unhistorical, uncritical fundamentalist view. Long before this, Arnold had quoted Spinoza's reply to those who, regardless of the history of the biblical texts, upheld their literal authority: "It is you who are impious, to believe that God would commit the treasure of the true record of himself to any substance less enduring than the heart!" (Super, 3, 180). Quoting the whole passage, Howard Lowry (51) declared: "He who has mastered this thought of Spinoza and followed its ramifications has mastered half the religious teaching of Matthew Arnold. The other half is Jesus Christ, his perfect temper, his perfect intuition."

To come back to *Literature and Dogma,* Arnold says: "Our mechanical and materializing theology, with its insane licence of affirmation about God, its insane licence of affirmation about a future state, is really the result of the poverty and inanition of our minds" (Super, 6, 152). Religious experience is verifiable; miracles and a materialized theology are not, and are in any case irrelevant. The traditional distinction between natural and revealed religion is false, "For that in us which is really natural is, in truth, *revealed*" (195). Even in these days of sometimes radical reinterpretation of Christianity it continues to be said that Arnold's religion is not religious because it is not founded on belief in a real object outside the self; and he has been much derided or damned for transforming God into *"the not ourselves which makes for righteousness"* (Super, 6, 196, etc.; on 190, n.1, prayer is "an energy of aspiration towards the eternal *not ourselves . . .*").[6] In the traditional concept of "right reason" (so

---

[6] For one able critic, J. Hillis Miller, "The empty phrases repeated so often in Arnold's essays are a way of keeping the void open after the disappearance of God. Even when these phrases have a meaning, that mean-

often invoked in *Culture and Anarchy*), what Hooker called "the general and perpetual voice of men" establishes values which for the humanist are "transcendent within the human order alone" but have "redemptive power" akin to the Christian: "These values for the Humanist are absolutely real, absolutely valid and absolutely binding because, and only because, they can be proved in human experience to exceed in dignity and power the inferior perishable values of the world."[7] Granted Arnold's impatience with metaphysics and his rejection of the God and Christ of theology, he clung with religious passion to the redemptive gospel and example of Christ; and his positive creed, far from deifying man, was energized and warmed by humility, self-renouncement, and continual striving.

Arnold's view of religion had many critics, temperate and intemperate, in and after his own day. The most familiar one is probably T. S. Eliot (whose great religious poetry is untainted by polemical dross). From the high, solid ground of Anglo-Catholicism Eliot looked down, with rather un-Christian scorn, upon the undergraduate Philistinism of Arnold's religious ideas, and he gave thoroughly prejudiced and misleading accounts of them. Even our meager outline refutes the assertions that Arnold wanted "to get all the emotional kick out of Christianity one can, without the bother of believing it," that "The total effect of Arnold's philosophy is to set up Culture in place of Religion, and to leave Religion to be laid waste by the anarchy of feeling." The philosopher F. H. Bradley is said to have "knocked the bottom out of *Literature and Dogma*" (Bradley apparently had not read the book), and his perverse and facile gibes are pronounced "final."[8] Another comment, which exemplifies a tiresome view of

---

ing is negative." *The Disappearance of God* (Cambridge, Mass.: Harvard University Press; London: Oxford University Press, 1963), 265. For Arnold the phrases were neither empty nor negative.

[7] Dorothea Krook, *Three Traditions of Moral Thought* (Cambridge University Press, 1959), 6. Miss Krook (without reference to "right reason") discusses Arnold (202–25, etc.) under the heading "Christian Humanism," though she somewhat qualifies the adjective; she sees *Literature and Dogma* as a great "prophetic book."

[8] Since some of Arnold's most sympathetic critics regard Bradley's onslaught as devastating, one example of perversity may be cited. In the *Contemporary Review* 24 (1874), 808, Arnold had said: "For the constitu-

numerous great Victorians, is that, "Like many people the vanishing of whose religious faith has left behind only habits, he places an exaggerated emphasis upon morals."[9] One might have thought that a devout Christian would have more respect for the religious goodness that Arnold so earnestly preached and practiced, and would have discerned the difference between that and mere "habits" and "morals."

In 1883, when the book had been ten years before the public, Arnold summed up common opinion in a sentence of that new preface which has already been cited: "The sole notion of *Literature and Dogma*, with many people, is that it is a book containing an abominable illustration, and attacking Christianity" (Super, 6, 142). The "abominable illustration" was the likening of the Trinity, in the popular notion, to the three Lord Shaftesburys (Super, 6, 459), certainly a lapse in taste and tact. Although it was, Arnold said, "part of a plea for treating popular religion with gentleness and indulgence," his momentary levity invites the comment he had made on the Evangelical Dean of Ripon's reference to Bishop Temple as the total leper and Dr. Pusey (the leader, with Newman, of the Oxford Movement) as the partial leper: "A piece of polemical humour, racy, indeed, but hardly urbane, and still less Christian!" (Preface to *St. Paul and Protestantism*, Super, 6, 110, n. 1).

In *God and the Bible* (1875) Arnold replied to the chief critics of *Literature and Dogma*, explaining and defending his position, his urgent desire to reassert the essential truth and value of the Bible and to save what is precious from being blighted or killed.

---

tion and history of things shows us that happiness, at which we all aim, is dependent on righteousness" (*God and the Bible*, 1883, p. 29; cf. *Literature and Dogma*, Super, 6, 181, etc.). Bradley, whose attack was apparently based on two of the *C. R.* articles which were to become *God and the Bible* (he cited nothing else), replied that "what is ordinarily called happiness" does not follow virtue, that "in every-day experience" the opposite is so; and, quoting earlier words of Arnold's in mockery, said that he was talking clap-trap (*Ethical Studies*, London, 1876, p. 283). It should have been obvious to any reader that Arnold was not using "happiness" in the ordinary shallow sense into which Bradley twisted it. Eliot's phrases are in "Arnold and Pater" and "Francis Herbert Bradley," *Selected Essays* (London: Faber; New York: Harcourt, Brace, 1932).

[9] *The Use of Poetry and the Use of Criticism*, 106.

He thought that the book contained some of his best writing (Russell, 2, 313).

The preface to *Last Essays on Church and Religion* (1877) also starts from the reception of *Literature and Dogma*. Whereas in England that book is generally regarded as "revolutionary and anti-religious," liberal intellectuals on the Continent are astonished that an English liberal should seek to revive what is dead.[10] In reply Arnold maintains that Christianity will survive because of its "*natural truth*" and because conduct is three fourths of life. The teaching of Jesus and the facts of experience agree in recognizing that obedience to the lower self brings death and misery, that obedience to the "higher self, or reason" brings happiness and life, that "self-renouncement *is* joy." The contrast between the two selves is conspicuous in regard to "the two great Christian virtues, charity and chastity, kindness and pureness" (at present one of the two does not appear to be in high esteem). But, as Socrates taught, virtue and knowledge are interdependent, and if on the one hand the Bible and Christianity must be reinterpreted, on the other—here we recall *Culture and Anarchy*—the mass of people, who cling blindly to the untenable, must be persuaded to seek enlightenment and transform themselves. This double transformation

can be accomplished only by carrying the qualities of flexibility, perceptiveness, and judgment, which are the best fruits of letters, to whole classes of the community which now know next to nothing of them, and by procuring the application of those qualities to matters where they are never applied now. (158)

The long first essay, *A Psychological Parallel*, begins with the fundamentalist insistence on all or nothing, St. Paul with miracles or no St. Paul. Arnold's discourse has the interest of revealing his high admiration for the Cambridge Platonists, particularly John Smith. They (and John Hales along with them) live, or should live, by virtue of "their extraordinary simple, profound, and just conception of religion"; for that long-obscured conception "the hour of light has at last come." Situated between Laud-

[10] *St. Paul & Protestantism . . . and Last Essays on Church & Religion* (New York: Macmillan, 1883), 159–60.

ian sacerdotalism on one side and Puritan dogmatism on the other, they saw Christianity as "a *temper*, a *behaviour*." "Their immediate recompense was a religious isolation of two centuries" (the situation was repeated, in Arnold's age, with High Church Tractarianism and evangelical Dissent). Although Arnold slights the Platonists' full acceptance of traditional beliefs, he is quite right in stressing their concern with "the profound *natural truth* of Christianity," the one "ground which will not crumble under our feet." Arnold's strategy and title are explained by his argument that, although St. Paul believed in miracles and Smith in witchcraft, neither man founded his religious and moral faith on such things but on verifiable experience of good and evil, on the attainment of righteousness. The second half of the essay is concerned with the wrongness of dogma and literalism and with Jesus' own free and loving use of "the common wording and imagery of the popular Jewish religion" for the expression of higher meanings.

Before leaving the Platonists—whose influence Arnold discerned in his beloved Bishop Wilson—we might record some bits from the *Aphorisms* of Benjamin Whichcote, a book Arnold mentions. These may, better than further comment, suggest the nature of the classical-Christian tradition of "right reason" which, as we saw, was so constantly appealed to in *Culture and Anarchy* and is the basis of so much of Arnold's religious and ethical thought."[11]

14. If we consider, what is *becoming reasonable Nature*; we shall have a *Rule* to guide us, as to Good and Evil.

76. To go against *Reason*, is to go against *God* . . . Reason is the *Divine* Governor of Man's Life; it is the very Voice of God.

100. Both *Heaven* and *Hell* have their Foundation *within Us*. . . .

220. Religion is intelligible, rational, and accountable. . . .

221. The *Moral* part of Religion never alters . . . The Moral Part of Religion does *sanctify* the Soul. . . .

[11] *Moral and Religious Aphorisms By Benjamin Whichcote*, London, 1930. The aphorisms are numbered.

291. Religion doth not *destroy* Nature; but is built upon it.

440. Religion is a good Mind, and a good Life.

586. Morals are owned, as soon as spoken; and they are nineteen parts in twenty, of all Religion.

591. Religion is . . . the being as much like God as Man can be like him.

742. We partake of the *Death* of Christ; by passing into the *Spirit* of Christ. The great work of Christ in Us lies, in implanting his own *Life* [Lively Nature] in the lapsed degenerate Souls of Men.

743. Morality is not a *Means* to any thing, but to Happiness: every thing else is a Means to Morality.

853. The *State* of Religion consists in a divine Frame and *Temper* of mind: and shews it self in a *Life* and Actions, conformable to the divine Will.

969. Nothing is more *Spiritual*, than that which is *Moral*.

Arnold's final witness, the subject of two lectures included in *Last Essays*, was Bishop Butler, whose *Analogy of Religion* (1736) and *Sermons* had long been magisterial textbooks of rational Christianity. Arnold could welcome a cleric who "well says that even religious people are always for placing the stress of their religion anywhere other than on virtue;—virtue being simply the good direction of conduct" (165–66). In *God and the Bible* (139–40) Arnold had quoted Butler's sermon on *The Ignorance of Man*:

"If things afford to man," says Butler, "the least hint or intimation that virtue is the law he is born under, scepticism itself should lead him to the most strict and inviolable performance of it; *that he may not make the dreadful experiment of leaving the course of life marked out for him by nature, whatever that nature be, and entering paths of his own, of which he can know neither the danger nor the end.*" What can be more solemn and grand?

Arnold had gone on to say, as he hoped one day to show, that the greatness of Butler . . . is in his clear perception and powerful use of "a course of life marked out for man by nature, whatever that nature be." His embarrassment and failure is in his attempt to establish a perception as clear, and a use as powerful, of the popular theology. But from Butler, and from his treatment of *nature* in connection with religion, the idea of following out that treatment frankly and fully, which is the design of *Literature and Dogma*, first, as we are proud to acknowledge, came to us; and, indeed, our obligations of all kinds to this deep and strenuous spirit are very great.

In *Bishop Butler and the Zeit-Geist* (*Last Essays*) Arnold criticizes Butler's psychology as "arbitrary" and "fantastic" (we recall his early sonnet) and pronounces the traditionally "unanswerable" *Analogy* thoroughly unsatisfying. But he comes back to what the *Zeitgeist* leaves invulnerable, Butler's reliance on right reason, "the law of virtue written on our hearts" (237), his conviction that "religion and Christianity do somehow 'in themselves entirely fall in with our natural sense of things'" (303–4), that "our nature" is "the voice of God within us" (264). And Arnold states once more his own conviction, which has Jesus' authority (282), that

as man advances in his development, he becomes aware of two lives, one permanent and impersonal, the other transient and bound to our contracted self; he becomes aware of two selves, one higher and real, the other inferior and apparent; and that the instinct in him truly to live, the desire for happiness, is served by following the first self and not the second. (281)

Finally, we might add two relevant utterances of a later and greater religious and philosophic sage, Coleridge, which Arnold cited (at second hand, though he knew a good deal of Coleridge) in his note-books: "Faith is allegiance of the moral nature to Universal Reason, or the will of God" (quoted twice); "An approving conscience is the sense of harmony of the personal will of man with that impersonal light which is in him, representative of the will of God" (quoted three times).[12]

Arnold's note-books, which were not intended for publication, cannot be left out of the briefest discussion of his religious and

---

[12] *The Note-Books of Matthew Arnold*, ed. H. F. Lowry, K. Young, and W. H. Dunn (New York and London, 1952), 40, 50, 72.

ethical thought or his general character and temper. These hundreds of private jottings, which cover the years from 1852 until his death, are not all fortifying and cherished bits of wisdom. There are items from *The Times* and the *Saturday Review*, from Mr. Roebuck and Sir Charles Adderley, and, also recorded for public use, occasional notes of Arnold's own. Along with a minute record of official engagements and expenses there are private resolutions about times for working and reading, and much light is thrown on his interests by the annual lists of books to be read which, from at least 1845 onward, Arnold drew up as guides for the best use of his scanty leisure. But the great preponderance of literary entries consists of religious and moral aphorisms and observations. To many modern readers Arnold may seem to have been naive in copying down such things, but, like a multitude of Renaissance humanists, he had a sincere and practical faith in the directing and energizing power of pregnant statements of human experience and aspiration—a faith reflected in the repeated key phrases of his published works. While he was doubtless not at all concerned about precedents for such a private compilation, he had many, in the published collections of Erasmus and the commonplace books of a multitude of Renaissance writers (Ben Jonson and Milton, for instance) which lay behind the essays of Montaigne and Bacon and many other works; these writers were not naive. For all the man-of-the-world urbanity and wit of Arnold's prose, the deep seriousness of his religious books is borne out by the great predominance of religious and moral entries in the note-books and the meditations they imply. A very large proportion of them come from the Bible and the classics (notably from Stoic ethics), but they range widely, from Bishop Wilson to modern writers, mainly French and German, especially Goethe, George Sand, Sainte-Beuve, Michelet, and Renan. It may be observed that in the earlier years nothing is so often repeated—and often at the beginning of a year—as one or other of two phrases from Thomas à Kempis' *Imitation of Christ*: *Semper aliquid certi proponendum est* and *Secundum propositum nostrum est cursus profectus nostri*; and, throughout, no book except the Bible is quoted so much.

While it has long been a commonplace that Arnold's religious

books are "dated" (as of course their biblical scholarship is),
it should be remembered that he was doing the special task
which he saw as urgent at that time; and one may think that
his gospel remains in essence wiser, richer, and far more exacting than the numerous prescriptions for a sick society now current.[13] For an expression of his limited but unconquerable hope
of progress through enlightenment, through moderation and wisdom, through "imaginative reason," we cannot do better than
recall an essay already cited several times, that on Lord Falkland (1877). After his picture of the violent conflict between
single-minded parties in the Civil War, Arnold takes leave of
his hero in one of the few passages in his prose where emotion
is allowed half-poetic eloquence:

But let us return to Falkland,—to our martyr of sweetness and light,
of lucidity of mind and largeness of temper. Let us bid him farewell,
not with compassion for him, and not with excuses, but in confidence
and pride. Slowly, very slowly, his ideal of lucidity of mind and largeness of temper conquers; but it conquers. In the end it will prevail;
only we must have patience. The day will come when this nation
shall be renewed by it. But, O lime-trees of Tew, and quiet Oxford-
shire fieldbanks where the first violets are even now raising their
heads!—how often, ere that day arrive for Englishmen, shall your
renewal be seen!

[13] A compendious and specific statement of Arnold's reinterpretation of the
central Christian dogmas, which William Robbins calls "the last and most
effective summary . . . of the essentials of his ethico-psychological position," appeared in A Comment on Christmas (quoted by Robbins, The
Ethical Idealism of Matthew Arnold, 1959, pp. 30–31, from the Works,
London, 1903–04, 11, 323).

# Conclusion

ARNOLD IS sometimes discounted or dismissed on the ground that his attitudes and ideas were only those of an Englishman of a particular class in a particular period, so that he is now a figure of limited historical interest. This mode of judgment—which obviously might be used against any writer of any age and which implies that Arnold was a mirror rather than a critic of his world—suggests the more positive fact that he is an eminent example of a man who speaks with something more than personal authority. His note-books, which we just looked at, are only the last of many reminders that, whether or not he had any awareness of it, Arnold was a lineal descendant of the Christian humanists of the Renaissance. Like them, he combined devotion to the ancient classics with a firm belief in the ennobling power of great literature. Like them, he believed in the transforming possibilities of education, in gradual enlightenment; and, like the greatest humanists (Erasmus, Budé, Vives, Rabelais, Montaigne, Milton, and others) and unlike modern authors and scholars, he did not disdain to write—in his case at the cost of hundreds of days—about the substance and methods of education, education for the many, not for the few. Like the humanists, he saw the end of education and life in wise and virtuous action, and envisioned a peaceful, harmonious society which would rise above individual, nationalistic, and religious struggles for power. While Arnold did not accept the supernaturalism of the Christian religion, he was close to Erasmus and the Cambridge Platonists in exalting the "philosophy" and the imitation of Christ. It might be added that it was Erasmus and Sir Thomas More who brought back into literature one of Arnold's most effective weapons, irony.

For emancipated and rootless moderns, such an affinity may only confirm the view that Arnold, whatever his sophistication, belongs to an obsolete world which has nothing to say to us and ours. For others, who would not brush aside the experience and wisdom and art of two and a half millennia in order to start again from scratch, Arnold may seem to be a modern voice of a central tradition who might well be heeded by the inhabitants of our darkling plain. " '*The fashion of this world passeth away*; and I would fain occupy myself only with the abiding.' There speaks the true Goethe, and with that Goethe we would end" (*Mixed Essays*, 235). Arnold was, to be sure, a complex mind, informed and conditioned by a world more complex than that of the old humanists, but his basic attitudes and ideas, whatever their complications and whatever their minor inadequacies or inconsistencies, have the further strength of coherence and clarity. His poetry is coherent even in its negations and conflicts as well as in its aspirations. His views of literature, education, society, and religion, of criticism and culture, all coalesce in one ideal, "the humanisation of man in society." That, he knows, cannot be achieved overnight; but it cannot be achieved at all unless it begins in the individual person's self-scrutiny, self-enlightenment, self-transformation. This ethical, intellectual, and aesthetic process is much more difficult than unquestioning acceptance of the raw self, which, Arnold would say, seems at present to be the unacknowledged creed of a multitude of people from the extreme left to the extreme right, and which promises nothing but continuing conflict and confusion. Since Arnold's time obstacles on the endless road toward "perfection" have multiplied in number and magnitude, but it may be thought, at least by those who lack confidence in salvation through psychology and sociology, that his diagnosis and prescription remain dynamically valid—unless we prefer passive acquiescence in the evolutionary doctrine that man is the missing link between the apes and humane human beings.

# Suggestions for Further Reading

◇❀◇❀◇❀◇❀◇❀◇❀◇❀◇❀◇❀◇❀◇❀◇❀◇❀◇❀◇❀◇❀◇❀◇❀◇❀◇❀◇❀◇❀◇❀◇❀◇❀◇❀◇❀◇

COMPREHENSIVE LISTS OF works and studies are in *Bibliographies of Twelve Victorian Authors*, ed. T. G. Ehrsam, R. H. Deily, and R. M. Smith (New York, 1936), and *The New Cambridge Bibliography of English Literature*, ed. George Watson, vol. 3 (Cambridge, 1969), 465–83, etc. *The Victorian Poets: A Guide to Research*, ed. F. E. Faverty (2nd ed., Cambridge, Mass., and London, 1968), contains (164–226) a full critical survey by the editor of modern scholarship and criticism concerning Arnold's verse and prose. Many of the books named below include bibliographies.

Some indispensable editions of poetry, prose, and letters are listed under Abbreviations at the beginning of this book. While Allott's annotated *Poems* is used here, the edition of C. B. Tinker and H. F. Lowry (London and New York, 1950), with textual notes, is also authoritative. There are various volumes of selected poetry and prose.

Critical studies of more or less general interest are listed in the following paragraphs; bibliographical data are not given for books already cited in footnotes (see index). Countless good articles and essays must be omitted; a number have been mentioned in footnotes and their authors' names are in the index.

Arnold forbade a biography, and there is none yet. (There are of course the several volumes of letters, which have been quoted so often in this book.) More or less biographical material is given in most of the following general studies, all entitled *Matthew Arnold*: the large standard work by Lionel Trilling (1939 and later edns.), which retains its vitality and distinction; and the small books by Sir Edmund Chambers (Oxford, 1947), J. D. Jump (London and New York, 1955), Fraser Neiman (New York, 1968), and Michael Thorpe (London, 1969), who deals wholly with the writings.

Arnold's poetry has been studied in many substantial and valuable books, which have multiplied in recent years: C. B. Tinker and H. F. Lowry, *The Poetry of Matthew Arnold: A Commentary* (New York and London, 1940), which includes interpretation with much on personal background and sources; Louis Bonnerot, *Matthew Arnold Poète* (1947), a very full "biographie psychologique"; a section of E. D. H. Johnson's *The Alien Vision of Victorian Poetry* (Princeton, 1952); W. Stacy Johnson, *The Voices of Matthew Arnold* (New Haven, 1961); A. Dwight Culler, *Imaginative Reason* (1966); G. R. Stange, *Matthew Arnold: The Poet as Humanist* (Princeton, 1967); Alan Roper, *Arnold's Poetic Landscapes* (1969). S. M. Parrish compiled a *Concordance* (Ithaca, 1959), the first ever done with an electronic computer—a technological achievement Arnold might perhaps have condoned.

Some studies, mainly of the prose, are: E. K. Brown, *Matthew Arnold: A Study in Conflict* (1948); W. F. Connell, *The Educational Thought and Influence of Matthew Arnold* (London, 1950); F. E. Faverty, *Matthew Arnold the Ethnologist* (Evanston, 1951); G. Tillotson, *Criticism and the Nineteenth Century* (London, 1951), which includes several essays; J. H. Raleigh, *Matthew Arnold and American Culture* (Berkeley and Los Angeles, 1957); Vincent Buckley, *Poetry and Morality: Studies on the Criticism of Matthew Arnold, T. S. Eliot and F. R. Leavis* (London, 1959); William Robbins, *The Ethical Idealism of Matthew Arnold: A Study of the Nature and Sources of His Moral and Religious Ideas* (1959); Leon Gottfried, *Matthew Arnold and the Romantics* (1963); Patrick J. McCarthy, *Matthew Arnold and the Three Classes* (New York and London, 1964); W. D. Anderson, *Matthew Arnold and the Classical Tradition* (1965); W. A. Madden, *Matthew Arnold: A Study in the*

*Aesthetic Temperament in Victorian England* (Bloomington and London, 1967); D. J. DeLaura, *Hebrew and Hellene in Victorian England* (1969); Fred G. Walcott, *The Origins of Culture & Anarchy: Matthew Arnold & Popular Education in England* (1970). John Holloway analyzes Arnold's persuasive strategy and tactics in a chapter of *The Victorian Sage* (London and New York, 1953). T. S. Eliot's essays and lecture were cited in footnotes.

Among innumerable studies of Victorian attitudes and currents of thought are these: Basil Willey, *Nineteenth Century Studies: Coleridge to Arnold* (London, 1949; New York, 1966), and *More Nineteenth Century Studies: A Group of Honest Doubters* (1956); J. H. Buckley, *The Victorian Temper: A Study in Literary Culture* (Cambridge, Mass., 1951; repr. 1969) and *The Triumph of Time: A Study of the Victorian Concepts of Time, History, Progress, and Decadence* (ibid., 1966); W. E. Houghton, *The Victorian Frame of Mind 1830–1870* (New Haven and London, 1957); Raymond Williams, *Culture and Society 1780–1950* (London, 1959); G. Kitson Clark, *The Making of Victorian England* (London and Cambridge, Mass., 1962); A. O. J. Cockshut, *The Unbelievers: English Agnostic Thought 1840–1890* (London, 1964); Raymond Chapman, *The Victorian Debate: English Literature and Society 1832–1901* (London and New York, 1968).

# Index